THE HEALING JOURNEY
New Approaches to
Consciousness

CLAUDIO NARANJO

THE HEALING JOURNEY
New Approaches to
Consciousness

PANTHEON BOOKS
A Division of Random House
New York

Chapter I, "The Healing Potential of Agony and Ecstasy," first appeared, in slightly different form, on pages 94–111 of the *Journal for the Study of Consciousness*, Vol. 2, No. 2, 1969, edited by Dr. C. Musès.

Library of Congress Cataloging in Publication Data

Naranjo, Claudio.
  The Healing Journey.

1. Hallucinogenic drugs. 2. Psychopharmacology. 3. Psychotherapy. I. Title. [DNLM: 1. Hallucinogens—Therapeutic use. 2. Psychotherapy. WM420 N218h 1974]
RC483.5.H3N37   616.8′918   73-7026
ISBN 0-394-48826-1

Manufactured in the United States of America

FIRST EDITION

Dedication

To Franz Hoffman, Emeritus Professor of Physiology and Director of the Center for Studies in Medical Anthropology at the University of Chile, Santiago, who sponsored my career as research psychiatrist in psychopharmacology and shamanism.

And

To all the experimental subjects and patients of whom I have written—who did the same.

CONTENTS

PREFACE by Stanislaus Grof   ix

FOREWORD: PROBE INTO INNER SPACE   XV

I   THE HEALING POTENTIAL OF
     AGONY AND ECSTASY   3

II   MDA, THE DRUG OF ANALYSIS   26

III MMDA AND THE ETERNAL NOW   78   *clan T MDMA.*

IV   HARMALINE AND THE COLLECTIVE
     UNCONSCIOUS   124

V   IBOGAINE, FANTASY, AND REALITY   174

INDEX   229

ABOUT THE AUTHOR   236

PREFACE

With the increasing knowledge about the nature and dynamics of emotional disorders, it becomes more and more obvious that for most of them no overnight cure will be discovered in the form of a new and miraculous tranquilizer or antidepressant agent. The symptoms of these disorders are usually deeply anchored in the personality structure of the patient, and their causal treatment requires systematic psychotherapy that can trace the involved problems to their original sources.

According to the statistics, emotional disorders in most of the countries of the world show a continuous increase. This presents a very serious dilemma from the point of view of effective therapy and prevention. A systematic psychotherapy such as psychoanalysis or analytically oriented therapy is an extremely time-consuming procedure. It is financially accessible to only a small fraction of the patients; and even if this could be overcome, the number of psychiatrists and psychologists would have to be increased many times in order to meet the demand for this specialized treatment.

It is understandable that under these circumstances much effort has been invested in developing methods that could intensify and shorten the psychotherapeutic process. None of the approaches that have been suggested in the past has met the ideal criteria required for brief but effective psychotherapy.

In recent decades, two relatively independent streams of experimentation and research seem to have yielded promising results. The first of them is the use of chemical agents as adjuncts to psychotherapy, which after the inconclusive and, as a whole, disappointing era of barbiturates and amphetamines has experienced a real renaissance after the discovery of LSD and some other psychedelics. The second important innovation is the development of new and rather powerful modifications to psychotherapeutic techniques such as encounter groups, Fritz Perls' Gestalt psychotherapy, Lowen's bioenergetics, marathon sessions, Ida Rolf's structural integration, Desoille's *rêve éveillé*, Leuner's guided affective imagery, and so on.

Claudio Naranjo is an outstanding representative of both major streams, and in his synthesis of drug-assisted psychotherapy and the new experiential techniques, he seems to offer an interesting solution to the problem of brief therapy.

For many years, he has been closely related to the Esalen Institute at Big Sur, California, which has been the cradle of many of the new experiential techniques. He ran a number of weekend seminars and experiential workshops for Esalen and had a mutually enriching interaction with its staff members, who were pioneers in various new techniques of psychotherapy. As a direct disciple of Fritz Perls, Claudio has mastered Gestalt therapy, used it successfully in his work, and made original contributions in this field. His activity has not, however, been limited to California only, and he is well known as a lecturer and seminary leader in many growth centers all over the country.

Claudio Naranjo's experience with drugs is even more impressive than that with new psychotherapeutic techniques. Over the years, he has experimented with more than thirty compounds—mostly psychedelics and amphetamine derivatives—as adjuncts to psychotherapy. He made a special journey by canoe up the Amazon River to study *yage*[1] with the South American Indians. He brought back samples of this drug and published the first scientific description of the effects of its active alkaloids. Although he has worked with all the classic psychedelics, his unique contribution is in the area of new or less known psychoactive drugs. During recent years, commuting between the United States and his native Chile, which imposes fewer restrictions on drug research, he was able to experiment with many new compounds that are not known to professionals in the United States. With several of these drugs, he has done real pioneering work and published the first existing scientific descriptions. At a time when experimentation with mind-altering drugs is carried out mostly by teenagers and lay persons, and the professionals base their opinions on sensationalist newspaper headlines, Naranjo has been able to continue sober and highly qualified psychiatric research.

Besides being one of few professionals systematically working in this field, he was able to make several important and original scientific contributions. Because of his rich experience with various drugs, he had enough experimental background to develop the beginnings of a taxonomy of altered states of consciousness. Even if much more experimental work is required in this area, he seems to have laid the foundations for future selective and specific drug-assisted psychotherapy. In the future, it may be possible to choose from a series of available psychoactive drugs the substance that will be best suited to the patient's particular problems and combine it with the most appropriate psychotherapeutic technique. The possibility of such a selective approach in the future is evident from the delineation of the specific effects of various drugs described in this book. It is also very clearly illustrated by the condensed case histories.

Probably the most significant contribution of Claudio

---

[1] A South American vine, containing harmaline and other alkaloids, used by shamans as part of their initiation and practices.

Naranjo's experimental work is the investigation and introduction of new drugs, distinctly different from the classic
psychedelics. These drugs seem to be much easier to work
with; they do not produce hallucinations and do not have
deep disorganizing effects on the mind like LSD, mescaline,
or psilocybin. The condition produced by these drugs can
be exploited for depth analysis, but at the same time they
are much more easily manageable both by the patient and
the therapist. It seems appropriate that Claudio Naranjo
does not include them automatically in the old category of
hallucinogens or psychedelics, but coins for them new and
specific terms such as "feeling enhancers" and "fantasy
enhancers."

A description of all the positive assets of this book would
not be complete without mentioning Naranjo's profound
sophistication in regard to old religious systems. It has
helped him to bridge the gap between ancient wisdom and
modern science on the one hand and the seemingly irrecon-
cilable conflict between dynamic psychotherapy and spiritual guidance on the other. The modern reformulation of
the concept of the healing potential of agony and ecstasy
and the discussion of the relation between emotional growth
in psychotherapy and spiritual growth under the guidance
of a religious teacher belong to the most interesting sections
of his book.

The richness of the clinical examples illustrating the
effect of the described drugs, as well as the various techniques for handling difficult therapeutic situations, add a
new dimension to the book. They seem to have a value
independent of the drugs that have been explored and make
this publication a practical handbook of advanced psychotherapy.

As a whole, Claudio Naranjo's book makes extremely
informative, stimulating, and exciting reading. It is a must
for all serious students of behavior sciences interested in
innovations of psychotherapy, in psychopharmacology, and
experimental psychiatry, as well as in psychology of reli-

gion. Because of its unusual clarity, it will also be an indispensable tool for intelligent laymen seeking reliable information in these fields.

STANISLAUS GROF
Chief of
Psychiatric Research

Maryland State Psychiatric Research Center
October 1970

FOREWORD: PROBE
INTO INNER SPACE

This book was completed in the earlier part of 1970, while I made preparations for a journey that, I thought, could be (and in a sense has been) of no return. I was leaving behind thirty-seven years of a life shaped by the study of music, philosophy, and medicine, and by the pursuit of the philosophers' stone. I had been an "eternal student," one always dissatisfied and wanting to reach beyond boundaries, to the point that my scholarship involved the postponement of other aspects of my life. I had not done much (or, in a sense, anything), since I was so busy wanting to know more. On this particular occasion, however (that is to say, before embarking for Arica, Chile, on July 1, 1970), I needed to settle my accounts with life just as if I were about to die; I needed to make my will, so to speak. An aspect of this was giving expression to what I learned, but scarcely communicated, during my life as a medical doctor devoted to clinical research in psychopharmacology. I felt that as an experimenter—that is, one who chose as his subject the study of the unknown—I had the duty to communicate my observations. Only in this way, I felt, could I close the door to this chapter of my life, if the experience that I had amassed could become useful to others. Perhaps I was being compulsively philanthropic or possessed by self-importance in thinking in such a manner. As I consider the book again, however, after it has aged for several years in a drawer, I think that it may well turn out to be a useful work, since little has been written for general audiences in the field of pharmacologically assisted psychotherapy, and information about the feeling and fantasy enhancers of which I speak has been limited to a few papers in scientific journals.

Although I completed this book in 1970 in California, the work described in it was carried out mostly between 1965 and 1966 in Santiago de Chile, where I also wrote the MDA chapter and conceived of the book on the four drugs. I was at that time a research psychiatrist at the pioneering Centro de Estudios de Antropología Médica at the medical school of the University of Chile. The creation of this department had been under the initiative of the emeritus professor of physiology, Dr. Franz Hoffman, who had thirty years earlier founded Chile's first institute of physiology. He was a man who, in his sixties, discovered that physiological research was not everything, and as his eyes were opening to the transcendent, he suddenly woke up to the painful reality of the dehumanization of medicine. The Center for Studies in Medical Anthropology arose in an attempt to diagnose carefully this process of dehumanization, to investigate its theoretical and practical aspects, and to repair it. How the pursuit of this goal led me to the research described in these pages could be a long story and yet one most simply condensed in the statement that Dr. Hoffman believed in an organismic rather than organizational approach in the direction of the Center, and this, in him, implied the faith that the greatest good would result from the support of individual initiatives and styles. My own initiative and style was that of exploring the possible vitalizing effects of drugs which seemed, momentarily at least, to open avenues of essential expression and to hold in abeyance an individual's ingrained perceptual schemata and conditioned habits of response.

I am deeply thankful for the occasion that Dr. Hoffman

and the University of Chile gave me to do what I wanted most to do during nine years of my life—years that were not only productive in themselves but also the foundation of all later understandings. Only the atmosphere of great relaxation afforded by this working context allowed me to confront fully what I did not know; its lack of distractions permitted me to obtain firsthand experience in things; and its lack of external pushes or pulls exploded me, paradoxically, into the present probe into inner space, an activity which I frequently experienced at the time as a trusting yet risky leap into the unknown. The only aspect of the book that I might now, several years later, be tempted to change is a tendency to consider my "cures" too definitive. I would now prefer to consider them important steps toward the goal of dissolution of compulsive character or conditioned personality structure.

The four pharmacological agents that I discuss in this book fall into two classes: feeling enhancers and fantasy enhancers, both of which have in common the characteristic of being non-psychotomimetic psychedelics. The two words "non-psychotomimetic" and "psychedelic" evoke, beyond their specific denotations, contrasting connotations. "Psychotomimetic" and "psychedelic" have been the terms generally employed by different individuals and in the context of characteristic attitudes. "Psychotomimetics" (i.e., substances that induce states that mimic psychosis) was a concept arising from the hope, in the minds of medical and scientific people, that psychosis might be experimentally induced and controlled in such a way that it could be thoroughly understood and an answer found for its healing.

Since this possibility involved a danger, however, the word soon took on the connotation of a warning, a red signal, and, by extrapolation, a negative value. "Psychotomimetic," therefore, came to be the "uptight" word for "psychedelic." "Psychedelic" (deriving its meaning from the Greek *delos*, "manifest," and thus synonymous with "mind-manifesting"), the term introduced in the Fifties by Dr. Humphrey Osmond, one of the pioneering researchers into the new field, retained the connotation of positive value. In contrast to "psychotomimetic," which remains the language of the professional, "psychedelic" became the language of the layman—who was, at the time, more inclined to see the positive aspect of the experiences elicited by the new drugs. Throughout this time, a controversy simmered, boiled, and then almost evaporated without solution: Are the drugs in question essentially "psychotomimetic" or essentially "psychedelic"?

Fortunately, the Sixties saw the introduction of substances in which the psychedelic and psychotomimetic properties are not coexistent. Because of the fact that the four drugs with which I have dealt in this book are non-psychotomimetic psychedelics (which is to say, mind-expanding substances that do not elicit psychotic manifestations, except in a metaphorical or Pickwickian understanding of psychosis), they offer a very special interest to the clinician. They stand in a domain of their own, which lies between that of substances that are not psychedelic enough (in the true sense of the term) to be useful—such as scopolamine, amphetamine, or pentobarbital—and that of substances that are too psychotomimetic, difficult to handle, and potentially hazardous.

Due to the nature of the experiences brought about by feeling enhancers and fantasy enhancers, the session protocols from which I quote throughout the book are not qualitatively different from those of my psychotherapeutic practice in general during the same period. Their distinguishing characteristic, when contrasted with the background of my general practice, is their experiential density, the degree to which they are pregnant with significance. It might be said that the pharmacological agents employed had acted as psychological catalysts or lubricants, removing the obstacles, facilitating an attitude of openness to experience.

I would like to point out, however, that the results I have described are not independent of a personal ingredient and are not necessarily obtainable by anybody employing the four drugs in psychotherapy. Intuition, experience, and research data in the literature lead me to accept the widely shared view that psychotherapeutic results are inseparable from a personal ingredient. Furthermore, I am aware that it has been my *state*, rather than my accumulated skills and information, that has been the most determining influence in the sessions I have conducted. One of the most important aspects of psychedelic drugs, whether or not they are potentially psychotomimetic, is that they open a person up to subtle influences—which may be a blessing or a curse.

If the drugs described in this book come to be accepted by the medical profession, I believe they should be subject to some control that will ensure that they are used by those with psychological, experiential, and technical qualifications, as has been proposed by Professor Joel Elkes at Johns Hopkins and also by the staff of the Maryland State Psychiatric Research Center in their program for the training of astronauts of inner space.

Although they are not reported here, I did use controls in my research that contribute to the substantiation of my description of the distinctive qualitative effects of the four drugs. I have reported the harmaline research in a chapter on harmaline alkaloids published in *Ethnopharmacological Search for Psychoactive Drugs*, edited by Bo Holmstedt and published in 1967 by the Department of Health, Education, and Welfare in Washington; more detailed information on MDA has also been published before, in *Psychopharmacology* 5:103–107, in an article that appeared in 1971. I have not published the data corresponding to the other two substances, which lies at present in a storage room in Chile in a mountain of paper that fills several boxes. I therefore apologize for saying no more at this point than that I have given ibogaine and MMDA to a sufficient number of people to whom I have also given LSD or mescaline or

MDA or harmaline to satisfy me about the consistency of the reports. I can also add that 99 per cent of those who have experienced the effects of either ibogaine or harmaline have regarded the effect as so unmistakably distinct from that of feeling enhancers and ordinary psychedelics that they have regarded such an experiential criterion as sufficient evidence of an objective difference in the drugs' effects. I personally share with Gordon Allport the view that psychology will shift more and more from a one-sided statistical-mindedness to the detailed naturalistic study of individuals.

I believe that self-awareness is contagious, and moments of self-discovery, once adequately communicated, can be a gift of consciousness to others. Nothing other than this has led to the current popularization of psychological literature. The true language of psychology is not Latin, but plain romance. If I have not been mistaken in asserting that the experiences recorded here are pregnant with significance, let them then become part of our common awareness, and may they contribute to the awakening of the individual reader.

A final and brief word: my indebtedness to Frank Barron, Leo Zeff, Stanislaus Grof, Michael Harner, Carlos Castaneda, Don Juan, and the shamans of the world.

I hope and wish that this book may contribute to the attainment of peace, joy, and harmony on earth.

CLAUDIO NARANJO

Kensington, California
March 1973

THE HEALING JOURNEY
New Approaches to
Consciousness

THE HEALING
POTENTIAL OF
AGONY AND ECSTASY

DRUGS IN PSYCHOTHERAPY

THE ASSOCIATION BETWEEN THE occurrence of altered states of consciousness and personality changes has probably been known in all times. Shamans of many regions induce trance states to effect healing; mystics often experience "visionary" states at the time of their "conversion"; patients in the later stages of psychoanalysis sometimes hallucinate or exhibit other transient psychotic manifestations.

The deliberate use of altered states of consciousness in the therapeutic endeavor falls mostly within the domain of hypnotherapy and that of the utilization of psychotropic drugs. Also recently there has arisen an interest in the notion of "positive disintegration" (Dabrowski) and the value of psychotic experience when properly assimilated, drug experience being by far the method of widest applicability.

The first drugs to be extensively applied to the facilitation of therapeutic intention were barbiturates and amphetamines. An intravenous barbiturate was first employed by Laignel-Lavastine (1924) as a means of "revealing the unconscious," and later became the basis of the procedures known as narcoanalysis (proposed by J. S. Horsley, 1936), narcosynthesis (Grinker), and others.

The first use of a central stimulant as an adjunct to psychotherapy seems to have been J. Delay's "amphetamine shock," followed by Jantz's "Weckanalyse." Before this time, Myerson (1939) had described the combined use of intravenous benzedrine and sodium amytal, but interest in this procedure increased notably in the Fifties, when intravenous amphetamines came to be more frequently used.

After the stimulants and depressants, the hallucinogens became an object of interest as facilitators of psychotherapy. The clinical experimentation of Federking (1947) with small or medium dosages of mescaline were followed by that of Abramson, who advocated the use of small dosages of LSD-25 in the course of psychoanalytic treatment by drug-induced state of mind, and that of Sandison, who brought to bear a Jungian outlook on the process.

The following years saw not only the appearance of qualitatively similar drugs (psilocybin and other tryptamines), but of dissimilar ways of approaching the state of mind elicited by them. Outside the medical field, many became impressed with the intrinsic spiritual value of the "psychedelic experience" and felt more interest in this than in any therapeutic application. In particular, Aldous Huxley had a great influence in calling attention to the religious and aesthetic aspects of these drugs. Others saw such states as not unrelated to the question of behavior change, but in fact as the key to it, and thus designed their procedure and setting so as to maximize the likelihood of peak experiences. This, for instance, was the way in which Hoffer and Osmond approached their treatment of alcoholics in Saskatchewan and how the Harvard group conducted their rehabilitation project in a Massachusetts prison.

The drugs that I am dealing with in this book are only

some of those discovered or rediscovered in later years, and suggest that we are seeing only the beginning of the possibilities of elicitation of specific states of consciousness other than the habitual one. On the other hand, the drugs we already know—stimulants, depressants, hallucinogens, and those to be described in the following chapters—indicate that it is not *one* particular state of mind that can be advantageous to psychological exploration or therapeutic interaction: any one of a series of artificially induced alterations in the habitual pattern of an individual's personality may constitute a unique advantage in the breaking of vicious circles in the psyche, bringing into focus unknown domains of feeling or thought, or facilitating corrective experiences, in which underdeveloped functions are temporarily stimulated or overdeveloped ones inhibited.

The four drugs with which this book deals fall, both chemically and in terms of their subjective effects, into two groups. That of the phenylisopropylamines, comprising MDA and MMDA, is characterized mainly by its effects of feeling enhancement, sharpening of attention, increased fluency in associations and communication. The other, that of the polycyclic indoles (ibogaine, harmaline) could well be called, for its effects, "oneirophrenic," the term that Turner suggested for the harmala alkaloids. Their effect on most subjects is that of eliciting vivid dreamlike sequences which may be contemplated while awake with closed eyes, without loss of contact with the environment or alterations of thinking. Yet the quality that makes the drugs in both groups valuable to psychotherapy is that of facilitating access to otherwise unconscious processes, feelings, or thoughts, a quality that deserves to be called "psychedelic" in the sense of the word intended by Osmond: "mind-manifesting." Since they differ from the hallucinogens in that they do not bring about the perceptual phenomena, depersonalization, or changes in thinking characteristic of the latter and yet share with them an intensification of awareness, they might well be called non-psychotomimetic psychedelics.

Not only are there clear differences between the various types of psychotropic drugs, but individual characteristics in the effect of each and a variety of possible syndromes that each can elicit. Sometimes it may be hard to discern anything in common between different possible reactions to the same drug, but in other instances we may discover that what appears to be very different is only a different presentation of the same process. Just as the ego loss brought about by LSD may be experienced as an ecstasy of unity with all things or a desperate clinging to a tenuous identity, fear of chaos and of madness, so, too, the realistic enhanced awareness of the present brought about by MMDA may be experienced as a serene fullness or, for one who is not ready to confront the moment, tormenting anxiety, shame, guilt.

The number of typical syndromes elicited by each drug is more than two, for it also depends on personality types, and each will demand some specificity in the optimal psychotherapeutic approach. Yet much of the therapist's attitude toward the situation will depend on his understanding of the dimension implied in the above-cited contrasts. It is a polarity of pleasure-pain, as well as personality integration vs. disintegration at the moment, and with this I want to deal in the following pages.

PEAK EXPERIENCE VS. ENHANCEMENT OF PATHOLOGY

Apparently, all psychoactive drugs, from barbiturates to ibogaine, may cause either pleasurable states of mind or unpleasant ones, states that seem more desirable than the usual ones and others that are marked not only by suffering but by lack of good thinking, appropriate actions, or accurate perception of reality. Huxley has described something of the characteristic "heaven and hell" of mescaline, and those words have become standard to many

who are familiar with the effects of the LSD-like hallucinogens. Yet there are as many heavens and as many
hells as there are drugs. What a given individual's reaction is along the continuum may partly depend on his
constitution. Thus, Sheldon has remarked that the active,
forceful somatotonic tends to react to alcohol by becoming more active or aggressive, the more sociable viscerotonic, more emotional and talkative, and the introverted
cerebrotonic, more withdrawn and brooding.

Yet, whatever the personality traits that may often be
predisposing to a given reaction to a given psychoactive
drug, it is clear enough for those discussed in the book
that a given individual may show reactions of different
types on different occasions of administration and also at
different moments in the course of a given session. Moreover, it seems fairly certain that the elicitation of a "heavenly" or a "hellish" experience depends greatly upon the
person's attitude at the moment, the surroundings, the
relationship to the therapist, and the latter's intervention
during the session. And since this allows for some measure of deliberateness in the choice of an experience of
one type or another, it is desirable to understand what
value each of these may have to the aim of psychotherapy.

What is the nature of these experiences, in the first
place—the "positive" and "negative"—and what is it that
makes them pleasant or unpleasant? The gamut of peak
experiences, in ordinary life as in psychopharmacological
conditions in general, comprehends a variety of states
which, I would suggest, have in common their being
moments in which intrinsic values are discovered or contacted.

There are several ways in which we use the word
"value." More than indicating different *kinds* of value,
these point at altogether different psychological processes
that may give rise to value judgment. One of them I
would propose that we call "normative" value, for here

"value" consists of the acceptance or rejection of something (person, action, object, work of art, and so on) according to a pre-established rule. Such a rule may be implicit or unconscious, i.e., the process of matching the ongoing perception of something against it. It may consist of a given standard of "good taste," a notion of what a good person should be like, what the good life consists of, and so on. In this value-ascribing process, "value" is an idea-feeling-action depending on the nature of past experience or conditioning.

But when we like the taste of an apple, when we enjoy breathing fresh air, or have a true experience of beauty, love, or mystical rapture, "value" is not something computed from the match or mismatch of the ongoing experience with a standard, but the discovery of something which seems to live in the moment and was possibly unknown before. And, moreover, norms have generally found origin in such discovery of value before any norm existed—"And God saw that it was good."

The variety of experiences of intrinsic value may be understood as a continuum or progression going from the simplest level of sensuous delight to the most encompassing level of mystical rapture. The former is the domain of true pleasure, which is to be differentiated from most of the experiences that we *usually* regard as pleasurable. These constitute not so much the discovery of intrinsic value but the relief of tension end-points of displeasure (thirst, hunger, etc.). Enjoyment of sense impressions is not bound to need or instinct, but, like all intrinsic value, is experienced as something pertaining to the "object" itself (the color, the taste, the sound, and so on) and therefore seems gratuitous. It could well be regarded as the most elementary form of love, in that it entails an appreciation, a saying yes to reality in its detail, in its fabric, or in its stuff, rather than in its specific shapes or beings constituted by it. This is the quality that, in the domain of sound, Stokowski has called the *body* of music, in contraposition to music's "soul," and has a beauty of its own, much as does a person's body.

But the soul of art is in the domain of beauty proper, which differs from pleasure not only in quality but in its object. Whereas the latter consists in the enjoyment of isolated sense impressions, in beauty it is a whole that is appreciated: an object, symbol, or person certainly endowed with sensory qualities but not definable in terms of these. And so, just as good music may be played on an instrument with poor tone quality, a worthless painting may be made with the most beautiful colors.

What a sensory quality is for pleasure and what a whole configuration is for beauty, a *being* is for love. And as a *thing* is more than its sensory qualities, a being is more than its *some-body*. As a person *has* a body or is expressed through the body, the spirit that conceives a work of art speaks through it but is different from its particular shape. And the more we go into a work, the closer we get to an encounter with the spirit of the author conveyed by his style. Truly, one of the deeper experiences in the perception of art is one of love for the being expressed in it—whether that of Bach, Dostoevski, Van Gogh, or whoever has created out of a "spirit" and not just decorated space and time at random. (But to meet such a spirit truly, we must be one, rather than a succession of random happenings in that place that we call "I.") And when we love an object, it is also a being for us, beyond its physical appearance, which may be beautiful or not. It was perhaps a love of all things that made Gauguin say, "A thing is not always pretty, but always beautiful." I am not saying that there is *in* the objects some sort of object-soul, but only pointing out the quality of our own possible experience. In one instance, the object is just an aggregate of physical qualities, and in the other, we personify it to some extent and relate to it as a being, an individual, sometimes implicitly, as when we wash a dish with loving care, or more or less explicitly when we don't want to be parted from a dear old sweater.

Just as *a being* is the object of love, *being* in itself is the object of the feelings conveyed by the words holiness and sanctity, the wonder of existing, no matter in what form—the miracle and gift of that affirmation that created this world: "Beingness," as Huxley translates Eckhardt's *Istigkeit*.

And just as we are not gifted to find beauty in all forms or love all beings, we are also limited in that we can sense beingness only through certain beings, certain things, sounds, persons; these stir our intrinsic religiosity, which may or may not be related to the idea of God or conventional religious conceptions.

If peak experiences are those in which intrinsic values are met—those ranging from the most elemental affirmation of the perceptual data, through beauty and love, to the affirmation of experience in itself, the common ground of things—then what is the other end of the heaven-hell continuum?

Superficially or descriptively, this corresponds to the enhancement of syndromes that are well known in psychiatric tradition: psychosomatic or conversion manifestations, reactions of anxiety or depression, amplifications of character pathology, transient delusional states or catatonia, and so on.

More deeply, I would like to propose that these states are only the end products of a negation of intrinsic values. Valuing, appreciation in all forms and on all levels, is a pro-life force that not only affirms the world but constitutes our only way of truly living. And as there is this yea-saying to life, there is an active nay-saying, a denying force that draws a curtain over the intrinsic joy of existence, renders us incapable of loving and "unfaithful" to the feelings that would lead us to worship existence in itself.

A drug only makes an aspect of a person's psyche

more manifest. According to whether the individual is able to accept it or not, he will be in contact with a value or in conflict between his enhanced tendency and his denying sub-self. Such conflict can naturally lead to repression, substitutive symbolic expression through body or mind, reactive formations, anxiety about letting go.

Such experience is not without value, though, because it entails such an unusual and often dramatic clash of the forces within the personality that the conflict may thus be exposed, understood, and eventually resolved. Exposing the conflict—a conflict that is basically that of being or not being, that between being for or against oneself— amounts to exposing the "monster" in the mind in whom the denying force originated. Resolving the conflict, which is achieving unity, may be likened to the slaying of the dragon in classical myths and the acquisition of his power, or, alternatively, to a taming of the beast, by virtue of which its dying energies are now put to the service of life.

The process of "descending" into the pathological, chaotic, and destructive as a means of personal integration is not a discovery of contemporary psychotherapy. We may find it, for instance, explicitly recognized by Dante in the conception of his *Divine Comedy*. The poem begins when the author, in the middle of his life, finds himself lost "in a dark forest" he has entered "while asleep." He envisages the "high mountain" in the distance and wants to climb it and thus reach his highest goal. But this is not possible. Three fierce beasts (different transformations of the same one) successively obstruct his way. His guide then appears to tell him how such a "direct path" is impossible and that he must first go through the underworld.

Then Dante tells how he followed his guide and had to contemplate one after another the different aberrations of man until, much later, having gone through hell and purgatory, he is told how these constitute "diseases of love"—"the love that moves the sun and the other stars."

And the process which Dante describes in the *Comedy* is most relevant to what we may say on the utilization of "hellish" experiences elicited by drugs. It is the traditional understanding of the contemplative way in spiritual development. All passions are seen and recognized as different from the "I," the center of one's own existence. Not without stress or pain does Dante bring himself to face the different scenes of hell, and on occasion he is unable to remain conscious at the shock (*"e cade como corpo morto cade"*), but he maintains a detached attitude and leaves everything behind.

Awareness, or consciousness, is, in fact, the single element that most psychotherapists in our day would indicate as the essential motor of transformation. Awareness of our processes is that which may bring them under our control, make them "ours." And, paradoxically, in the act of being aware we are not only "it," but a more encompassing entity that may continue to exist with or without "it." "Spirit is freedom," says Hegel. This is the difference between Dante's hell and paradise, as well as that between the beginning and end of successful psychotherapy. For hell and paradise do not differ in the forces there portrayed—just as there is a hell of lust, there is also in the *Comedy* a circle in paradise where dwell the loving spirits, and to the hell of anger corresponds that of militant spirits; to the one of gluttony, that of those who are gluttons of celestial manna, and so on. The difference lies only in that what in hell is manifested as a "passion" (something "suffered" passively) is in paradise a "virtue" —from the Indo-European *vir*: force, energy, and also from the Latin *vir*: man.

The transforming effect of consciousness on the life processes is a transmutation by which they become more and not less what they are. It is as if the state of consciousness depicted as "hell" were one in which our energies, not knowing what they really want, missing their true aims, had lost their natural channels. When every part of man "remembers" what it truly wants, sickness turns into health, and what was once a parody of life becomes something which had been a mere shadow.

The voyage through chemically opened hells is not different in essence from the age-old way of self-knowledge nor from the process taking place through exposure to the modern insight therapies. There are technical differences in the three cases, but the main difference is in the intensity of the process, so that under the effect of drugs months may be dramatically packed or condensed into hours. The process is still the same as in all "ways of growth": an act of acknowledgment of what has been avoided or pushed away from the boundaries of awareness. Since what we avoid looking at is what we fear, this must be an act of courage. And since much of what we do not allow into our field of consciousness is painful, uncomfortable, or humiliating, the acquisition of such self-insight may partake of these same qualities. The pain or anguish of some drug experiences may be thus understood as the condensed, concentrated pain or fear of months or even years of self-discovery, and may be the unavoidable price that a person has to pay for seeing his reality.

Experience tells us that such a reaction is temporary, the end of the *via purgativa* being self-acceptance, but it is doubtful that such an end may be attained without starting at the beginning, exposing the wounds that are to be healed—conflicts to be reconciled, self-hatred to be re-examined, shame and guilt to be worked through, and so on.

The fact that healing does take place proves that the "problems" and sources of suffering have been in a sense illusory.

If the chemically elicited intensification of awareness brings about an enhancement of pathology, this is only because "normality" is partly maintained at the cost of psychological anaesthesia, and "adjustment" ordinarily is in the nature of a denial rather than a transcendence of inner turmoil. Yet a further step in awareness may show that all this pathology now laid bare could thrive only in the dark, and the conflicts causing it were the result of confusion-unconsciousness itself.

The paradox upon which psychotherapy rests is that the suffering that we avoid is merely perpetuated through avoidance. Only by moving toward fear and confronting the monster that is the source of agony can the discovery be made that there is no monster there to fear. This sometimes finds dramatic expression in sessions in which an individual feels that he is actually going to die, but, in the moment of giving in to death, wakes up to the ecstasy of enhanced aliveness; or in others where he feels that he is going crazy, but, when he is finally able to surrender control, he discovers that this was only a catastrophic expectation of his, that the Pandora box was really empty and his urge to control obviated.

We may conceptualize the process as one of insight into the distinction between reality and illusion, as one of "positive disintegration" (Dabrowski) or, behavioristically, as one of reconditioning and "desensitization" through exposure to the avoided in an atmosphere of support, or any number of ways. For practical purposes, though, it seems clear that the best that the therapist can do is stand by the traveler in hell as Virgil did by Dante, reminding him of his goal, giving him courage to step ahead and see, pushing him even, when he wants to retreat in fear. I believe that the realization that hell is no hell must come from inner realization and not from well-intentioned reassurance and brainwashing, so I find myself again and again saying to my patients, "Stay with it." Staying with it is the way of going through it, whatever it is.

Still, beyond hell there is purgatory, and Dante's symbols may be as relevant to the therapeutic process in this as in other points. Hell is a state of helplessness and hopeless suffering; purgatory is one of chosen suffering for the sake of a goal. In the first, man is a victim; in the second, a penitent. In hell, man merely contemplates his reality, being, so to say, flooded by the evidence of his awfulness. Purgatory begins when open-eyed vigilance is not threatening any more, but it is still a challenge to act. This is the beginning of the *via activa*, in contrast to the *via contemplativa*, and the pains of purgatory are in the nature of the friction between a being's expression and the ingrained hindrances of his personality. It is a confrontation of that which can only be confronted or brought into awareness through the challenge of moving against it. In Dante's imagery it is the climbing of a mountain. In psychological terms, it is the courage to be, to express one's essential nature in spite of opposition. In the psychotherapeutic context, and particularly in that involving psychoactive drugs, action usually proceeds in the very limited social context of the relationship with the psychotherapist, but can be extended into the abstract media of art or the potentially unlimited domain of imaginative representation. The importance of action carried out in the medium of visual imagery or dramatic representation accounts for the stress given to the techniques of Gestalt therapy and of the guided daydream in the cases to be presented throughout this book.

It may seem obvious that the process of inner change should begin with the inevitably painful contemplation of those aspects in the present distorted psychological reality that are to be transformed. Yet there is much to be said of a complementary approach in psychotherapy— that of promoting the growth and expression of the healthy aspects of personality rather than the destruction of the old patterns, the development of a firmer grasp on reality rather than the analysis of the phantom world of questionable pictures and interpretations of existence. In the domain of drug therapy, this becomes the issue of utilizing the peak experiences.

Among psychotherapists using LSD and similar drugs,

it seems clear that there has been a tendency for some to seek one-sidedly the elicitation of peak experiences and to consider the "bad trip" as an accident that they do not take as a challenge to work through. On the other hand, there are those who are skilled in handling pathological manifestations and conflicts but feel at a loss in the face of blissful episodes that have no place in their conceptual framework.

If both the agony and the ecstasy of drug experiences have a potential for psychological healing, it is important for us to know the place and promise of each in the treatment of an individual and the best way to deal with each when it occurs in the course of a session.

Technical as the issue seems, I think that the question as to how these two types of experience are related is only a particular instance of a more encompassing one on the relationship of psychotherapy as we know it to the spiritual disciplines and the spiritual quest as described by mystical writers or teachers.

When it comes to the understanding of drug experiences, the attitudes or beliefs about the relationship between psychotherapy and the spiritual quest vary as much as when human experience at large is the issue. The most widespread tendency, though, is to see them as unrelated, either one or the other being all-important. Thus, there are those who stress the "transcendental" side and regard psychotherapy as a rather trivial matter and those who either look on everything "mystical" with suspicion or see it as of cultural interest though irrelevant to the higher goal of healing the mind. Psychotherapists who see the relevance of spiritual disciplines to their field of endeavor (like Fromm, Benoit, or Nicoll) or religious thinkers interested in psychotherapy (like Watts) are a minority, and their number diminishes when we look for those who have definite notions as to how the ideas and procedures of these different domains are related, and not just divided interest.

In my own view, "psychotherapy" (rightly understood) and "mysticism" or "esotericism" (rightly understood) are but different stages in a single journey of the soul, different levels in a continuous process of consciousness expansion, integration, self-realization. The central issues of both are the same, though the phenomena encountered, psychological states dealt with, and techniques appropriate to them may differ. Some of these issues, as I have detailed elsewhere, are, aside from the growth of consciousness, that of contact with reality, the resolution of conflicts into ever more encompassing wholes, the development of freedom and the capacity to surrender to life, the acceptance of experience, and, most particularly, a shift in identity leading from the enactment of a self-concept to the indentification with the real self or essence.

The relationship between the quests for sanity and enlightenment might be seen as that between the minor and the major mysteries of antiquity. While the former aims at the restoration of "true man," "original man," the goal of the latter was the transcendence of the human condition, the acquisition of some degree of freedom from the needs or laws that determine ordinary human life by assimilation to a radically different state of being. The gap between strictly human consciousness, even at its fullest manifestation, and this "other shore" is at the root of symbols such as that of a bridge or ocean to cross or a ladder to climb (not merely an earthly mountain), and, particularly, those of death and rebirth, which may be found in all mystical and religious traditions.

"Original man," "natural man," is the goal of psychotherapy. This is man freed from "original sin," man that does not turn against himself but fulfills his potential in affirmation of himself and existence. Such is the man that Dante, in his monumental synthesis of the culture of antiquity and Christianity, places at the summit of purgatory: earthly paradise. Paradise, yes, but still not heaven, for this lies beyond the sub-lunar world of Aristotle; its "circles" are those of the planets, the sun, and the fixed stars.

Just as in Dante's journey, only after reaching the fullness of the ordinary human condition (attained after hell and purgatory) can he soar above the earth, so most spiritual traditions recognize the need for a *via purgativa* before the *via unitiva*, the need for man to realize his true nature as a human being before he can aspire to realize his divine nature, for him to establish order and harmony in his life before his soul can become receptive to the "supernatural"—which is only that part of the natural which lies beyond his ordinary understanding and awareness.

Yet these stages are not clear-cut in practical reality, for ecstatic and visionary experiences can take place before the human personality is ready to live up to, or even understand, their content. Toward these exalted states we find that spiritual schools of all lands display a rather ambivalent attitude. On the one hand, the yogi guru warns the disciple not to become fascinated by the acquisition of special "powers" that may sidetrack him from the true aim; the Christian mystic warns monks about the fascination of "visions" and emotional rapture; the Zen master regards hallucinatory experiences during meditation as *makyo* ("from the devil"); and, in general, we find references to danger being associated with contact with the occult by the "unprepared." Preparation in this context does not mean knowledge as much as a personal development without which the way of mysticism becomes that of magic: a quest of the supernatural in the service of the ego rather than one for a supernatural order to which the ego may become subservient, the living understanding of a greater whole in which the individual may find his true purpose.

On the other hand, these experiences of heaven without purgatory, *samadhi* before enlightenment, grace before mystical union, exceptional states of consciousness before the attainment of full spiritual maturity, are not only sought after by specific practices but regarded as seeds of transformation.

I think the same twofold point of view may be brought to bear on the peak experiences that a number of psychoactive drugs may elicit in some persons. More often than meditation disciplines or rituals, they can bring about heaven without purgatory, the states of insight into universal truths which are at the core of religious mysteries, unaccompanied by insight into, or change in, the individual's faulty personality. The individual may use such experience for ego inflation or for personality change, for self-justification and stagnation, or as a light to show him the way.

Much as can be said of the therapeutic value of peak experiences, I think there is an advantage to the point of view (presented in greater detail in Chapter III) that personality change is *distinct* from peak experiences, whatever the relationship between them may be. Any one of them may be a step toward the other, but it may be important to keep in mind that a "mystical experience," for instance, only *facilitates* psychological healing (by giving the individual a higher perspective on his conflicts, for instance), and psychological health only provides a more receptive state for the deeper experience of reality constituting the core of peak experiences.

The fact that "mystical experience" sometimes brought about by the agency of drugs of one kind or another seems to have a lesser bearing on the individual's life, in general, than spontaneous experiences of the same type (or those that have resulted from a systematic spiritual discipline) has often invited the question whether the two are really of the same nature.

It is only natural to expect a spontaneous religious experience to be more permanent than one facilitated by an external agent, for the mere occurrence of the former indicates a personality that is compatible with it or its implications. The greater the external influence—chemical or other—that is necessary to bring it about, the more one can assume the existence of psychological obstacles to it, and a gap between the values, motivation system, and point of view of the ordinary state and those characteristic of the non-ordinary. Yet if we picture the artificially induced peak experience as a momentary release from the prison of the ordinary personality and its built-in conflicts, we may speak of its value as that of giving the prisoner a taste of freedom and a perspective on life richer than that of his lonely cell. Such an experience will contribute to his permanent liberation by reinforcing his incentive, shattering his idealizations of prison life, giving him valuable orientation and information from outside sources as to what to do to gain his freedom. Much of this depends on the prisoner's activity while the door of his cell remains temporarily unlocked. He may, in one case, not even push the door open, being too sleepy or scared of life beyond the walls within which he has become accustomed to living. Or he may walk out to get some food from a neighboring room, or just go for a walk and enjoy the landscape. Alternatively, he may be concerned above all else with using his time to secure his permanent freedom. He may find help, or instruments, to bring in and remove the bars when he finds himself locked in again, or he may busy himself with making a duplicate key for the lock.

In other terms, we may understand the artificial ecstasy as a state that is made possible by the transient removal of obstructions to the flow of a person's deeper psychic life and his experience of reality. Such removal of obstructions may be compared to the anaesthesia of higher cortical control elicited by alcohol, NO_2, lack of oxygen, and so on, resulting in disinhibition of impulse or affect. Yet, if this neurophysiological model is correct, the site of action of the drugs dealt with in this book must be different from that of depressants, for it is a different quality of disinhibition that takes place.

Yet this experience of freedom from habitual obstructions in awareness and action is only a preview of an eventual overcoming of such blocks or a restructuring of dysfunctional patterns within the personality. Though both may be experientially the same, in one case we are facing a conditional freedom, and in the other, a freedom in wholeness, which is a freedom *in spite of* difficulties. Going back to the prison analogy, it is as if, in the former case, the guard has just been put to sleep but not overcome or killed, as the ego is shattered with the mystic's enlightenment, as the "old man" or "outer man" dies when the "new man" or "inner man" is born at some point in the successful spiritual quest.

Much of what has been said above applies to some extent to experiences elicited by certain spiritual disciplines, environments, or personal "contagion." Simple retreat from the world, for instance (whether that of a simple life, or that of the monk and the Indian *sannyasin*, who have given up all attachments), falls into the same pattern of avoiding certain hindrances, distractions, and conflicts that detract from the possibility of peak experiences. It is certainly a greater challenge to maintain a state of centeredness and genuineness in the midst of pushes and pulls of family life in an urban setting than in a cave in the Himalayas. And yet retreat may be of invaluable help for one who needs to find himself before he knows what he wants from others and what he wants to do with his life. Likewise, in many forms of meditation, body and mind are relieved of the habitual inner agitation that precludes the desirable inner states that are being sought. Here, too, peak experiences are made possible by the suppression of stimuli in which they would ordinarily be drowned. Yet such transient experiences obtained in solitude and silence while facing a white wall with a mind empty of thoughts are not mere evasions of the complexities of life, but a source of strength to return to it and deal in a better way with the problems that it poses.

In drug-elicited peak experiences it is sometimes clear

that a similar withdrawal from conflict areas has proceeded quite spontaneously, and we may approach such moments in the same light as those arising from meditation. Their negative aspect is that they constitute a healthy contact with reality in only a narrow range of experience, bypassing the domain where lie the personality defects. Their positive aspect is that such avoidance of difficulties may be functional, consisting a necessary step toward the achievement of *partial* integration. Once some centeredness has been achieved, the following step will be that of extending it into the periphery of personality, just as the ultimate end of meditation is its extension to ordinary life in the form of an enduring self-awareness and depth. Avoidances may be suspected as an underlying condition of what I like to call partial peak experiences— those that, though intense, cover only a fragment of the range of qualities. Some persons, for instance, exhibit vivid aesthetic and religious feelings but have a gap in the area of human feelings that would be expected to lie between such qualities in the value continuum. Were personal relationships considered at that point, ecstasy would probably be dissolved, engulfed in anxieties and resentments, but the individual unconsciously wards off such inner disturbance in order to afford clarity in other areas of experience. For others, the gap or avoided area may be different. There are persons who may see everything as beautiful except themselves, so that the thought of their personal life or the sight of their reflection in a mirror can turn their heaven into hell. For others, it may be the perception or thought of people in general that is avoided, such as in Huxley's famous first mescaline session reported in *The Doors of Perception*. In still others, everything can flow beautifully so long as their eyes are kept closed and contact with the environment avoided, and in still others external reality is enjoyed, but isolation and closing of eyes is avoided because of the anxiety that arises from the unfolding of fantasy.

Such avoidances are essentially an expression of phobic areas in the everyday personality, and, as in psychotherapies in general, there is a choice between two strategies to deal with them: bypassing the blocks in order to develop the sane aspects of the individual, or facing the blocks by plunging into the turmoil of distressful and avoided feelings. The first choice, in drug experiences, might be conceived as a short-circuiting into heaven, after which the situation on "earth" is not essentially changed or understood better. The second is the choice of dealing with earthly difficulties with only slight chances of being able to rise above them, but with more chances of effecting change. Again, the choice between the two kinds of experience might be likened to the choice between the intrinsically valuable one of looking out through an open window and that of attempting to open a window next to it that is at present closed. The outcome of the latter choice will possibly be no more than a few inches of light instead of the wide view of the landscape that could be perceived from the window that is already open, but there will remain the lasting benefit of one more place in the house from which to enjoy the world.

This is not to signify that the first kind of experience does not have value in bringing about change in personality. The fortifying virtue of intrinsic value can give a person the strength and even the desire to remove the blocks to increased experiencing of value. The sight of the goal is what stimulates the wanderer, as the drawing closer to it brings it better into view. Moreover, just as a young oak needs protection from rabbits, yet the mature tree can serve to leash an elephant, so the avoidance of conflict may have its place while emphasis is laid on the development and expression of the healthy sides of personality. Eventually, this healthy growth, stimulated through peak experiences in the course of therapy, artistic endeavor, or life situations, may invade and replace the disturbed domains of the individual's functioning.

So here we have two approaches to the process of psychological healing that are opposite and yet compatible and even complementary.

The peak experience is what Christian theology regards as grace: a gift that can come to both saint and sinner, and that the individual can either use or fail to use. The experience of psychological disharmony, on the other hand, is the challenge of the *via purgativa*, the mountain to be climbed. The higher the pilgrim is on the mountain the more likely he is to receive the ever-downpouring gift from heaven. The greater the gift of grace received, the stronger will be his sense of direction, his hope and faith, his will to climb.

Both approaches are well documented in the spiritual practices of mankind. Some stress the direct seeing of reality and dispelling of the phantoms of illusion. Others stress attending to the experience of the moment, illusory as it may be, for only attention to it will show that illusion is the reflection of reality on the rippled surface of the mind and will lead from the reflection to the original light. From my own experience, I have developed great faith in the person's own motivation to follow any of these paths at a given moment and respect for his natural rhythm in alternating from one to another. At times, he will need centeredness above all else; at others, feeling in touch with his true feelings and impulses, he will want to explore the world from these, carrying them into realization. His groundedness in the peak experience will turn hell into purgatory for him, but if in his outgoingness he feels lost, he will again need to withdraw to the center. The rhythm may become evident in a single session or during several. Initial ecstasy may make purgatory possible for some. To others, the gift of grace may be unavailable at first, and they will reach serenity only after repeated confrontations of the terrifying, along with the discovery that there is nothing to fear.

I tend to distrust the one-sidedness of drug experiences

both in the direction of joy and suffering, thinking that the one may involve avoiding the issues and the other a bias in favor of personal striving and hard work. What I do when prompted by such suspicion is probably best told by the clinical material in the forthcoming chapters.

CHAPTER II

MDA, THE
DRUG OF ANALYSIS

MDA (methylenedioxyampheta-
mine) is an amination product of safrol, just as MMDA
is obtained from the amination of myristicine. Safrol and
myristicine are essential oils contained in nutmeg; they are
somewhat psychoactive and quite toxic. As is the case with
MMDA, MDA has not been found in nature, but the hypothesis has been put forward that both might be produced
in the body by amination of their parent compounds, which
would in turn explain the subjective effects of nutmeg,
already acknowledged in the Ayur Veda,[1] where it is desig-
nated as *mada shaunda*—narcotic fruit.

The psychotropic effects of MDA were accidentally
discovered by G. Alles,[2] who ingested 1.5 mg. of the
chemical for the purpose of assessing its effects on circula-
tion. Alles' experience was mainly one of heightened introspection and attention, but at the time of the onset of
subjective effects he saw illusory smoke rings about him,
which led him to believe that MDA would be a hallucino-
gen in sufficient amounts. From my own research with the
drug, this does not quite appear to be the case. In a first

[1] Ancient Hindu scripture dealing with medicine and the art of
prolonging life.

[2] The discoverer of amphetamine.

study designed to describe its effects in normal individuals, not one of eight subjects reported hallucinations, visual distortions, color enhancement, or mental imagery,
while all of them evidenced other pronounced reactions:
enhancement of feelings, increased communication, and
heightened reflectiveness, which led to a concern with
their own problems or those of society or mankind. Further experiments with MDA in neurotic patients in the
context of psychotherapy have confirmed such effects, but
here physical symptoms were of frequent occurrence, and
visual phenomena were described by most individuals at
some point of their experience. Yet the most characteristic
feature of the experience of these subjects was one which
we will here call age regression. This is a term employed
to designate the vivid re-experiencing of past events sometimes made possible by hypnosis, wherein a person actually loses his present orientation and may temporarily believe himself to be a child involved in a situation of the
past. Age regression brought about by MDA differs in this
last respect, however: such loss of awareness of the environment and the conditions at the time of the experience
seems to be more typical of hypnotic regression, whereas
in the MDA-elicited state the patient simultaneously re-
gresses and retains awareness of the present self. Yet in
both instances the person more than conceptually remembers the past, as he may vividly recapture visual or other
sensory impressions inaccessible to him in the normal
state, and he usually reacts with feelings that are in pro-
portion to the event. This is the same process termed "returning" in dianetics, and which can range all the way
from hypermnesia to repetition of a past experience in
which not only the old feelings are again felt but physical
pain or pleasure and other sensations, as the case may
be.

Age regression has been observed by some psychotherapists using LSD or mescaline, and others, using the term
more loosely, claim that this is a constant aspect of such

experiences, in that there is a shift to the pre-verbal mode of mental functioning characteristic of early childhood, and a temporary suspension of schemata and behavior patterns.

Regression with MDA is something more specific than a change in the style of mental operation and reactions, in that it entails the remembering of particular events. This may occasionally be brought about under the effect of other hallucinogens or without any drug, particularly when sought after through therapeutic maneuvers. Ibogaine, in particular, lends itself well to an exploration of events in a patient's life history for the richness of feeling with which these can be evolved. Yet with MDA regression occurs so frequently and spontaneously that this can be considered a typical effect of this substance, and a primal source of its therapeutic value.

I believe that case reports rather than generalizations convey the subtle understanding of a drug's effect that is needed for its utilization in psychiatry. It is from such that I have learned whatever I may have to say, and I think that I can say it best by recording some of the events I have witnessed as a psychotherapist, obscure as these may at times be. In what follows I shall summarize the essentials of some instances of MDA therapy chosen as the most effective in bringing about changes in the patient's personality. As it will be seen, all of these entailed a dawning of new insight by the patient into his own life history or some aspect of it. In this, the healing process differed from what is observed in most instances of harmaline, MMDA, or even ibogaine therapy.

The first case presented here is actually the first in which I used MDA for a therapeutic purpose. The patient is an engineer in a high management post and a professor of business administration who had studied psychology for professional reasons and, in so doing, come to realize that life in general—and his in particular—could develop, and become richer and deeper. When questioned on his reasons for wanting psychotherapy, he emphasized a feeling of not having developed or achieved what was in his potential to develop, his life being limited in scope: "Both my professional and love life have been controlled by accident. I have had little influence on the course of my life." This he attributed to his insecurity, which manifested itself in doubt of his judgment and actions, which in turn left him at the mercy of external pressures. "This may be pleasant for those who live with me, but I am not satisfied. I need more direction on my life, and for this I need to be more unyielding." His insecurity, too, made him vulnerable, so that he was sometimes hurt by little things—mostly criticism from his wife. He felt little affection or regard for her, and had considered a divorce, but felt too attached to his children to leave the house. To the question of what he would want to obtain through psychiatric help he replied: "I want to know where to go in view of what I have. I want to be better, useful, and achieve new happiness. In the most intimate part of myself I have always been unsatisfied. I want to be sure of my worth. That is my greatest problem, which prevents me from deciding and takes away the direction from my life. And I want to understand how this state came about."

I proposed to the patient a treatment which would entail a preparatory period of approximately two months with weekly appointments (during which he would write an autobiography), which would be followed by a day-long MDA session and group therapy thereafter. The autobiographic account that he wrote was quite careful, and it is interesting to contrast some of its views with those at the time of the MDA session or later. I shall quote isolated fragments. Of his parents he says:

"My mother was a sensitive, hardworking woman with a lively interest in things. She had a deep love for her family, which translated itself into a constant desire for progress and well-being for all of us. She was always investing effort to this end. I loved her deeply.

"My father was a tough, good, honest man. Sure of himself, generous at times and selfish at others. A hard worker, raised in the constraint and discipline of a Spanish village. His life was guided by some simple rules of conduct and certain ethical principles that are broad and true."

The first childhood memory which he describes is a dining room:

"I lived in a house with adequate comfort. What I remember best is the dining room. This was large, rather elegant or at least that of a prosperous bourgeois. Very pleasant. It had a hanging buzzer, a highly polished mahogany table, a cupboard with glass doors full of lovely cups.

"During meals I remember that my greatest problem was French bread, which, having holes, could have worms inside and was therefore not good to eat. With regard to the people, I remember my mother, vaguely, some maids, some uncles, my paternal grandfather. For all of them I was a good boy, and it seems that they pampered me a lot, since I was practically an only child for a long time."

He ends the story of his childhood with the following paragraph:

"It seems that I had a wet nurse in this house, for they say my mother did not have milk. I remember this nurse most clearly at a later stage in life."

Of the period between this and the beginning of school he remembers financial difficulties at home, his great sadness about dropping a necklace of his mother's in the fireplace, watching a maid having sexual intercourse, speculating on female genitals and pregnancy, and the birth of his brother when he was six. Of the whole period he says: "I was just one more poor boy," which is in contrast to his pleasant memories of his first year in an American school, and the following in an English school, in both of which he felt appreciated by the teachers and enjoyed playing with his classmates.

Out of the twenty pages of his biography he devotes only five to his life before school, but these proved to contain what is most relevant to the events during the MDA session. The rest of his writing deals mainly with school and work, and only briefly mentions the death of his mother, when he was in the first year of the university and his rather loveless love affair, ending in marriage. Several events point to a lifelong feeling of shyness and prohibition in face of women and sex, which he is well aware of, and he ends the story of his life by pointing at his insecurity and underestimation of himself and his family, which, he believes, originated between the time of his first memories and school, but he doesn't know how.

One and a half hours after the ingestion of 120 mg. of MDA, the patient felt normal except for an exceedingly brief change in visual perception at the end of the first hour, when the shape of a hill in front of the house resembled to him that of a lion. Aside from this phenomenon, lasting not more than ten seconds and which would seem a rather normal fantasy (though he perceived it as unusual), he evidenced no further symptoms of being under the influence of a drug. The situation persisted after the intake of an additional 100 mg. of the chemical and another hour and a half of waiting, so I interpreted this to be a case of subjective resistance to the impending experience rather than physiological insusceptibility.

It was my own fantasy that the patient kept a very formal front, while another part of him was having the "drug experience" without "his" even knowing it. The verbal kind of communication that we were having did not seem to put him in touch with his ongoing experience at the moment, so I turned to the non-verbal level. I asked him to let his body do whatever it wanted most at the moment, without questioning it, and he went back to the couch which he had left minutes before.

He reported a slight feeling of weight on his body, a desire to lie down with all his weight and let his exhalation be more complete. I asked him to give in to this desire and purposely exhale with force at each breath. As he did this more and more forcefully, he felt first the need to contract his abdominal muscles, later his whole body, flexing his legs and thighs, spine, arms, and head. I kept coaching him into carrying this impulse to the extreme, until, about three minutes later, rolled into a fetal position, he exploded into laughter. The "drug session" proper suddenly began. Though his English was far from fluent, and I had not heard him speak it before, it was in English that he now spoke, as he laughed and expressed delight at feeling himself all over. Even on the following day, he spoke English while describing the experience:

"I was strictly myself. It's very funny that I wanted to speak English, and I was laughing at the man, the man that I was. In that man that I felt was laughing was another fellow. It was deep, deep, deep inside of me, when I was . . . my real self."

I am transcribing from a tape recording, and the faulty English leaves room for some ambiguity, yet it is clear that his deep pleasure was in *feeling himself*, which is what he was literally doing: "I felt my shoulders, the muscles on my arms, my abdomen, my back; I went on feeling myself —my legs, my feet. *It was me!*"

"And I was a right man, a beautiful man in a certain way, extremely masculine. Man, it is a good body . . . reflects what he is inside."

Throughout his entire life he had felt inadequate, he had doubted himself in all ways, and now he knew that he had felt himself to be ugly. He had even believed that something was wrong with his feet. Now he knew how illusory this was, how it was all based on his lack of perception of himself. About a month later, he would say of this experience:

"This feeling myself and finding myself in each part of my body, which was a materialization of myself, was something I loved, and at the same time I suffered. I loved it because it was myself, I suffered because I had for such a long time looked down on and postponed myself, even regarded myself as evil—in terms of an awkward and limited conception of myself. I felt sorry for myself."

He kept feeling his body, as he talked, for about a half-hour, and soon (much against his ordinary style) he had removed his shoes, opened his shirt, loosened his belt. He commented on how he took delight in feeling normal, symmetrical, well built, and how his organism was a successful embodiment of himself in all his individuality and uniqueness. Then he talked of touch as being the most reliable of the senses, the one that permitted the most direct contact with reality in all its richness. He digressed on the limitations of other senses and of the intellect itself, of analysis and logical constructions when it came to the grasping of ultimate reality. What would this pure and simple act of fully knowing be? This was possible only in God. What wonder and infinite beauty there was in God! Original and final being in whom everything was initiated and to whom everything naturally flowed. He talked excitedly in English for two hours without interruption as he contemplated the evolution of man in his search for God— the Greeks, the Romans, and Phoenicians, the Middle Ages in Europe, the Renaissance, capitalism, the estrangement of modern man and the need for solutions.

At this point, his enthusiasm was clouded by a different feeling. He looked as if he were searching for something and said, "This encountering of myself is painful!" I repeatedly instructed him to express and elaborate on his experience of the moment, but this he rejected more and more: "It is not this, it is not this moment, but something in my past. Something happened to me, and I don't know what."

At this stage, I had to leave the room for some minutes and I advised him to write during this time, as this would keep his thinking more organized. So he did, in large handwriting, about ten lines to a page, with not a few words in large capital letters, such as I, AM, and I. After nine pages, he became preoccupied with a recurrent mistake he had made, which consisted of writing "m" instead of "n." It was this that was bothering him when I came back, and he continued to write in my presence as we talked. "The great problem of the 'n,' " he writes on the fifteenth page, "which is it, 'm' or 'n'? I feel anxiety. I find that N is in ONE. One, one. ME. (I had written NE). Anxiety. Anxiety about my sins. Sinner. Anxiety. Anxiety. I turn to GOD. WHICH ARE MY SINS. The N. I get anxious.

"The bread with worms that I saw as a boy in the dining room. I still see it. It had holes, and in them were worms [*gusanos*].

Gusano
UN
UNA
NANA"

His associations have taken him from letter "n" to the disgust at worms that he had imagined in the dining room bread and then to his nanny, his wet nurse. Now he clearly evokes his feeling for this nurse. He writes: "Affection with some DESIRE. I tremble."

He feels the urge to understand something which he anticipates as very important in connection with his nanny, and, as he writes, he realizes that the substitution of "m" for "n" means substituting Mama for Nana. When he discovers this confusion, he writes several times: "Nana and not Mama. Nana and not Mama." He then remembers more of his nanny—how she took him out for walks when he was only two to three years old, how he slept with her and caressed her; how unconditional her love was, how at ease he felt with her. He remembers her appearance, her fresh face, her black hair, her open laughter. And as he remembers her, he feels sadder and sadder, sad at having lost her, of not having his nana any more. "Nanny left," he writes. "Alone. Alone. Alone. Anxiety. Mother was part, not all. Nanny was all. She left. Came to see me later. Loved me. Painful wound. I am. With pain. I am more myself. I am myself. I am myself with my nanny. How sad that she left. She gave me so much for nothing. No! Because she loved me, more than her own son. Poor boy, he lost his mother! She loved me so much! She left, and I remained alone among others. Mother. Searching for love."

He could now see all his life as a begging for love, or rather, a purchase of love in which he had been willing to give in and adapt to whatever others had wanted to see and hear. Here was the reason for his lack of direction in life, his submissiveness. He had lost something so precious, and felt so deprived! His thoughts now turned to the period when he was left "alone" with his parents. The change from Nana to Mama involved moving from the kitchen to the dining room. He felt constrained here, uncomfortable, unloved. Intimacy and warmth were now missing in his life; he was not unconditionally accepted as he was any more, but had to adapt, live up to certain demands, have good manners. Yet there was something in his feelings at this stage—feelings he was experiencing again in the session—which he could not grasp adequately or even feel clearly. There was more than pain, more than love for Nanny and loneliness. He felt anxious, and in this anxiety lay something which he tried to understand better. "What did you feel toward your parents?" I kept asking, and no clear reply came at first. Then it was the question, "Why did they let my nana go? Why did my nana leave me? Why did you let my nana leave me? Why?" It seemed to him that she had been fired. Mother was jealous, perhaps, because he loved her best, or because his father had an affair with her. "And what do you feel in the face of this, now that they have fired her?" His anxiety increased. "Did you accept this without protesting? If you did, perhaps you felt guilty . . ." And now he has it: guilt. This is what he felt. Guilt for not having stood up for his nana, not defending her, not leaving with her. Now it seems to him that this was the point. He wanted to leave; furthermore, he was planning to leave the house, but his parents did not allow him to. "It was horrible . . . a sense of weakness, weakness!" But now he also remembers that after this he pretended to be weak, he just played the good, weak boy, because when he didn't, there was something very disgusting, something very unpleasant that they did to him. "They came up with all this stupid thing of guilt and hell. I had a very real conception of the world, clear and clean. I feel it . . . and then came a host of demons, devils of another world, pain of punishment . . . things that weren't in my scheme, and were imposed on me. Who did this?" His maternal grandmother? This is not clear. He goes on reminiscing about the threats of punishment, sin, hell, and devouring fire. "I had great trouble in believing that. To me, fire was fire, and if people went to hell, there was no blame. And the person would have no body, and therefore nothing in which he could suffer. So this was a lie, a trick, a trick. For what? To make me behave. Ha, Ha! A trick to make me behave. So I would be a bastard rather than be mistaken. I would be a bastard, but a real one!"

As he goes on talking of fire and hell, now he suddenly evokes the image of glowing coals on which he inadvertently dropped a necklace, and the sorrow of not finding the pearls any more. Now he understands that sorrow. It was not his mother's necklace, as he had believed, but his nanny's. It belonged to that woman who had given so much, invested so much effort, having nothing, and who was so ill-treated. And then somebody had spoken of hell. A maid perhaps?

"No, I am certain it was somebody else, somebody who argued with authority. I believe it was my mother . . . my mother! It was my mother. She was lying to me. Yes, it was my mother. How awful! How stupid! And she made me live this guilt! And this striving to be what I wasn't, and the fear to be what I was! What narrowness and stupidity! What insistence on making me to her taste, damn it! She didn't have a child to *have* him, but to *make* him. To make him into her image! And she forced me into this stupid thing of sin and hell. They could not be good and fair without this stupid thing. What an idiotic lady! What a status-seeking woman, damn it! No authenticity. Perhaps there is more . . . a postponement of values. What for? To play the sweet young virgin, to play the lady. And my father is a bastard, too, for that; they both exploited an image. Ouch, how tough it is to see your parents shrink! How small do I see them now! It seems that they joined forces against me. Not against me, but against Nana, against life. Now I remember how they regarded me as unintelligent. I was very perceptive, intelligent, and I could fool them, ha, ha! Yes, using precisely their arguments, the arguments they used to put me down, more than put me down. Terrible! This is more terrible! They subordinated my life, the life of their favorite son, to such a pile of rubbish!"

This is far from the picture of his parents and the feelings that he expressed toward them in his autobiography. He had even remembered the dining room as beautiful. His intuition was right in telling him that something had gone wrong with him at an early age. A complete change had occurred in his feelings in that these were buried and replaced by a set of pseudo-feelings acceptable to his parents. No wonder that he felt limited and unfulfilled!

The session started at noon, and at 3 a.m. the following morning the patient went to bed. He went on thinking about this throughout the next day, and around noon he dictated to a tape recorder, interrupted by outbursts of weeping, a description of what had occurred to him the previous day and what he was feeling at the moment. This is how he ends:

"I have to reflect upon this: Why do I think my nurse suffered so much? Or was it myself that really suffered? She was so detached from so many things that it is possible that she did not suffer when told to leave. She just felt sorry for the boy who remained alone. That was her only sorrow. And for me the sorrow was staying alone, completely unadjusted. I suffered indeed, from a brutality. I suffered because my nana was leaving, I suffered because she was fired. I suffered for remaining alone. I suffered because she was unfairly treated, and I suffered from my impotence. Not being able to do anything! It was losing a part of myself. What lack of consideration on the part of my parents! Lack of care, mismanagement, selfishness. They did not love me at all. Sheer theatrics. Sheer theatrics. Perhaps in the course of time they have seen how satisfying it is to love a son, and they have loved him, but I think that I was not loved at the beginning. I was pampered, it is true, but the feeling of love was only with my nana.

"Now came the problem that I had in appearing as a master with a mask, in order to be accepted in this new environment. It was my home, it is true, but it was new, since my nana was not there. And I then understood that I could have a lot of things by pretending to be good and weak. That was the mask I wore. I think I wore it until yesterday. I have always wanted to appear different from what I am. And I have always doubted what I am, doubted my qualities. And now I see that I have always worn this mask, and I know how to adjust it to people and circumstances. This I learned very early, to be a good boy, because otherwise . . . Ah! Now I remember that they once told me that I had sucked the milk of a *huasa* (ignorant peasant), and that was why I was so crude. I feel honored to have taken my nana's milk! It is milk, milk, milk, milk, milk, of real breasty breasts! Of a really womanly woman! They said such things to degrade me. They thought their boy was crude, that he had the inclinations of a *huaso*, and therefore they inhibited me or pushed me around so that I would not seem too much like one. I gradually gave in, it seems. A child is flexible, very flexible. I really didn't notice that I was giving in, then. Now I understand the trouble they took to put me into those schools. These were truly good, but they were a means of social climbing. They wanted me to feel guilty for having nursed from a peasant's blood. What a way to degrade my nana! That blood was the noblest of all!

"They slowly managed to make me betray this. And this is my other sorrow: having betrayed my feelings, not having seen her any more, not having told her how I loved her, not having loved her any more—though deep down I always have loved her, and I have lived with gratitude for her. Only with her have I experienced love in my life. Somewhat with my mother, later, but not the same. And this, which was so strictly mine, I forgot and postponed. This is the root of the sorrow: having abdicated from myself. I found it: *the sorrow of having abdicated from myself*! I won't take it any longer. I am going to be what I am and whatever I may be!"

I believe that this is a remarkable document, in that it coherently describes a few hours that effected a radical change in a person's psychological condition. In it is portrayed a process that is the aim of psychotherapy, and one that is normally achieved over a long period of time. Drugs can facilitate the process, but even with their help it is exceptional to witness a "one-day cure" of the extent shown in this instance. Many people were surprised to see the changes in the patient's expression and demeanor on the following days. He stopped using eyeglasses, except for reading, and the style of his dress lost its formality. Subjectively, his feeling of his own body changed, in that he retained some of the heightened physical awareness and pleasure experienced with MDA, and not only his eyesight seemed to improve but his auditory discrimination. In his thinking he felt more security, as he could maintain the certainty of certain things, and this showed in his work and professional dealings. He felt an abundance of energy which was unknown to him, except in childish play, which he could now remember from his early years. Life was now basically enjoyable, and he knew to what extent he had lived in a state of depression. As to the lack of direction that he felt in his life, this was replaced by a desire for further personal development and a concern for human development in general, which he has successfully been serving in creative ways through his profession.

This definitely fits with the picture that he gave of his nurse when he was able to remember her, but for one who knows him well it is hard to find better terms to describe *him*. It would seem that the qualities which he was projecting he was now able to express. This he did first for himself, in his quest for self-perfection, and for his children, in the quality of the company he gave them. Then came his active concern for society, in his work, and only at the end of a year did he feel real love for his wife. (This step was the outcome of a session of harmaline and MDA which could be described only at great length. Since it represents in many ways an elaboration of the one summarized here, I have omitted it from this account.)

I feel that one of the values of this case history is in the light it sheds on the relevance of the past and its explanation to the healing process in emotional disturbances. It can be seen that it is not remembering the facts that is important, nor even remembering feelings, but the change in *present* views and feelings which is involved in acknowledging and confronting reality, present or past. The patient's view of his present, before therapy, was part of the "mask" that he was wearing, part of a role he had learned by which he became a "good" boy having a good boy's feelings toward his parents. These feelings could be maintained only by "forgetting" the facts which did not support them, facts which would give rise to other feelings, not compatible with his role. Living up to his artificial self-image—the self-image created to meet his parent's demands—meant giving up his own experience, ignoring what he had seen, heard, felt ("abdicating from myself"). This was probably taking place in every aspect of his perception, not only in the interaction with people but in the ordinary use of his senses. And this was evidenced by the improvement in his eyesight after therapy, his discovery of unseen nuances and unheard sounds in nature. Wearing a mask seems to be an all-or-nothing affair. It cannot be kept just for the parents; it sticks so close to the face that it also interferes with the sight of nature and the hearing of music. By the same token, it is an all-or-nothing affair for a person to be himself—that is, to use his own senses, think his own thoughts, feel his real feelings. There cannot be both programming and a free flow of feelings and thoughts. Only an openness to the unknown within permits the discovery of every instant—as with the god in Apuleius' story who would stay with Psyche only on condition he not be asked who he was.

For this patient, "being himself," opening up to his own feelings, whatever the circumstances, meant opening floodgates which were built to defend the landscape as he saw it. Early in his life he knew that a view of his life like the one he grew up with could be maintained only at the cost of suppressing reality. This he must always have known unconsciously (even though he consciously ignored it, as he did all the rest) and he therefore kept his conscious life in a watertight compartment. This explains his resistance to the effects of MDA.

And since his defensive system was a highly intellectualized one, it is understandable that a non-verbal approach was the most successful in bringing him to a position of spontaneity. As he himself commented early in the session, even the perception of his body had been replaced by an *a priori* image of himself, but this was surely a less guarded area and more safely questioned than his life style, character, or feelings for other persons. Once a direct contact with reality was established, and it was really "he" who was feeling the true sensations of his body, the gates were open, and he was in touch with a chain of associations that could potentially lead him to any experience on the same level of reality.

It may be useful to think of the healthy individual as a system in which all parts are in communication and therefore every action, feeling, or thought is based upon the total experience of the organism. An aspect of such availability of experience is remembering—either overt, conscious remembering or the implicit memory involved in taking past experience into account as a clinician does when making a diagnosis, or a hiker before taking a leap. This does not happen in neurosis. Here a person's feelings or behavior are not based upon the totality of experience, but part is "shut off" so that he lives in a fragment of himself at a time. In most adults some narrowing of personality has taken place, so that the psychological island on which they live is not the whole territory into which they were born. And since childhood is the time of the greatest spontaneity and unity, it is childhood memories in particular that become dissociated from present experience.

It can be seen from the above case history how incompatible it was for the boy, at a given age (probably three to four), to feel sadness and anger and at the same time to be accepted by his parents—the only support he was left with. He could only suppress his feelings by suppressing the thoughts that caused them—i.e., forgetting. Remembering was then a threat to his security, to his feeling that he was acceptable to the grownups. Yet the adult man who came for therapy is not in the same situation any more. His active forgetting, his defensive structure, has persisted in him as a useless remnant of his biography, a scar, an anachronous device that protects him from a danger that long ago ceased to exist. For there is no real threat to him any more in thinking one way or another about his parents. The world is large, and he does not need them any more as he did when he was three years old. Freud said that neurosis is an anachronism, and in that fact lies the possibility of psychotherapy. In a way, this can be conceived as an exploration of the feared and avoided regions of the soul, whereby it is discovered that there is nothing threatening or to be avoided in them.

There may be sorrow, or anger, as in the present instance, but only through a fearless acceptance of such can the sum of a person's experience be integrated into the whole of a healthy personality.

The cure of this patient can be viewed as a shift from a way of being and feeling as he once learned that he "should" be or that it was convenient for him to be, to his "true" being—that corresponding to the imprint of his life experience on his constitution. It can be seen that his neurotic pattern—"mask," idealized self—consisted of a replica of his parent's distorted perception of the boy and their own aspirations for him, at a time when he felt alone and greatly needed their love. A salient aspect of this was that they saw him as crude and unintelligent and wanted him to be well educated, well mannered, and refined. So they forced him to withhold anything which would be "vulgar" and forced him to regard culture as a "must," without which he would have felt like a worthless simpleton. The compulsive quality of the process made it something rigid, which turned him into an over-formal, unspontaneous, wordy intellectual incapable of enjoying simple things. Such a process of substituting an image for life, a set of "shoulds" for true experience, lies at the root of every neurosis, however different the circumstances may be that lead to the building of the mask and however unique its features.

What seems unusual in this patient's history is the neat demarcation line between a time of normal development in an atmosphere of love, and that in which he was faced with the demand of adapting to disturbing influences. It is conceivable that such a shift from Nana to Mama which caused a parallel shift from "being" to "appearing" may have been a source of difficulty for the boy in his speech, since he must have sought his nana in his mother and must sometimes have called her by the wrong name. And as Nana and associated thoughts became forbidden to him, the word itself, like Mama, must have become loaded with the conflicting feelings.

It was a happy though blind intuition which I had in advising the patient to write, thus allowing the buried conflict to emerge through decades onto his writing pad. The channels between his past experience and the present one of writing letters had been opened by the agency of MDA, but it surely would not have become apparent through the highly automatized activity of adult speech. One can conjecture as to what might have happened if the patient had not been led into writing. Would his repressed feelings and memories have gained access to the present by another, different route? Could it be that once the associative channels are open, unification takes place along the path of least resistance—as when water falls down a mountainside, changing its course to accommodate the obstacles in its way?

The following histories may suggest an answer:

The first concerns a thirty-five-year-old man who had been engaged for years in the discipline of a spiritual school in the hope of becoming a more complete human being. He expressed this hope in his first interview, pointing out that to be really a "man" would imply qualities such as a will, responsibility, freedom, which he was far from having developed. However true these thoughts may have been, it soon became apparent that the patient's feeling of not being a complete man involved a specific fear of his being a homosexual, which he hardly dared confess to himself, let alone to his spiritual guides. Such fear was part of a persuasive feeling of insecurity, as there was a constant implicit assumption in him that if he were to be spontaneous, others would see him as effeminate and "unmask" him. This insecurity spoiled his relationship with people, especially in his profession as a physician, and it had become his greatest concern. "I want to be sure that this insecurity is based on illusory fears, and that I am not a homosexual, or whether I have reason to fear . . ."

The following is the autobiographical information most relevant to his symptom—according to the patient's account prior to the MDA treatment:

"From information given to me repeatedly and with much emphasis by members of my family, my mother had to spend the nine months of her pregnancy in bed since she had a heart disease that later led to her death [when the patient was nine]. When I was born, the midwife was upset at the difficulty of the delivery and she twisted my right foot. For that reason, I was not able to walk until I was approximately five years old, at which age I was cured after many treatments.

"All these circumstances that surrounded my birth caused my parents to give me a lot of care, and they thus spoiled me, made me nervous and stubborn, which in turn made my older brother very angry. He did not dissimulate his irritation, but was constantly bullying me and calling me 'little pansy' and 'sissy.' I suffered very much for this and was permanently crying, since he was six years older and much stronger, and I could not fight him, and the times in which I tried to defend myself I got the worst of it. I would get so mad at him that on some occasions I threw knives or scissors at him and hurt him. In spite of what I have said, my brother was my father's favorite, since he pointed to him as an example of intelligence and manliness, and always encouraged him and approved of what he did. This was never the case with me.

"Since my brother did not let me play with him and I had no friends, I had to spend my time with my sisters— especially with the older of them, whom I love very much and to whom I am very close. From this relationship, I think, I picked up the effeminate manners for which my brother scorned me and which gave me problems during the first years of school.

"As to my mother, though I believe that she loved me, she never expressed this affection, in contrast to my father, who was much more expressive than she was."

About one hour after the intake of 100 mg. of MDA (a small dose for this patient), he reported some dizziness, and nothing further developed for the following fifteen minutes. At this point, I asked him to look at my face and report on whatever he saw in my expression. At once he felt that my way of looking at him was similar to his stepmother's, so I asked him to pretend I actually was his stepmother looking at him with the expression that he perceived. How would he translate this expression into words? What would "stepmother" say to make her attitude more explicit? "Sissy!" she would say. "Sissy! Sissy! Always running after your father, attached to him like a little girl." Now I asked him to answer her as he would have answered as a boy if he had dared to say what he felt. "I hate you! I hate you!" For the following five minutes or so, I asked him to shift from one role to the other and thus sustain a dialogue with his stepmother, which led to further expression of his feelings of being victimized, his helplessness, his need for his father as his only protection from her attacks. At this point, a reminiscence gradually began to dawn on him. "Something happened with the gardener—there was a gardener in the house—and something happened, I don't remember what—it was in the garage, *that* I remember—I see myself sitting on his lap—can this be true?" Then there was an image of the gardener's penis and his sucking it, then a feeling of his face being wet, all of a sudden, and his perplexity. All this had something to do with little pictures which came in cigarette packages, and he gradually remembered that this man gave them to him in exchange for sexual manipulations. And he did not want them for himself . . . no, for his sister . . . yes, for his sister he would do this, so that she would have these little prints for her collection . . . for she was competing with his older brother, he now recalls, and his brother . . . (now he remembers the important part) . . . his brother caught him! He remembers him looking into the garage, and he remembers his own fear—his brother would tell his parents!

It took about five hours to reconstitute the whole situation brought about by the long-forgotten episode. Most of his insights and memories are summed up in the following pages written on the following day:

"When I was caught by my brother I was very afraid. I ran to my sister and told her I had been discovered and that Fernando, who did not love me, would tell mother on me. She was very afraid of my father and was so frightened he would beat her that she begged me to plead guilty and say that I had liked what I had done. 'Please, you are the king of the house, they will not beat you, but me, yes.' I believe she was affectionate to me in order to get my father's love in exchange.

"When Fernando caught me, he thought, 'Ha, ha! The king of the house is a sissy! I am the only man.' My mother was in a rage. 'I will beat you! Why did you do it?' 'Because I liked it.' 'Ah, so you liked it!' and she filled my mouth with pepper. I kept saying, 'I liked it, I liked it, and I will tell Daddy on you!' She became more angry and thought, 'Just like his father.' 'Aha, so you liked it!' And she sprained my foot.

"My sister: 'Poor little fellow! What have they done to you because of me, because you would not tell on me? They have sprained the foot of the king of the house. Poor little kid.'

"Younger sister: 'So you are to blame! See what they have done to Roberto on your account. You are bad. I am going to tell on you.'

"Father: 'See what Sarah did! How did you dare get the boy into this? It is you that is to blame!' And he hit her with a ruler on the soles of her feet. 'Don't beat her, Daddy. I liked it, I liked it!'

"Mother: 'What have I done? I sprained his foot, and my husband will get angry. Forgive me, Roberto, I didn't know what I was doing.'

"I: 'You stink, Mother, why don't you bathe? Don't pick me up at school, Mother, because I feel ashamed of you. I want my father to go. He is nice, you are bad. You don't love me, you sprained my foot.'

"Mother: 'There goes the pansy again. He wants to go with his father, the two of them are of the same kind. Weak. The only man in the house is Fernando. He is my son, he is like me.'

"I: 'So that hurts you to see that I am a pansy. That is what I am going to be, and I will tell my father every time you call me that.'

"Father: 'What a bitch I married! What has she done to her son! I can imagine what she thinks of me—just the same as of him. In truth, the only man in the house is Fernando, who resembles her.'

"Fernando: 'My father loves Roberto best, but after telling on Roberto I have Mother to myself.'

"Younger sister: 'After telling on Sarah I have Father for myself. Poor little kid! How sad it is that they have sprained his foot. See, Daddy, how I love Roberto, too.'

"Fernando: 'Pansy, pansy! The only man in the house is me.'

"I: 'Daddy, Fernando called me a pansy.'

"Father: 'Don't bother your brother, Fernando. Don't you see that he is nervous since the accident with his foot?' "

The form of this document is reminiscent of the actual course of the session, in that I asked him to impersonate the different individuals in his family and express the feelings of each in face of the situation. When all that has been quoted was clear to him he became concerned with the vague recollection of a later event. The process of gradual reminiscing was similar to the previous one—the room where his mother lay in bed, his future stepmother talking to the nurse, something about the dosage of a medicine, his wish that his mother would die, and his guilt thereafter. By the time the effects of the drug had worn off, he definitely felt that he had killed his mother by giving her a greater number of drops than those prescribed, but at the same time he doubted the reality of the whole episode that he was "remembering," which in turn was rather vague.

During the following two days, the patient could do very little else but ponder on the events discovered under the influence of the drug. He alternately accepted them as true or distrusted their reality, deeming them illusions caused by MDA. On the other hand, he felt that the process that had begun with the session was not complete and insisted (unsuccessfully) on remembering more of the circumstances associated with his mother's death. As time went by, the feeling of reality of the sexual episode increased, and this paralleled the disappearance of his doubts with regard to his masculinity. His security (self-assurance) also increased greatly in his contact with people in general, and he felt that he could be more spontaneous, though now he was burdened by an unconscious feeling of guilt. He did not care much whether he was a homosexual or not and for the first time in his life could discuss the matter openly with others. His real guilt now lay in feeling that he was a murderer and that he could not confess. A dream that he had some days after the session impressed him very much. In an episode of this he was at his mother's funeral, and tigers came in through the window. He felt that these were expressions of his own anger, an anger that he had buried very early in his life, and only now was beginning to sense through a curtain of symbols and memories.

The change that took place in this patient's understanding of his life and feelings may be noted by comparing the first paragraph of an autobiography written before the treatment with the beginning of another version of it written about a week after the session. Before the session he begins as follows:

"I was born on the 1st of August of 1930 in the home of a businessman who was very respected in our circle and belonged to one of the oldest families in town."

This is an attitude reminiscent of that which the previous patient displayed in speaking of the dining room at home. There the subject initially ignored his real feelings for this place, which had been the major torture room of his life, and had replaced them with pride in his parent's social standing, conveyed by the polished table and fine cups. In this opening, too, the patient highlights his parent's "respectability" and, in so doing, looks at them in terms of the values which were most important to them. Into these values they have also molded him to a very high degree, as he, too, has had to "abdicate from himself," and when a child abdicates from his real feelings and thoughts he is left at the mercy of external influences. For this particular boy, "being himself" meant such frustration and anger at his mother and older brother that he could not possibly cope, especially in the absence of a strong father to take sides with him. His father did show some understanding for his son, and so we can understand the boy's great attachment to him, but he was weak and submissive. After the session, the patient no longer speaks of him as a respectable man who took great care of him and was expressive of his affectionate feelings, but says, "I see him as a very weak man whom I have always dominated—whom I have even scolded on many occasions. He does not know what he wants and is very cowardly. That is, he has all the defects that I see in myself. I have never been able to speak openly with him because he is very gossipy and would not hesitate to tell others of my affairs. He never supported me in anything."

This view of his father is without doubt closer to his real feelings, and the shift in point of view is probably related to the fading away of his perception of himself as homosexual. It may be expected that, as he grows more open to his real feelings, he will experience less need to be supported by father or father-figures in the masculine world. He is one step closer to this, but a sense of guilt still prevents him from reconciling the unknown state of his childhood with his present view of his mother. It is enlightening to trace the feelings toward the women in his family throughout the time of his treatment. All that he says of his mother in his first autobiographic report is in a paragraph that has been already quoted: "As to my mother, though I believe that she loved me, she never expressed this affection, in contrast to my father, who was much more expressive than she was." His frustration here is almost unexpressed, not only in that he does not speak of his own reaction, but in that he does not blame his mother. Instead, he constructs the view that a character trait of hers—not being expressive—caused her not to show her affection.

Elsewhere in his account, he tells of his reaction to his mother's death: "When I was nine years old, my mother died from a long-standing heart disease. I remember, or I believe recalling, that I did not cry and that I did not want to leave the house of a cousin where I had been sent to keep me away from the funeral rites, and where I was having a good time."

Of his stepmother, he openly says, "I hated her. This woman never loved me and she separated us from one another—except me from my older sister, who always showed me great love and whom I love very much."

During the session it became apparent to what degree this older sister represented a mother substitute and was so important to him that he not only agreed to the gardener's manipulations for her sake but was able to blame himself for it and thus protect her from being punished. Yet it also became clear that it was a poor substitute for his mother's love, since he did not really experience it as true affection but as a role she adopted and a manipulation to attract her father's love. In view of such later insight, we may regard the patient's initial statements of mutual love with his sister as self-deception, at least in part, and as the outcome of a desperate need to believe that somebody loved him.

On the day following the session, in addition to the writing that has been quoted, he jotted down the following remarks on his mother and stepmother:

"When my mother died, I did not cry. On the contrary, I was happy that she died. I got along better with my stepmother, until my father separated us."

From this it would seem that much of the hostility previously experienced toward his stepmother was the displacement of repressed hostility toward his mother, and as he could now acknowledge some of it (implied in the fact of having felt happy at her death), his (retrospective) feelings toward his stepmother improved. A similar displacement seemed to be taking place in his anger toward his father, since he initially blamed his stepmother for bringing about separation in the family, and he now sees that his father separated him from her. That his stepmother acted like a screen on which were projected the unacceptable feelings toward his parents is further confirmed by the course of the MDA session, which began with the perception of his stepmother's expression in my face, but the dialogue with her turned it into one with his mother as he proceeded.

In the autobiographic pages written a week after the session the patient says the following of his mother: "I remember her as a woman of exceptional strength. I think she was very good, but at the same time lacking in affection, or at least in the expression of it. I recall that I kept asking her whether she loved me, and she would answer, 'Leave me alone, I am very tired!' Every once in a while she gave me a kiss, but I don't remember her as ever having *caressed* me." As to his stepmother, he sees her as "a lazy and dirty woman; she used to beat me and drive my brother to beat me all the time. My sisters used to defend me. If I cried or told on her to my father, she called me a sissy. She spared the food, and I think that the incipient TB which I had was related to this—or so my father thought, at least . . . I hated her as I never hated anybody else, and she took her revenge by calling me sissy, stupid, lazybones . . . But I also feel sorry for her. How must she have suffered with such a pack of monsters as we were!"

It can be seen that the patient's views and feelings have reverted to some extent to those prior to the session. Not completely so, though. In his last statement about his stepmother, there is an implied recognition that she was the target of his own irrational reactions, and he conceives of her attacks as a revenge. On the other hand, there is some difference between the original statements about his mother and the foregoing: ". . . lacking in affection, or at least in the expression of it. I recall that I kept asking her whether she loved me, and she would answer, 'Leave me alone, I am very tired!' " Here there is a distinct acknowledgment of his insecurity and frustration, and the notion that his mother did not love him is closer to being accepted and expressed. The way in which he constructs the sentence ("lacking in affection, or at least in the expression of it") is a miniature replica of the process whereby the contents of the session as a whole are being repressed again and restrained. First comes a clear statement, then what appears to be a rationalization, a justification of the mother that may be understood as a means of holding back the unacceptable feelings that he would have if the former statement were certain. This was typical of him throughout the process described here. Under the effect of MDA, he would vividly describe a scene (sperm wetting his face, for instance) and then become concerned with its reality. "Can this be true? Did this actually happen? No. This is just my imagination. I cannot really remember this. I was too young to remember anything. But then why do I see this so clearly? And everything seems so coherent! If this is true . . . Yes, it must be true. Can it be true? What do you think, Doctor, can this be true?"

Long sequences of this nature took place between successive steps in understanding or remembering, and, as I have mentioned before, the days following the session were followed by intensive questioning of the same type.

Soon after working with this patient, I left the country for two months and expected to see him again upon returning, but he now felt that the help received in the meantime from a fellow therapist of mine was all that he needed and that he would rather concentrate on the spiritual quest as before. I have met him accidentally on occasion since, and it is my intuition from the quality of this contact that the process initiated on the day of the session was never completed. Even so, the treatment was effective in affording the patient the symptomatic relief that he sought, in giving him greater self-reliance (which made his relationship with others more satisfactory), and in bringing about greater spontaneity in his life.

This patient's hesitancy in accepting the truth of the events recalled while under the influence of the drug illustrates a reaction frequently observed in the period following a therapy session. It would seem that repressed memories can be accepted only when a parallel change in the patient's attitudes to or interpretation of them takes place, in such a way that they are no longer threatening to his present "balance." In truth, the implicit fear of change that makes a patient ward off certain events or experiences is an intimation of a secret recognition of the instability of his present situation. Like the fear of high places in those who unconsciously want to fall, the fear to remember bespeaks a wish of the organism to fall back into the truth, a hidden desire to see.

It would seem that MDA may be instrumental in inducing a state where nothing is threatening, and where the person can unconditionally accept his experiences, for his security lies elsewhere than in an image of himself. After such a phase is over, the information in the person's consciousness may clash with his current views, or elicit reactions (like condemnation of a parent) that he cannot allow himself. The result may then be anxiety or horror at the events remembered, denial of their reality, or amnesia with regard to the whole episode. For change to occur, time has to be allowed, so that the gap between the reaction to the critical event and the patient's personality structure can be bridged, as was successfully achieved within twenty-four hours by the subject of our first illustration. When assimilation of the critical event is insufficient during a session, the process may continue for the following day or month or be resumed in a *subsequent* session with the drug.

The following case is particularly illustrative of the operation of defenses after successive MDA sessions and shows how in each one of them the patient was able to see more of his past and also integrate more into his post-session awareness. The patient is a thirty-year-old stutterer who had been in psychotherapy for two years and who had experienced considerable improvement in his symptoms. He was referred to me by his therapist because she felt that the lack of emotional contact in the present therapeutic relationship was precluding further progress, and she hoped that a drug could help the patient in dropping his over-intellectualized and normative approach in the therapeutic encounter.

When questioned as to his own interest in further therapy, the patient explained that stuttering was no longer his main concern, but irritability at home, an absence of feelings, and a lack of contact with things in general. "I feel that I don't touch the ground while I walk, but float above it; I don't feel fully in touch with anything." He often used impersonal phrasings at the first interview (i.e., "*There is* tension in my arms"), and when I called this to his attention, he explained: "*This* is my essential concern: I want to be able to speak in the first person!"

One of several psychological tests used prior to the treatment proper was the HPT,[3] consisting of a series of human photographs to which the subject is invited to respond in terms of what he likes or dislikes in them. The most remarkable feature of his responses was the rejection of many faces which he perceived as criminal. He related this feature in his reactions to his own unconscious perception of himself as delinquent, as evidenced in dreams in which he was persecuted by the police.

The most salient datum in the patient's history, as remembered by him before the treatment, was that his stammering began at the time of his first year in school, of which he recalled very little. He had very few memories prior to this time in his life—his mother going to the clinic to have his younger brother, himself naked for a sunbath and hiding from a new maid, his parents buying him a gift. Of the next school he remembered vividly a blond little girl that loaned him a pencil. He said that throughout his childhood he used to lock himself in his father's closet and secretly give in to fits of rage and crying until he could not stand the heat any longer. He described the relationship to his parents as normal and uneventful and said that he used to tell his mother everything until he was twelve or thirteen, when he changed in this respect, and she complained of his loss of confidence in her. At school, he was a rather good student, but avoided sports. Since the age of fourteen, he had taken an active part in different Catholic youth organizations. He had two brief love affairs before marrying, one at sixteen and the other at twenty. He met his wife at the university and established a good friendship with her that still endured after six years. He had now been married for four years and had two children, for whom he felt much tenderness.

[3] Human Preference Test, by the present author.

After the ingestion of 150 mg. of MDA the patient's first symptom was anxiety, a fleeting wish to cry, which he controlled, and then a sensation of his arms and chest being smaller, thinner. "Does this suggest anything?" "Being a child, I suppose."

For the next hour or so, he enjoyed the music greatly and playfully moved his arms and legs to its rhythm. "Supple, as if I ran naked in the wind."

Aside from the experience described, most of the content of the seven hours that the session lasted was related to the patient's mouth. At first he felt that his jaw was clenched and tried to open it more and more with the help of his hands. He constantly felt his face and jaws. Then he initiated movements that suggested those of sucking, and when this was called to his attention, he intentionally engaged in sucking movements for a long time. All along, he felt that his jaws were tense and painful and kept feeling them. His lower and left molars were hurting, too, and this persisted until the following day. At another moment, he felt like opening his mouth wide and pulling his tongue out, and for some time, with his mouth wide open, he felt like exhaling forcefully. Then he felt cold, started moving to the music again, and went on opening his mouth, pulling out his tongue, or sucking. He explained (in English) that he had been concerned with his jaws earlier in his life, since at the time of puberty he did not want to masticate with force for fear of distorting the oval shape of his face.

The patient's first words, at some point in the second hour after the initial symptoms, were to say that he realized that he had never been loved, that this might have been so, but he never really believed and felt with certainty that somebody cared for him. After this, he spoke English and continued to use this language for the rest of the session, in spite of having only learned it in school and being far less fluent in it than in Spanish. On one occasion he spoke French, too, and at several points in the session he commented with surprise on the fact of having forgotten the Spanish language—but this did not seem to trouble him. He spoke a few sentences in Spanish again after imagining his father as the back of a seat with a metal frame. I asked him to talk to his father and he said in Spanish and with some resistance, "Why do you go away?" "Why don't you stay at home?" "Why don't you embrace me?"

Knowing that the patient's stammering had started during his first year of school, I questioned him about this period of his life, and he recalled a certain day on which a bunch of children unjustly blamed him for having pushed a smaller boy. One of them threatened to punch him in the mouth, but he could not quite remember whether he had actually been hit. He spent approximately an hour reflecting on the scene. He imagined himself with his mouth full of blood, tended to believe that he had begun stuttering on this very day, and thought that he must have felt a victim of great injustice and very helpless.

After this day and for the following month, the patient noticed a surprising effect of the session on his movements, which became supple and unusually coordinated. He felt it as he played the guitar and the recorder, as he worked in carpentry in his spare hours, and at night, when he no longer felt the usual discomfort of not knowing where to put his arms before sleeping. Aside from this physical effect, he felt unusually warm toward his children and patient in dealing with the events of family life. When presented once more with the HPT, two days after the session, his responses were very different from the week before; the main theme in his rejections was predominantly not that of "delinquent" traits any more, but half of his comments referred to expressions in the mouth area of the faces depicted. Those most often mentioned were fear and a wish to cry, too much showing of the teeth, or falseness. In such emphasis of the mouth and rejection of feelings expressed in it, the testing situation paralleled the subject's experience in the MDA session, during which the mouth had been the center of attention in terms of both physical sensations and fantasy.

Despite the well-being experienced by the patient, the therapeutic process described above suggested itself as incomplete for the following reasons:

1) Incomplete expression of feeling: At the beginning of the session, the patient felt like crying, but did not give in to the urge. At the end of the day, he feared that he might feel suicidal, but again felt only on the brink of sadness. These brief experiences, his life history (crying in closets), the lack of any intense feelings throughout the session, and the rejection of sad expressions in the test showed that he was still not ready to accept or even know his own emotions.

2) Incomplete recall: Symptoms of regression during the session (sucking movements, shrinking of the body) strongly suggest that the patient's mind was unconsciously wanting to come to grips with episodes in the past, and this is further confirmed by the school scene that he remembered in part. Yet here, as in the case of feelings, the patient only comes to the brink of remembering an episode, the existence of which he is able to sense. The emotions which he imagines that he had when bullied at school (crying, rage, impotence) match those that he perceived and rejected in the HPT.

3) Incomplete insight: The patient's experience indicates that he has grown up with a feeling of not being loved, that he missed his father, and that at least once he was permanently affected by being unjustly blamed and attacked by other children. This in turn suggests that he was facing the latter situation much on his own, without expecting any support from his parents or teachers. Again, this whole picture matches the feelings of anxiety and sorrow fleetingly experienced during the day of the session and subsequently perceived by the subject as foreign to his habitual views and feelings. The following day, he considered this experience of helplessness a mere theoretical possibility, to say nothing of his perceiving in his parents'

past behavior anything which would corroborate such feelings of aloneness or make them understandable.

On the whole, it can be said that the treatment with MDA led to the envisaging of a panorama that was not quite revealed. The patient was advised to attend weekly group therapy meetings to achieve greater awareness and expression of his feelings, and after three months he took part in a group session with MDA which I summarize here:

Early in this session, the patient, who sat next to one of the girls of the group, had asked her whether she wanted to be alone. When she nodded, he dropped to the floor, where he lay on the cold tiles. The cold led him to experience sensations known to him from some illness—cold and vomiting, *alone and helpless, unable to ask for help*, abandoned. He said he understood that it was a feeling of rejection that made him feel nauseated, cold, and alone. He then went onto a bed at one end of the room and gave in more and more to this feeling. He made soft moaning sounds which became longer and louder until they turned into insistent howls. After about half an hour of shouting, this became increasingly articulated. The first words were: "NO! NO! NO!" Then some minutes later, it was "Not mediocre! Not mediocre! Not mediocre!" And later still, he threw back insults at an imagined accuser: "Mediocre! Mediocre!" and then "Criminals! Assassins!" for a long time. He started hitting the bed, and later the wall, with his fists. In the process, he realized that the real target of his anger was his father. Then there were references to his teeth. "They fall by themselves! Mommy, they fall by themselves!" Interspersed with "No! No! Daddy! Daddy!" He called on his father for help as he was being forced into something by his mother and finally ended, softer, with the repeated utterance, "I have no Daddy, I have no Mommy."

The process lasted some four hours, after which he forgot everything. When witnesses informed him of what they had heard, he was able to recall to some extent what he had said or done, but not the situations of the past that he was reacting to. This is what he writes on the following day: "I think that the yelling was for several situations at the same time, in each of which I felt in a similar position —not being able to count on the protection and love of my parents, either because they denied it to me, because they were not at hand, or because I did not feel that they were close enough or that they could help me. Such situations could have been an experience at the dentist, being attacked by the children at my first school, or some illness during which I felt very badly and alone."

I am not reporting on all the experiences of the patient in the group, but it is interesting to note that throughout the day he felt an intense desire to be protected and caressed by other group members—along with an inability to ask for it.

Comparing the patient's first MDA session with the second, it is obvious that on the second he was able to recall and feel more (of his aloneness, frustration, and need), but at the expense of subsequent amnesia. In spite of the latter, I felt that the depth of the experience itself showed a relaxing of defenses and that this one might constitute a bridge to a following session in which his memories and feelings could be integrated into his conscious life. This was supported by the patient's responses to the HPT two days after the session. The change here was striking once more, and along with the rejection of weakness, a new theme became apparent, a type of critical, sardonic, and detached expression which in at least one of the pictures he associated with his father's.

The next session took place one month after the second and started out feverishly and with a lot of yelling. He seemed to be going through the same experience as in the previous session, but the situation that inspired his feelings was different. This began to unfold gradually as he gave in to his rage. "Your son is a thief. Your son is a thief.

Your son is a thief," he wrote on the following days—and after that, anger, defense, hatred: "No! No! It is mine, I found it lying on the floor! It is mine, mine, mine! I have not stolen it! I have not stolen anything! I found it. Criminals! Criminals!"

By the middle of the third hour he explained how he remembered that in his first or second year of school he found a small jewel (a diamond apparently), which he kept without knowing its value. He was accused of theft and he swallowed the stone. He clearly remembered that he was given an enema and forced to vomit, in order to retrieve the jewel. Now he had the fantasy of still having something inside. He vaguely distinguished two packages. A small one behind his sternum, and a larger one below. He opened the smaller one and found the diamond. "The other, which I scarcely saw and forgot, is still unopened," he stated later, and added: "In having discovered all this, I felt free from something very big and heavy, as if I could breathe deeply and for the first time in many years. But this desire to breathe deeply and violently pointed at something which I was not able to grasp." During the rest of the day, he interacted with others instead of withdrawing, as in the past group sessions. After the effects of the drug had worn off, he said goodbye to the other group members, and while doing so was brought to the verge of tears. Especially when saying goodbye to me, he felt very moved and kissed me on the face as a son would kiss a father. This was a dramatic contrast to the feelinglessness which had made him seek treatment.

On the following day, he was overcome by an intense sense that he really had no father or mother, and this made him feel as if he had killed them. He felt, too, that the pieces of a huge puzzle were falling into place: dreams, fears, life situations. Yet in the course of the week it seemed that a curtain was being drawn over his sight, his feelings were dampened again, and the story brought to mind during the session appeared to him as less and less real.

One further session was proposed to the patient for reasons similar to those which precipitated the previous one, and it is worth reporting that this particular one was to be both the least remembered and the most effective. In brief, during the first hours of the session, the patient felt like a woman and enjoyed this role; after this, he discovered that early in his life he had taken on a feminine identification on the assumption that he would thus attract his father's love. To be a woman meant, principally, to be feeling and sensitive, like his mother. But at some point in his life he had told himself, "Men do not cry,"—this phrase came up repeatedly in his MDA experiences—and he became anaesthetized. On this occasion, too, his feelings state led into a brief period of feelinglessness, incoherence, and then indifference. "The value of this was to see a caricature of myself," he later said. "What I am always, to some extent, I was then to the extreme." What happened in his unconscious while he was feeling like a woman or being incoherent or indifferent is hard to know, but only after this session did the patient feel that he had taken a definitive step toward emotional sanity. A fleeting state of anxiety made him realize that this was the condition in which he had lived all his life before the treatment and which he had not even remembered for some months. And furthermore, it seemed to him that the whole world had changed, even though he felt himself the same person. When questioned on the nature of the change, he said that it was difficult to put into words, but was something like "being related" to others. "I don't have to control others, for I no longer depend on their acceptance or rejection. I can accept them regardless of whether they accept me or not. If they do, fine; if not, too bad; but I have no need to spend energy in a sort of CIA activity to detect how I am to others." In addition, his efficiency at work has improved, according to his estimate, 1,000 per cent.

Some months after the beginning of his treatment, he summarized these changes in a letter, on the occasion of my last days in the country. Toward the end, he posed the question: "What happened during the last session that brought about the crystallization of this delicate upper crust of sanity, which I nevertheless feel is permanent? I could go on answering, 'Nothing . . . simple. While I was there, the world was replaced by a different one.'

"Some facts I see. During the first stage of the session, I lived in a closet, my hell. But now that I remember, the most unpleasant feeling that I can remember is that of rejection, and, reflecting well, that this was not so painful after all. Hell was nothing but the release of much feeling, and much of this was quite pleasurable. In the second stage, I could see myself as I have lived for years: incapable of loving."

This is how the person that suffered from feelinglessness ends his letter:

"Claudio, friend, I know that I cannot give you anything like what you have given me. I know that you have not even expected this letter. I know that you have not even expected the affection which you know that I can only feel in spite of myself. I know that you *accepted* me knowing that I hold a faith that teaches giving what you give, and which I imitated out of compulsion. I know that you are happy about me.

"Now you leave. I shall not thank you. That would be adding a flower to your garland, which you leave behind. I want to say to you what my father never heard, what I could never say to him, for I had no chance, or he did not give it to me, who knows?: I love you.

"My wife, my sons, others that meet me will never know of the friend that you are, but if they knew, they would have to smile, with the same smile that I now have, hidden, for a long time, for this occasion.

"Have a good trip."

The above-cited accounts of MDA therapy show both the episodic hypermnesia that the substance can elicit and the counteractive defenses that may set in, in the face of unacceptable self-knowledge.

In the interplay of remembering with anguish and forgetting or becoming confused, perceiving one's life and not daring to face it, lies the specific hell or purgatory of MDA, a counterpart of the better-known hells of mescaline or harmaline. But the picture of the effects of MDA would not be complete without a view of its specific paradise.

With many drugs, we find that there is a typical field in which a peak experience is expressed, when it does occur. This is, for instance, the domain of transcendence and feelings of holiness for LSD, that of beauty for mescaline, of power and freedom for harmaline, of loving serenity for MMDA. One may ask whether there is anything that could be regarded as the typical positive experience of MDA, and what this is like.

In an overview of some thirty sessions with the drug, I find that the most characteristic feature of those that convey a sense of completeness, depth, and integration is something that I would describe as an enhancement of the experience of I-hood.

In fact, just as the standard psychiatric term "depersonalization" has been used in connection with the state of mind often brought about by LSD-25 or mescaline, one could here use the converse term "personalization." Instead of the "egolessness" of ecstatic oneness with the world elicited by the former, there is here an emphasis on individuality and on the uniqueness of a given life. Indeed, some of the subjects have at one point or other in their session come upon a shared realization which they expressed emphatically with an identical statement: "I am! I am! I am I!"

This trait in "good" MDA experiences appears amply illustrated in the first case history presented in this chapter. Let us consider once more the terms in which the patient described his experience at the onset of effects of the drug, as he enjoyed feeling himself: "I was strictly myself." "I was laughing at the man that I was." "I went on feeling myself—it was *me!*" This experience resumed after some hours, while he was beginning to remember his childhood events, and he wrote in big letters, covering a complete sheet of paper, "I AM MYSELF."

One aspect of this experience is that it entails the sensing of the immediate reality. In contrast with the person under the effect of LSD, who is prone to see gods or devils, impersonal forces being manifested through his personal existence, here the individual's consciousness is centered on the unique qualities of his tactile, proprioceptive, auditory, and other sensations. And these by no means show demons or abstract principles, but the subject's particular reality. Records of MDA sessions abound in such discovery of particulars, which are often clues to unresolved past situations. A patient, for instance, noticed that his voice sounded fearful and submissive, as when he talked with his father, and this led him into a clarification of his past relationship to his father, followed by a greater freedom from such an anachronous pattern. He had probably always talked with this same voice, only he was not aware of this aspect of himself. Once he could *sense* himself, he could also become aware of his attitude, his past attitudes corresponding to the present one, and life episodes that brought them about. Thus it could be said that his perception of himself at the moment and his memory of himself in the past belong to the same *personal* domain and are linked by easy association chains. When one became the object of repression, so did the other, and the lifting of repression of both past and present went practically hand in hand.

The child's discovery of his individuality probably stems from the realization that he can control the movements of his body and exercise a will. In analogy with this, the adult rediscovering his I-sense in an MDA session often engages in some motor activity which is the embodiment and sign of his individuality. Moreover, on two occasions at least, such movements constituted an enactment of the playful spontaneity of a baby. In one of them, the patient started by engaging in wormlike movements that he felt were like those of a baby in a crib. Soon he started to make sucking movements, which he continued for some three hours, while other manifestations gradually set in. First, the sucking sounds, then the repetition of the syllable "ma," "ma, ma" again and again, then hitting the bed rhythmically with his fists as he shouted "ma, ma" louder and louder, and finally the word "I, I, I" repeated with the rhythm of his beating, with pleasurable forcefulness. Subsequently, and up to the time of the session's end, the whole panorama of his family relationships gradually unfolded.

Exactly converse was the sequence of events for another patient, whose *first* experience worth noting after MDA had taken effect was the sense of egohood: "I moved an arm and became keenly aware that *I* was moving it. *I* was there. What a wonderful thing, to be myself! I could feel every muscle, every part of my being, and all were I."

Shortly afterward, I showed him a photograph of himself with his father. His father was leaning on his shoulder in a gesture expressing both protectiveness and possessiveness. As soon as he saw it, he talked to his father in the photograph: "No, no . . . you are *you*, and I am *me* . . . No, no, no! I will not let you live my life, I will not let you lean on me. We are two different worlds, and independent of each other. I have been living your life, I have been carrying you inside and doing what you would, but this will not go on." He explained this further to me, discovering that, even in a love affair that he recently had, he could now see that it had been his father and not himself who was loving the girl.

A similar process went on as he looked at other photographs and evoked related memories. In face of each, he was aware of what his own feelings and interests at the moment were and where lay the distortion by which he was not being true to himself. Every time he could sense this he experienced great discomfort, until he relived the situation, experiencing not what had been but what would have been if he had been his real self, talking to the figures of his past out of a new stance that he now understood to be truly his own. Thereafter, he was able to enjoy a sense of unity again and the feeling of his own "I." "Only I live this instant, only I. I live an instant that is mine. Nobody has the right to live my life, and I am not to accept being burdened by extraneous life." "I don't want to lose this precious moment. To feel myself in the world, with others, is marvelous. Not the people, but oneself."

At one point, his attention turned to his masturbation at the time of puberty and his guilt about it. This was his view of it now: "It was important only because *I* was there, and in it I found my I, my support. Indeed, it was the only thing that *I* did, and this behind my own back."

This patient was a twenty-five-year-old man whose reason for consulting was a lack of spontaneity and freedom of expression that he was aware of in face of the persons about whom he cared most, especially his mother. When I handed him photographs of his mother he realized how she had manipulated him through her suffering and that he had failed to stand up for his real wishes and views. He lived out with intense feeling an imaginary encounter with her that ended in stabbing "her" with a knife on the floor in the midst of great anguish. He later wrote, "I remember what difficulty I had in killing you, Mother. I killed that life of yours that was living for myself. I could kill it so that I could then love you. I then gave you *my* love, and it was not your own love back, but that emanating from myself."

I thought at this point that there would be nothing else to deal with, since the patient's state was of contagious peace and balance, and the main issues in his life had been dealt with in the past five hours. Nevertheless, I kept showing him photographs. Most of them elicited inspired reflections, advice to his parents, objective appraisals. Yet when I showed him one of himself at one or two years of age he experienced disgust, relived an episode when his mother was forcing food into his mouth, and then felt that he was biting a breast. "Even then I was aware," he commented later, "that this was for my mother's lack of milk."

After a few minutes of silence, the patient's posture began to change and gradually became that of a fetus. There were no words, just a sudden spasm that he later explained as a reaction to an "imaginary" blow.

After three or four minutes more, he asked me to leave him alone for some time, since there was something into which he felt that he could not go with a witness. I was called in by him after five minutes or so, and he explained his recent experience. He felt that he had been present at the moment of the sexual act out of which he was born. He experienced his father as a tough male, and his mother as frightened.

I am impressed with the last events that I have recounted, regardless of their interpretation, because this was a young man who not only did not know about MDA but who also had never been exposed to psychoanalytic or other expectations of prenatal memories. Moreover, I know him as an exceptionally straightforward, honest person who sticks to what has meaning for him in his words, so that I can hardly imagine his weaving fantasies to put up an interesting show. Whether these are memories, and there exists an "I" independent of the structure of the nervous system that can remember what he described, I do not know, nor do I know anybody who does. Yet prenatal "memories" are a phenomenon of the human mind, observed in the case of analysis or hypnosis, and an account of MDA would not be complete without the description of this experience.

The uniqueness of this patient's session does not end

here, though. After a short time, the patient emitted a sudden cry and fell to the floor, raising his hands to his chest. After the event, he explained, "This was a death scene, and those stupid people had killed me." But now, for the first time in the last hours, he began to get restless, anxious, and uncomfortable. He expressed the feeling that he should not go any further, but kept hesitating. "I feel that this does not·belong to me any more, and it is not for me to know. I cannot bear the burden of another life." Yet, gradually, more scenes unfolded. He was a Nazi. He spoke fluent German in a voice that I had never heard in him before. He saw himself at a dinner table *"Hilde, bring mir die Suppe,"* he shouted. At another moment, he sang while crossing a field in the countryside.

Was all this a fantasy or a true recall of a previous existence? The patient had a German grandfather, with whom his family lived until he was four years old. Could this Nazi that he was identifying with have been his grandfather, or a transformation thereof in the child's mind? He could not answer my question. All that he knew was that he was feeling heavy. He felt afraid and nauseated at his own question, "Was that I? Myself? Was I that?" He felt burdened with guilt for that life *as if* it had actually been his. Finally, he decided that he would not take such a responsibility. He told his alter ego, "No. I cannot bear you. You are too heavy." Then he looked at the heater in the room and felt his own self once more—not just his ordinary self, but his recently acquired sense of "I": "Knowing that I listen, I do, I move, gives me an incredible power."

The issue became clear only after his arrival at home. He searched for photographs of his grandfather, and looking at them he felt again the same nausea that he had experienced while thinking of the Nazi. He saw his grandfather as dirty and lecherous. Then, looking at the photograph of a youth with a swastika, he later explained, "My face contorted, and I saw myself as on the day when I raped her." He felt a great relief and then set out to understand what had happened to him. Had he raped somebody? He was quite sure that physically he had not. Had he morally raped somebody? Had he destroyed somebody? Then memories started flowing from his mind. The way he had frightened his little brothers and enjoyed their fear, the way he had kissed that little girl . . . These and other recollections were the source, he now knew, of that feeling of dirtiness and nausea. For all that he was feeling toward his grandfather, he now felt toward himself. He now saw that he had been using the Nazi and his grandfather as screens to project his guilt upon, since he had been unable to take responsibility for himself.

In a note that he sent to me in the following days he ends with these words:

"I did these wrongs, and I must compensate for them with good.

"Here I am. *I*, with the responsibility for this *I*.

"I take it. I fully take responsibility for my *I*. I take my responsibility."

I think that this account is of interest not only for the light that it may shed on many other "past-life memories" obtained in hypnotic or mediumistic states, but in terms of an understanding of the effects of MDA, as is my concern in this chapter. As with hypnosis, the MDA state is favorable to hypermnesia and time regression, but it also appears to bring about the emergence of false memories ("screen memories") and particularly the identification with them in what may be seen as a state of temporary shift in identity. The quality of these age regressions or shifts in identity is more often than not that of dissociation, in that the ordinary personality tends to forget, deny, or feel an incompatibility between its premises and values and the validity of the events "recalled."

Yet, paradoxically, the experience of I-hood or individualized selfhood that crowns a successful MDA experience is the very opposite of dissociation. It is precisely a state of psychic cohesion or unity, out of which a person may say, as in the last example, "I take responsibility for myself."

The whole process, therefore, may be seen as one of integration via dissociation, or, more teleologically, one of dissociation in the service of integration. As in hypnotic states, only by forgetting his ordinary identity and pretending, so to say, that he is not there as a witness, can the person allow himself to experience his life from a different point of view, habitually suppressed. But this temporary lie of "This is not myself" is the way to the realization of the truth.

Just as a shift in identity to a previous lifetime was, in our last illustration, covering up (and indicating) aspects of his real identity in *this* lifetime, we may wonder whether this is not always the case with memories, however true they may be. For, in being concerned with the past, we are most likely being concerned with an indicator of our present. When our patient felt suddenly relieved of the heaviness that had set in on him in going beyond his birth, this relief was his reaction *now* to a change taking place in his *present* condition. This change was expressed to his consciousness at that moment as the notion of having raped someone, which takes the place of a disgust toward his grandfather or his previous life conduct and personality. Once his disgust is directed at *his own* actions, he is not disgusted or overwhelmed any more, but relieved, for he *can* take responsibility, and his crimes are not so great after all. More than that, we may be right in assuming that it is not his past actions that are so important, but his attitude at the moment. In his desire to atone for his sins, as he expresses it, he is *now* leaving behind him the inclination that he was apparently condemning in his past actions, but most probably rejecting in his present self. This, which appears to be an acceptance of the past in terms of a project for the future, is really a change in motivations or personality in the present.

Thus the illusion of otherness can be the link to an

awareness of selfhood, making the individual feel safe in temporary irresponsibility until he can discover that what he has hitherto rejected is bearable for him to accept; and the illusion of an issue being in the past can lead to the discovery of its survival in the present. In a similar way, the content of a memory can be a lie that leads to a truth. Our patient's pseudo-recollection of a previous existence here leads to the remembering of his grandfather's personality, to that of his "having raped somebody," and finally to the specific events that he was not acknowledging and that were the source of his disgust. How much of the "memories" recovered in other sessions is fact and how much symbolic substitutes I cannot tell, but the present case suggests a way in which we may look upon them. One thing that is clear is that a "false" memory, though factually wrong, is psychologically true. Consequently, the acceptance of it is in some measure equivalent to a coming to terms with the real events distorted into it. Thus, in our last example, the "realization" that the patient expressed by, "I see myself as on the day when I raped her" brought immediate relief. Moreover, a screen memory can, by virtue of its symbolic character, pack into itself an experiential meaning that no single memory of a fact from a person's life might convey. True, there are instances of traumatic events (an example of these is the separation from the wet nurse in our first illustration), but in many lives there is probably no single episode in which the abdication from self took place, but a series of micro-traumatic interactions. The imagined day of an imaginary rape, thus, is most probably condensing the guilt for countless occasions, of which those recollected are a sample. And that sample is enough to come to terms with the issue.

My respect for the power of symbols increased greatly one day in my early practice when I was unsuccessfully treating with hypnosis a woman with an acute case of vomiting. She was in the second month of pregnancy, and her vomiting was so severe that it was becoming a threat to her life. Her newly-wed husband had died about a month before, and a connection between his death and her present condition could be suspected but was not clear to us at the time. She was a good hypnotic subject, and because of the emergency I attempted suppression or substitution of the symptom; but as the days elapsed, the effectiveness of my post-hypnotic commands diminished. A colleague then suggested the initiation of a guided daydream in the trance state. I do not remember this clearly after the ten years that have elapsed since, but I do recall the crucial scene of it, in which the woman stood facing her husband and could see his stomach through his transparent abdomen. My colleague acted on inspiration and instructed her to take his stomach and eat it. She did, and upon waking up, her nausea was gone. An action carried out in fantasy, the "meaning" of which neither she nor we could rationally understand, had cured her of a vomiting so deeply rooted as to resist hypnotic manipulation and so severe as to threaten her survival.

Similarly, I am ready to believe in the therapeutic value of confronting memories that never took place in external reality. They are an embodiment of a psychological reality that may not be contacted at the time, at least not in that form. Yet this is not the last step. Once our patient had accepted the idea of having raped somebody, *he was ready to look into the facts*. He had accepted the worst. He had pleaded guilty to his worst accusations. Now he was not defensive any more, but open to his reality, ready to see.

What he saw may seem to us more innocent than his fantasy of a rape, but we must not forget that this time it was surely *he* who was the agent of the actions remembered, and the comparative mildness of the crimes is compensated for by the reality-quality or certainty of his memories and the measure of his involvement and responsibility. Screen memories, just like symbols, both reveal and stand as obstacles to a fuller revelation. They both disclose and cover up. Yet paradoxically, once the cover is lifted, we may find that nothing was hidden behind it. Or, phrased differently, what was covered up was nothing. For there can be no question as to the activity of covering up, no matter how empty the container. This paradoxical fact, I think, is one way of understanding the whole therapeutic process: daring to look at the skeleton in the closet . . . and finding that it is not there.

The willingness to become a patient in the psychotherapeutic endeavor is already an indication of a willingness to lift the lid of what appears to be a Pandora's box. Even more so is the decision to experience the effects of a drug that will rend the veils of the ordinary state of consciousness. Yet, drugs and all, I think that few are able to make the last step in "looking at the real thing." Looking at the symbol or dealing with it in a symbolic way is already a great challenge and without doubt a healing adventure. But even beyond the battle with the dragon is the discovery that the dragon was an illusion, which realization, by the way, is the real killing of it.

Our patient was now ready to see the worst in himself, after accepting the blame of being a rapist. What did he see? A certain measure of destructiveness in the way he had gone about finding his pleasure. His judgment of himself in this was severe, but his sternness had the taste of forgiveness: "Well, here I am, and I am responsible for myself. I take it." Essentially, he could take it. It was not unbearable to have made mistakes. It was far more tolerable to him to face his faults than the substitute that he had found for what he implicitly assumed to be a greater terror: the crimes of a previous incarnation, the meanness and lasciviousness of his grandfather, his own act of raping. As he gradually moved from his habitual avoidance of the issue, the crime was found to be closer and closer to home, but smaller. It never ceased to be a crime for him, but he found it far more tolerable to face it. Even more, it was exhilarating, and it added direction to his life. "I did those wrongs and must compensate for them with good . . . I take full responsibility for myself."

Thus we can frequently see a successful MDA session as a process of reaching a truth through the indications of error. For error is often in the nature of a shadow of truth, a shadow pointing toward its source. Yet, when we find the source, we find that the shadows of error are like those cast by the setting sun—much bigger than the object.

If the above is true, not only of MDA sessions but of psychotherapy in general, or even of life, there is a sense in which it is *particularly* true of MDA, when compared with the other drugs dealt with in this book. The domain to which the content of MDA experiences belongs is that of life events, and the truth relevant to it is a truth of facts. The domain of MMDA, as we shall see, is more that of feelings in the present than that of events in the past, and when we speak of feelings we do not think so much in terms of truth as in those of depth and genuineness. The domain of harmaline, on the other hand, is that of visual symbols of archetypal content, and here, too, we do not habitually speak of myth in terms of truth but in terms of beauty and revelation. Ibogaine is, of all the drugs, that most related to the direct experience of reality, according to the judgment of many who have been exposed to a broad range of psychochemicals. Still, such contact with reality has the quality of an ineffable experience at the moment, rather than a clarification of events. Of all psychotropic agents, MDA is the one which best deserves to be called a "drug of truth." An active concern for truth seems to be characteristic of it, not only in instances like those presented here, but in the reactions of more healthy individuals who have become concerned with their present lives. In such cases, the effect of the drug is frequently in the nature of the great urge to clear away the distortions that plague and impoverish human relations and to open up channels of communication that can make life among friends or family members more significant. Such disclosure does not occur (as with ordinary hypnosis or the effects of so-called "truth serums") as an act of disinhibition and irresponsibility, but as a consequence of an active interest in confronting and sharing the truth and a realization that much of the avoidance of such in ordinary life stems from unwarranted fear. Aside from the above fact, the reaction to MDA is by far the most verbal compared to other drugs mentioned in this book, and this contributes to its being a useful agent in the protentiation of group therapy. But with that I shall not deal here.

NOTE OF CAUTION:

The years that followed the writing of this chapter have shown that MDA is toxic to certain individuals and at various dosage levels; also that, as in the case of chloroform, what is a regular dose to many people may be a fatal dose to some others: a case of aphasia occurred in Chile, and a death occurred in California. Since individual incompatibility is consistent and bound to dose level, however, it is possible to ascertain it through progressively increasing test doses (i.e., 10 mg., 20 mg., 40 mg., 100 mg.). This should be done without exception throughout the time preceding any first therapeutic MDA session. Typical toxic symptoms are skin reactions, profuse sweating, and confusion; I have observed these in about 10 per cent of the subjects at dosages of 150–200 mg.

CHAPTER III

MMDA AND
THE ETERNAL NOW

Mmda is an abbreviation for 3-methoxy-4,5-methylene dioxyphenyl isopropylamine. Like MDA, from which it differs only in the presence of a methoxyl group in the molecule, it is a synthetic compound derived from one of the essential oils in nutmeg. The chemical similarity between these two compounds finds an echo in their psychological effects on man—in each case predominantly one of feeling enhancement. Their chemical difference is reflected in some qualitative differences in effect, however: MMDA frequently elicits eidetic displays, and not the past but the present becomes the object of attention for the person under its effect.

MMDA stands with MDA in a category distinct from that of LSD-25 and mescaline as well as from that of harmaline and ibogaine. In contrast with the transpersonal and unfamiliar domain of experience characterizing the action of these two groups of drugs, these feeling-enhancing isopropylamines lead into a domain that is both personal and familiar, differing only in its intensity from that of every day.

MMDA SYNDROMES

One possible reaction to MMDA, as to other psychoactive drugs, is a peak experience. How this experience differs from that brought about by other compounds will become apparent in the following pages. An alternative to the artificial paradise of MMDA is its hell. This is a reaction characterized by the intensification of unpleasant feelings— anxiety, guilt, depression—which may be regarded as a mirror image of the first, and constitutes, too, a clear syndrome. Yet these two types of reactions may be classed together in that they are essentially feeling-enhancement states, and contrasted to other states where the feelings are unaffected, and there may be passivity, withdrawal, and/or sleep rather than excitation. I find that both imagery and psychosomatic symptoms are more prominent in the absence of vivid emotions, so that I would tentatively regard this syndrome as one of feeling substitution. Lastly, there are occasions when a person reacts to MMDA with little or no productivity, both feelings and their equivalents being absent, a state that could well be regarded as the limbo of MMDA. In these cases, the effect of MMDA is one of even greater apathy or deeper sleep, so that I would suggest understanding them as instances where the repression of feelings does not even allow their symbolic expression, a state that can be maintained only at the expense of consciousness.

Broadly speaking, then, and for the purpose of deciding how to proceed in the therapeutic situation, I will consider the effects of MMDA as belonging to five possible states or syndromes: one which is subjectively very gratifying and may be regarded as a particular kind of peak experience; another where habitual feelings and conflicts are magnified; a third and fourth in which feelings are not enhanced but physical symptoms or visual imagery are prominent; and, lastly, one of lethargy or sleep. Psychosomatic symptoms or eidetic imagery may be present in any of these states, but are most prominent in the third and fourth (as feeling substitutes), while feelings are the most prominent part of the experience in the first two, and a state of indifference (possibly defensive in nature) sets in in the third and fourth and culminates in the fifth. In the latter, as in normal dreaming, there may be much mental activity, but this becomes difficult to grasp, remember, or express. These states may follow one another in a given experience, so that the reaction to MMDA may be initially one of anxiety and conflict until better balance is achieved or somnolence supervenes; or a session may begin with the pleasurable balanced state and then lead into one of emotional or physical discomfort, and so on.

ON THE ASSIMILATION OF PEAK EXPERIENCES

We have elsewhere remarked how the peak experience that may be possible under the effect of MDA is one affirmation of the individual aspect of the self, in contrast to that of LSD, where the typical experience is one of dissolution of individuality and the experience of self as oneness with all being. In the peak experience that MMDA may elicit, it is possible to speak of both individuality and dissolution, but these are blended into a quite characteristic new totality. Dissolution is here expressed in an openness to experience, a willingness to hold no preference; individuality, on the other hand, is implied in the absence of depersonalization phenomena, and in the fact that the subject is concerned with the everyday world of persons, objects, and relationships.

The MMDA peak experience is typically one in which the moment that is being lived becomes intensely gratifying in all its circumstantial reality, yet the dominant feeling is not one of euphoria but of calm and serenity. It could be described as a joyful indifference, or, as one subject has put it, "an impersonal sort of compassion"; for love is embedded, as it were, in calm.

Infrequent as this state may be for most persons, it is definitely within the range of normal human experience. The perception of things and people is not altered or even enhanced, usually, but negative reactions that permeate our everyday lives beyond our conscious knowledge are held in abeyance and replaced by unconditional acceptance. This is much like Nietzsche's *amor fati*, love of fate, love of one's particular circumstances. The immediate reality seems to be welcomed in such MMDA-induced states without pain or attachment; joy does not seem to depend on the given situation, but on existence itself, and in such a state of mind everything is equally lovable.

In spite of MMDA being a synthetic compound, it reminds us of Homer's nepenthe ("no suffering"), which Helen gives to Telemachus and his companions so that they may forget their suffering:

> But the admirable Helen had a happy thought. She lost no time, but put something into the wine they were drinking, a drug potent against pain and quarrels and charged with forgetfulness of all trouble; whoever drank this mingled in the bowl, not one tear would he let fall the whole day long, not if mother and father should die, not if they should slay a brother or a dear son before his face and he should see it with his own eyes. That was one of the wonderful drugs which the noble Queen possessed, which was given her by Polydamna the daughter of Thon, an Egyptian. For in that land the fruitful earth bears drugs in plenty, some good and some dangerous: and there every man is a physician and acquainted with such lore beyond all mankind, for they come of the stock of Paiëon the Healer.[1]

What the therapeutic implications of such an episode of transient serenity may be can be seen in the following case of a twenty-eight-year-old patient who was sent to me

---

[1] Homer, *The Odyssey*, trans. W. H. D. Rouse (New York: New American Library, Mentor Books, 1971), 49.

by another psychiatrist after six years of only moderately successful treatment.

The patient's reason for consulting, now as in the past, was chronic anxiety, insecurity in his relationships with people, and women in particular, and frequent bouts of depression. After an initial interview, I asked the patient to write an account of his life, as I frequently do, in view of both the value of such psychological exercise and the interviewing time that may thus be saved. As he was leaving, I said, "If nothing new comes up, come back when you have finished with the writing. But if you really put yourself into it, you may possibly not need me any more by then." The man came back after four months with a lengthy autobiography and reminded me of what I had said, for the writing had indeed been one of the major experiences in his life and felt to him like a new beginning. Reading it, I could understand that, for seldom have I seen anyone so explicitly burdened by his past, nor such a heroic act of confession, in which the author struggled page after page to overcome his sense of shame.

Much of this autobiography, from childhood onward, spoke of his sexual life, and it ended with a description of aspects of it in his present life which were related to his generalized insecurity. On the one hand, he was disturbed by the appeal which anal sexual intercourse held for him and concerned with the thought that women would regard this as a homosexual trait. On the other hand, he liked to stimulate his own anus while masturbating and felt ashamed for this aberration. When questioned about his own judgment as to how homosexual he might be, he said that he did not know of any homosexual inclination in himself, but that he could not dismiss an "irrational" fear that others would not see him as a truly masculine person. Whether his anal eroticism betrayed a latent homosexual trend he did not know, and he was frightened by the thought of it.

While awaiting the first effects of MMDA, the patient felt uneasy and somewhat afraid of looking ridiculous, but to his own surprise, he gradually entered into the state of calm enjoyment which is typical of the more pleasant experiences with the drug: "Like not needing anything, like not wanting to move, even; like being tranquil in the deepest and most absolute sense, like being near the ocean, but even beyond; as if life and death did not matter, and everything had meaning; everything had an explanation, and nobody had given it or asked for it—like being simply a dot, a drop of honey-pleasure radiating in a pleasurable space."

After some time, the patient exclaimed, "But this is heaven, and I expected hell! Can this be true? Or am I deceiving myself? Right now, all my problems seem to be imaginary ones. Can this be so?" I answered that this was possible and that if his problems were really the fruit of imagination it would be good to understand this very clearly, so that he could remember it later. So I suggested that he might compare his present state of mind with his habitual state and try to grasp the difference.

The difference was obvious to him. What the drug had done was to turn off the judgmental side of him that we had exposed in the previous appointments, the inner critic that would not let him live.

I said that now he knew what life was like when his "judge" was artificially put to sleep, but that he would wake up again—and then it would be the patient's choice whether to put up with him or not. He agreed, and I proceeded to confront him with his problems and photographs of persons in his family, in order to fix in his mind the views of his postponed, non-judgmental self. In doing this, he realized even more clearly the reality of his tendency to self-torture in his ordinary life. As he later said, "I had an intuition of it long ago in self-analysis. But now I see it more clearly than ever, and it is not just a cause any more, but a *character* with all its attributes. And its importance in my life and problems—I feel it now—has been enormous."

This insight did bring about a difference during the days following the session, for the patient no longer identified as much with his self-punishing criticism, but looked at it with some detachment, as if he had a life (his *own* judgment) independent of both the accuser and the victim.

Looking at a diary from which the patient has kindly permitted me to quote, it is possible to see that up to four days after the intake of MMDA there was an almost undisturbed carry-over of that state of mind first made known to him with the help of the chemical. On the fifth day, he felt depressed for a few hours, but recovered after writing in his diary. This writing dealt first with his depression and then with what he had felt when "I was at that center, the center of myself, and I knew that I would never lose this, for I needed only to breathe deeply, smile at the universe, and remember the bookshelves that I looked at that day." He continues: "I understood that a few seconds and an empty room are enough to justify a whole life. It does not matter any longer, then, to die or to lose an arm. It is not a matter of quantity. In zero minutes and with no things, life is as good as possible. In a minimal space and with no money, even without health, with no social success and all that shit." And he adds: "But I feel this even today. I am at some distance from the central point of the Aleph, but I continue to be at the center, my center that is still chaotic, but yet everywhere, and pure."

I think that the patient is being very accurate when he perceives that in spite of his being "centered" in the newly discovered domain of intimate joy, self-sufficiency, and indifference to frustration, he is nevertheless in a state of disorder. In other words, he does not confuse (as patients and even therapists sometimes do) the experience of transcendence with that of psychological balance and sanity. He is aware of negative emotions that he recognizes as part of his neurosis and he continues to react in ways that he knows are not the most desirable; but in the same way that "losing an arm" would not matter, he no longer tortures himself for such shortcomings. Instead, he experiences a less compulsive but perhaps more effective wish to "construct" and "make order" in his life, "like a duty of love, or holy labor."

As different as spiritual detachment and healthy psychological functioning may be, I believe that the latter may gradually develop in the presence of the former, making the therapeutic implication of such a peak experience an indirect one.

One of the ways in which a mood of serenity may result in further change is that it increases the possibility of insight, much as an analgesic can permit surgical exploration of a wound. Such insight cannot be possible insofar as the patient's sense of identity depends entirely on the integrity of an arbitrary idealized image of himself. But when our subject now says that "death would not matter," even though he is most probably exaggerating, he may be unknowingly stating a metaphysical truth; for "at the center" *death of the self-concept* does not matter.

How a "not caring" mood and attitude can lead to greater awareness may be illustrated by other passages of the same diary. The following was written three days after the session:

> Something could not come out of my throat. Anal masturbation: the great guilt, the supreme offense, that the Great Puritan does not forgive. The utmost degeneration, the worst garbage.
>
> It was necessary to discuss it with Dr. N., but it did not come out . . . the fact of having caressed my anus, having introduced objects into it while I masturbated with the other hand, having daydreamed of being penetrated . . . the great hole, the ass, the center of my hell . . . remained hidden, not deeming itself forgivable or understandable, seeing itself as something at which even a person like Dr. N. would feel disgust.
>
> I can shove that Great Inquisitor into my ass, shit or

piss on him—but all this is already giving it too much importance, the solution lies in understanding clearly and feeling that it does not matter too much, that it is, like the rest of the problems, a surmountable thing. And not something evil or horrible, or a sign of inferiority, but a transitory way out for a torrent that is transitorily stopped.

And he adds, three days later:

I have understood that the great guilt does not lie in anal masturbation but in being homosexual; and I feel dizzy at the thought of it, because it seems to me that this is the worst that could possibly happen to me.

The sequence of psychological events described above portrays a familiar process in psychotherapy, where by an object or concern (i.e., ways of masturbating) loses importance, while increased importance is attached to a more substantial issue (e.g., being homosexual). A detached, serenely accepting attitude is truly the power that makes the change possible, and petty conflicts may eventually lead to greater conflicts that enrich life rather than detract from it.

Here are further illustrations of the patient's increased ability to see himself:

I felt that nothing mattered. I thought about many things in the following days. I understood that my preoccupation about wearing comfortable clothes, clothes to my taste (I felt some shame when I retorted with this as the first answer to Dr. N.'s question as to what I wanted to do) stems from my mother's *imposition* on me to wear clothes which I found humiliating. I understood why I don't do things that I like or that I find convenient: because I consider them an obligation, and my mother has been telling me of my obligations for twenty-eight years. And I suspect that not wanting to phone my girlfriends when she or my father are around indicates guilt feelings about sex—and I also feel guilty about giving other women the love that I don't give her.

I do not believe it is just a coincidence that the passage telling of his insight into three different situations begins with a statement of the feeling that "nothing matters." For insight, we well know, does not depend on thought processes alone, but is one of the facets of change. Only when "nothing matters" could he accept being the "bad boy" that he never was and conceive thoughts in which he opposes his mother, for such thoughts are inseparable from his own self-assertion and rebellion.

The behavioral equivalent to the openness to insight described above is an openness to feelings and impulses which would be incompatible with the acceptable self-image. These become bearable now because there is something other than an image to rest upon—a "center," which gives the patient confidence to let go of his habitual patterns. If death does not matter, why would getting angry matter, or not doing the "right" thing according to previous conditioning?

The following passage is a good illustration of such increased spontaneity in behavior and constitutes a very exact parallel to the understanding expressed in the previous quotation:

> Once more I have felt rotten for living in this house where life is impossible, with such heat, with the old quack and his clients who keep ringing the doorbell, and the old woman nagging, nagging, nagging. Why don't I go with my car and get those chairs, and why don't I go and get the other crazy woman at the clinic on Saturday, and what would Uncle John say if he knew that I am not going to do this or that errand for her. (And how full of ants the house is, millions of them, and they fly! And they don't let me write.) But I told them: Fuck Uncle John and all the relatives and what they say! I shouted at her and pounded on the table once, twice, three, four times. And I told her not to expect me to go on listening to her just because this was what I had done for twenty-eight years, and so on. And she left with a bag. I thought that she was

going to her sister's house, but she has come back, so that it seems that she just went over to the laundry with some clothes. And I felt rotten—guilty at hating a shitty woman who has screwed me up and wants to go on screwing me up.

But enough! They will have to learn not to plague me in these last days that I'll spend with them.

The episode described above might be compared to the period of "worsening" that often supervenes at some point in the course of deep psychotherapy without drugs. In truth, the patient's hostility has only been laid open, and this may be the unavoidable price for him to pay for the possibility of experiencing it fully and understanding it, before he can leave it behind. The utter rejection of his environment portrayed in the patient's account may seem the very opposite of the unconditional acceptance of reality that is characteristic of "the MMDA state of mind" at its best. How can ants matter so much to one who has felt that not even death does? Nevertheless, the patient is accepting his own anger to a much greater extent than before, rather than repressing it and having it emerge in the form of symptoms. Such anger probably constitutes a defense against other feelings which he is still not ready to experience (the loneliness of not feeling himself loved or respected by his parents, for instance) and which are triggered by certain stimuli in the house, so we may expect that further progress *in the same direction* should bring such feelings into focus and make him less vulnerable to the heat in his room, the ants, his father's clients or his mother's demands. We might picture the psychological state presently described as one in which the "amount" of serenity remaining for the maximum of five days before is just enough to dissolve, as it were, one layer of the mental onionskin. But if this change remains, the same power will be henceforth going to work on the next layer.

A parallel may be seen between the unveiling of the patient's anger and that of his fear of homosexuality. Nei-

ther his irritability nor his sexual doubt is a manifestation
of health and psychological balance, but now he can at
least face them—and facing them he faces *himself* to a
greater extent than when he was concerned about the
clothes that he wore or what a woman would say of his
love-making. An indication that this is so is his evolution,
for even at a later hour the same day he was feeling as
well as he ever had, and for the following week had no
more downfalls than recoveries of a level of well-being
that had been unknown to him before. In these moments,
he would write passages like this one:

> I have understood that there is very little that matters. It
> doesn't matter that the car doesn't work, that a girl won't
> love us, that they won't give us the best appointments at
> the university, that they say that I am a homosexual, that I
> don't have a lot of money or a kingdom, that my parents
> will die, that Aunt Rose is as crazy as ever. It only matters,
> perhaps, to be able to breathe deeply and feel here, now,
> enjoying the air, and that fly. It doesn't matter not to be
> able to go to England, not to be a writer or a playboy.

And fifteen days after the session:

> And goodbye to the vicious circle, to the "ontological"
> boredom about everything, to problems, and psychother-
> apy. The Sargasso Sea is over, and the dark night and the
> storm; it is the end of anxiety up to the neck, depression,
> and shit in little spoonfuls. The sun is out, the sea is out,
> the world, and the fly.

The reader may have noticed how several quotations
in which the patient expresses his new understanding are
written in the past tense: "I understood"; "I felt." That
they are conveying the patient's state at the moment,
which he confirms personally, and the fact that they were
not written before (even though he produced a detailed
description of the MMDA session, which is not included
here) probably indicates that the understanding belongs

only to this moment, even though it was potentially present during the height of the effect of the drug. In other words, the state of feeling at the time of the session was one in which such viewpoints were *implied*, but which did not depend upon such views. The return process can be understood as one in which the remembered feeling is *translated* into *explicit* attitudes about specific issues. Or, using another image, the peak experience might be likened to a spot on a mountain top from which the surrounding panorama may be viewed; yet being on the top of the mountain does not supply more than the *possibility* of seeing, whereas this process of observation is different from that of mountain climbing. The particular view that can be seen from a given spot *implies* the viewpoint and makes it explicit, and in a similar fashion the particular insights that may be obtained from a given state of consciousness imply and express that level of awareness. Yet insight is distinct from the mental state from which it originates and constitutes the result of a creative act in which consciousness at a certain height is directed toward what lies below.

In other words, that "center" which can "justify life in an empty room" has to be brought into contact with the periphery of everyday life; the "heaven" of spiritual experience must be brought to bear on the "earth" of particular circumstances before real understanding can develop. And only then can life be created (i.e., behavior chosen) according to the point of view implied in the transient flash of understanding.

The reason it is difficult for the above synthesis to occur is that from the mountain top the valley may be invisible for a dizzy person who may feel inclined to look at the stones, or even to fall. And the atmospheric conditions are such that the mountain top can hardly be seen from the valley. Or, translating this into empirical terms, a person's present difficulties may be hard to bring to mind during the peak experience, when such reflection would be so desirable; or their unpleasantness may lead the person to avoid remembering them; or the particular state of mind that constitutes the peak experience may be disrupted by such thoughts.

On the other hand, when the person is closer to the issues of his daily life, to which he is most vulnerable, he may not be able to reflect on them at all, for he himself will be lost in them—like our patient with the bell ringing and the mother asking him to do things for her.

Since neither one of the alternatives is a complete impossibility, though, I believe that much value should be attached to the attempts at directing the mind, at the time of the "good" MMDA experience, to the conflicting situations in a patient's life, as well as to the patient's remembering his peak experience at the time of contact with his difficulties.

It is the latter that naturally occurred during the days following the session under discussion, and this explains the patient's use of the past tense, even when he was not only recalling, but re-experiencing, the taste of "centeredness" in face of given circumstances that he had potentially contemplated during the course of the drug's effect.

The way in which the patient alternates between "remembering" his experience of calm satisfaction and moments of despair (when he thinks that the treatment has been worthless) indicates that the state of mind reached under the facilitation of MMDA is not something that simply lasts for a given time and then is lost, but one that may be *learned*. Once a person has used his mind in that way, he has easier access to the same way of functioning. And in this learning, whereby a desirable attitude can be "remembered" not only intellectually but *functionally* (as the movements of writing and walking are remembered when we do them) after it has been adopted once, lies, I believe, one of the major justifications for the elicitation of an artificial peak experience. This could be likened to the guiding hand which holds that of a child to show him how to draw a letter, or those of the practitioner in M. Alexander's system, showing a person how to stand or sit so that he can feel the "taste" of rightness, or, in the conception of Mexican shamans using peyotl, the guiding hand of God. Once in possession of such discrimination or knowledge, it is up to the individual to remember it and put it into practice. An expressive passage on the role of learning when applied to a state of mind is the following recollection of Jean-Pierre Camus (quoted by Huxley in his *Perennial Philosophy*):

> I once asked the Bishop of Geneva what one must do to attain perfection. "You must love God with all your heart," he answered, "and your neighbour as yourself."
>
> I did not ask wherein perfection lies, I rejoined, but how to attain it. "Charity," he said again, "that is both the means and the end, the only way by which we can reach that perfection which is, after all, but Charity itself. Just as the soul is the life of the body, so charity is the life of the soul."
>
> "I know all that, I said. But I want to know *how* one is to love God with all one's heart and one's neighbour as oneself.
>
> But again he answered, "We must love God with all our hearts, and our neighbour as ourselves."
>
> I am no further than I was, I replied. Tell me how to acquire such love.
>
> "The best way, the shortest and easiest way of loving God with all one's heart is to love Him wholly and heartily!"
>
> He would give no other answer. At last, however, the Bishop said, "There are many besides you who want me to tell them of methods and systems and secret ways of becoming perfect, and I can only tell them that the whole secret is a hearty love of God, and the only way of attaining that love is by loving. You learn to speak by speaking, to study by studying, to run by running, to work by working; and just so you learn to love God and man by loving. All those who think to learn in any other way deceive themselves. If you want to love God, go on loving Him more and more. Begin as a mere apprentice, and the

very power of love will lead you on to become a master in the art. Those who have made most progress will continually press on, never believing themselves to have reached their end; for charity should go on increasing until we draw our last breath."[2]

What complicates this picture is that in the case of higher (non-instrumental) attitudes and ways of mental functioning, as in that of motor skills, the learning process is interfered with by the arousal of habitual patterns of response that are incompatible with the new. In other words, *remembering* the sane state[3] becomes possible only when specific stimuli are not eliciting the conditioned responses which the individual wants precisely to get rid of. Consider, for instance, one more quotation from our patient's diary:

> It is now one week since the session with MMDA, and today I felt alone again, in my bed, in my dark, hot room, in this sinister house, and I feel like escaping, like going someplace, to a movie perhaps, or to visit Alberto, or anybody, and I know that I will feel bad anyhow, for I won't be able to get out of myself, and I will be with them like a zombie, like a little boy crying inside, licking his wounds or masturbating, and introducing his fingers into his anus, hating his parents and dreaming that he is a king.
>
> And I feel all this today, only a week after having seen something of a definitive cure. And why? Because I didn't sleep well last night (after a quarrel with Alice), because garbage is accumulating in my soul again, because I came to wait for Ana's phone call. (Damn her! She slipped away

---

[2] Aldous Huxley, *The Perennial Philosophy* (New York and London: Harper & Brothers, 1945), pp. 89–90.

[3] In calling it "sane," I am assuming that this is the natural state and that only because there is such a thing as a natural state can it be manifested spontaneously and without learning. Learning becomes necessary only for its "realization," i.e., its translation into practical reality.

from me) That is it!! She screwed me up by not calling me. My security is down to zero again, and I continue to be one hundred per cent dependent on others.

The fact that the patient was temporarily precipitated into his neurotic pattern when the girl rejected him shows that such rejection had not really been taken into account when he felt himself so invulnerable. Only after being confronted with it and recovering from his fall, could he really say, as he actually did, "It doesn't matter if a girl doesn't love us."

I believe that in such confrontation with experience (or its possibility) lies the healing property, as well as the insight that gives permanence to the new condition. Such confrontation may take place during the session with MMDA, if the patient is led to consider the conflictive circumstances of his life, or later, when living is unavoidable. In the present case, I did lead the patient to a contemplation of his difficulties when he seemed ready to look at them with pleasurable calm, but I did not realize how he was dissimulating his avoidance of certain issues. This was his first concern afterward ("things that did not come out"), and he aptly describes the effect of the session, later, as "an antiseptic that eliminated the infection for two or three days, so I felt completely rid of my neurosis."

It is to be expected that the more the issues have to be avoided in order not to disrupt a "peak experience," the more unstable and short-lived such experience will be in the midst of ordinary living conditions. But I use quotes here for "peak experience" to imply that such an experience has an element of self-deception in it, in that it is possible only at the expense of repressing, or not looking at, what is incompatible with it. What can the validity be of feeling that we can accept death if we are unable to imagine it? Yet I believe that in most pharmacologically induced peak experiences there is a substratum full of issues that cannot be confronted.

We can ask ourselves, therefore, which may be the

more desirable: to take a directive attitude during the MMDA session and attempt to confront the patient with what he is avoiding, at the risk of disrupting a state of partial integration, or to let the patient experience as much as he can of his newly discovered centeredness, so that the taste of it remains while he later meets life as it comes.

In truth, there is not so much room for choice as it might seem. In my experience, only about 25 per cent of the persons react to MMDA with a spontaneous peak experience, while an additional 30 per cent arrive at it after working on their problems. In the latter instance, there can be little doubt that the experience has occurred *in spite of*, and as the result of, the resolution of at least some of the person's conflicts, which has generally been the object of most of the session. As to the former 25 per cent, it is generally my practice to allow the experience to proceed undisturbed for about two hours and then devote the remaining three to the examination of the patient's life and problems. In doing this, I am assuming that I can help the patient more by being present at this confrontation than by leaving it to him to experience in the following days, and that remembering life at the time of a peak experience may be easier than remembering it at the time of living. In actual practice, this does not violate the patient's inclinations, for he is either feeling open to whatever is proposed, in his accepting mood, or else feeling naturally drawn to such self-examination. This was true in the case (among others) of the man in our illustration who, after about two hours of enjoying his heavenly state, wanted to know where his hell was and to ascertain whether his present state was really valid or justified.

Sometimes, the crucial confrontation occurs spontaneously in vivid imagery, as was the case of a patient who had always felt insecure in his work as a manager, and would compensate by adopting a bossy attitude. Toward the end of his MMDA session, he imagined himself at work in the present state of relaxed warmth and really *learned* from such creative fantasy how this was truly possible, how his defensiveness was unnecessary and his undistorted expression of himself more satisfying and not inconvenient. There was very little talking with this patient, but his mood and behavior at work changed.

That there are limits to how much a person wants to confront at a given time is also true, and I think that the therapist's possibilities are more limited here than it would seem. The patient will not hear, or he will just pretend to hear, or his feelings will not parallel his thinking, his mind will go blank or be filled with distracting thoughts, and so on, and this will have to be accepted. Moreover, there may be a natural wisdom in the unconscious regulating process that controls the length of his steps toward integration. All the therapist can do in these instances is be available to offer what he can.

Another instance of such spontaneous confrontation in imagery is described by a patient in the following words:

> Then something significant happened. First I just felt something had happened, something was different. As if I had forgiven myself for something. Then I became convinced that the forgiveness was associated with the throwing-up some time earlier. Then I found myself in fantasy moving about within my office at the college. I discovered that I no longer was caught up in the self-flagellating depression that I had been in during the last week. I was free and at ease.
>
> Then I had moments of realization of a quality of peace of mind that I almost never have (in my anxiety, computing, rehearsing, manipulating, worrying, and other habitual states), and the quality was—and still is today, after fifteen days—a state of being able to let time pass with graceful ease, even to luxuriate and enjoy friends in the moment.

What is it, then, in practical terms, that the patient may be offered in such moments, when his state of mind could not be better? In general, I would regard the following immediate aims as conducive to the stabilization of a peak experience:

1. Explicitation or Expression of the Present State and Point of View

It may be assumed that the change that has taken place in the subject's feelings is not just a matter of metabolic processes in his nervous system, but that it entails an implicit change in the perception of people or relationships, or in his values. Since it is such changes that may support the new feeling state if they endure, it is desirable to make them as conscious as possible, and thus help him consciously discard the implicit distorted views that were supporting the symptoms. Thus somebody may no longer be seen as a persecutor, or the individual may discover his own worth in an area where he had been rejecting himself. The whole approach amounts to asking the patient *why* everything seems all right to him now (or why it is unnecessary to worry so that he may translate into concepts his implicit understanding).

In the case of the patient in our first illustration, this led him to a greater awareness of his self-punitiveness, as was mentioned earlier. Another realization that helped him in the expression of his new state of mind was the one he described in terms of "nothing matters," meaning really something like "nothing can take away from the joy of existing, which is an end in itself." The value of expression is that its products are like reservoirs of the experience that gave them birth and are to some extent the means of re-creating the experience. The fruits of expression are, like art, a means of making the invisible visible and fixing in a given shape a fleeting instant in the mind.

2. Contemplation of Everyday Reality

Most important here is the confrontation of stimuli (circumstances, persons) which are normally painful or elicit neurotic reactions. This is the opportunity for the discovery of a new pattern of reaction stemming from the integrated state, which would be less likely to occur after the peak of serenity is over, and where proximity to the given circumstance is too great. Confrontation in the mind before confrontation in reality takes place in a strategy which might be compared to that used by Perseus in his approach to the Medusa: he does not look at her directly, but at her reflection in Minerva's shield.[4]

Photographs are useful to this end, since the cues offered by them are valuable starting points for association with life experiences, in contrast with the stereotyped views that are often elicited by verbal questions.

Whenever a new approach or feeling is expressed which breaks the vicious circle of neurotic attitudes, the expression of it may be encouraged in order to *fix* it in the mind as part of the enlarged repertoire of responses. An imaginary encounter with a given person, in which a dialogue is produced, may be a useful resource, and also writing, which is perfectly compatible with the effect of MMDA.

The following illustration is from the report by a young man who had been in therapy for five years and was at the time of the session living through a chaotic and painful period in his marriage:

    . . . I remember lying on the carpet in the room, fully enjoying a warm, glowing, soft sense of well-being. Dr. N. came to me and suggested that we talk together. I told him

---

[4] Minerva is the goddess of wisdom, suggesting that the mirror-shield represents the mind.

about my love for Jeanne and the hurt I felt. He suggested I write down my feelings on paper. I wrote as though writing a letter to Jeanne. I told her how much I loved her. And that I was waiting for her. During this time, I experienced the most acute sexual response, especially in the pelvic area. I was thoroughly immersed in the joyful fantasy of loving Jeanne. Loving her in a quiet, tender way, caressing her ever so gently. I felt, perhaps for the first time, that my desire to be tender and loving toward her was the power that would break through her sexual anesthesia.

Their relationship improved after the session, since the attitude expressed in this letter persisted to some extent and replaced previous feelings of rejection and resentment. The act of expression (by committing these feelings to paper) can be conceived of here as a commitment, as well as a realization, in the sense of "making real" what was merely a feeling, living out what was only a possibility.

3. Exercising of Decision in Face of Present Conflicts

I usually ask the patient to make a list of the conflicts that he is aware of, or I make it with him before a session with MMDA, and this provides many questions to consider at the time of an eventual state of psychological harmony.

Conflict is perhaps the most central single manifestation of a neurotic disturbance, since it is the expression of a disunity or split in personality. In the exceptional moment of integration, when the usually incompatible fragments of the person's psyche are united, many of his conflicts will disappear. If the integrated attitude of the person is not rendered explicit at the moment, it will be lost more easily once the exceptional state is over; yet this is the occasion on which the person may know the attitude of his integrated self and learn what it feels like. When his self is not there any more, the memory of such an attitude will be one more thread in his fabric of experiential remembering—and perhaps the best possible advice as well.

HANDLING THE STATES OF FEELING ENHANCEMENT

Everything that I have elaborated upon up to this point applies to the kind of experience that ensues spontaneously in about 20 per cent of all instances after the intake of MMDA. It may apply in part to the similar experience which supervenes in an additional 30 percent of cases after therapeutic intervention, as conflict resolution and personality integration are achieved. But in about 50 percent of all instances, such feelings of "all-rightness," calm, and loving acceptance are not experienced at all, and in 80 per cent they are not present at the beginning of the session.

In such instances, the reaction to the drug may be predominantly that of an enhancement of certain emotions and/or psychosomatic symptoms, or one where imagery becomes the main object of attention. Each one of the possibilities constitutes a type of effect that calls for a distinct approach, and I shall presently deal with the predominantly feeling reactions. These feeling-enhancement reactions might well be grouped together with the "peak-experience" reactions, for the emotions are the focal point in both kinds of experience, yet both are in contrast in terms of the kind of feelings involved. As the peak experience constitutes MMDA's "heaven," the feeling-enhancement state constitutes its "hell." Instead of calm and loving acceptance of experience, the emotions of the second state are typically those of anxiety and discomfort, which render immediate experience unsatisfactory.

What the second type of experience has in common with the first is the relevance of the feelings experienced in relation to the present situation and to the immediate environmental and social context. I find such a "here and now" quality of the MMDA experience particularly suited to the non-interpretive existential approach of Gestalt therapy, which I have used—as will be seen from the forthcoming illustrations—almost free from admixtures in the handling of most sessions.

Experiences of discomfort are usually the outward expression of self-rejection or the fear of imminent self-rejection. Once this becomes explicit, the top-dog–underdog impasse can be re-examined to see whether the person can discover some value in his rejected side, whether his judgmental standards fit his true judgment or are in the nature of an automatic reaction, which can be dispensed with. Some examples may make this more clear:

A female patient has been encouraged to do or express whatever she wants during the session. When the drug begins to take effect she withdraws to her bedroom, where she lies down and listens to some music. After five minutes or so, she returns to the therapist in the living room and explains that she has not been able to enjoy these minutes since she has felt distressed at what she calls her "voraciousness"—she could not really listen to the music since she wanted a number of things at once, such as a drink, the therapist's presence, and, most of all, to be special.

Since her discomfort seemed to be associated more with her self-accusation of greed and voraciousness than with the unavailability of means to satisfy her needs, I inquired, "What is wrong with wanting more and more?" This comment proved to be more than superficially supportive, since it led her to an open-minded consideration of the question. When I later insisted that she state her wants and be increasingly direct, she found that in giving way to the expression of such wants she became more herself. What she initially labeled "voraciousness" soon came to be seen as wanting to be specially loved by a man. As I emphasized the humanness of this want, she saw the acceptability and even essentiality of fulfilling it in her life, in one way or another. "I've been going after my wants indirectly all my life, and the *indirectness* and lack of consciousness are what have fouled me up."

The process of increasing self-acceptance depicted in this illustration came about by the therapist's repeated invitation that she take sides with her rejected urges and acknowledge them as her own, rather than as something happening *to* her.

The following fragment of a retrospective account by another patient illustrates in greater detail the process of gradual unfolding of rejected urges in an atmosphere of support:

> . . . As I felt the first effects I lay down on my bed. Dr. N. sat next to me and suggested that I relax and let myself be carried by whatever I might feel. I began to feel much anxiety and a great desire to cry. Dr. N. told me to do so if I wanted, but I was resisting. I told him that I would not permit myself to do that, for it seemed ugly to me; that I disliked persons who indulged in self-pity and that I, who had chosen my way with so much struggle, felt that I had no right to feel unhappy.
>
> Dr. N. said that perhaps I had good grounds to feel pity for myself, so to go ahead and not mind crying. He said: Take a holiday for an afternoon and do whatever you feel like. I asked whether he would approve, and as he said yes, I wept bitterly. Dr. N. then asked me how would my tears explain their flowing if they could speak. I said they were flowing for the world's sorrow. He asked what that was. I said I imagined a great lake formed by the pain of every human being since the world exists, from the smallest, such as that of a child that falls down and cries, to the greatest. A ground of collective sorrow, in the fashion of Jung's collective unconscious. Dr. N. said he believed that I might be weeping for my own experiences, for concrete and definite things. That perhaps I had lacked something as a child, for instance, and this fact was still affecting my life.

I continued to weep and suffer, but with freedom and a feeling of relief. I had put a Vivaldi concerto on the record player. I felt the music very deeply and felt that through the music I could reach into the being who had produced it. I think Dr. N. asked me what the music was expressing, and I replied that this was Vivaldi's being, turned into a voice; a voice that expressed him totally. I marveled that he could have turned his inside out so completely.

As is usually the case, once the patient contacts her own urges before they could be supported and could con-she is turned inside out, she can read the expression of another being.

Such "turning inside out" in the last illustrations can be understood as an achievement of greater directness in the expression of wants. In both instances, it was important to point out to the patients how they were opposing their own urge before they could be supported and could consider the possibility of letting go of their opposition. Only when self-criticism is voiced can it be looked at in the face and reconsidered. So, questions such as "What's wrong with wanting more and more?" or "What's wrong with crying?" had to uncover the self-accusations of greed or self-pity before the patient's mature judgment could evaluate such automatic condemnation in a new light and make a decision. The end result is that unconscious desires become conscious and therefore a matter of intelligent problem solving.

Whereas the unconscious want is expressed in devious and symbolic ways, the satisfaction of which never quenches the underlying thirst, a conscious want can be fulfilled. Furthermore, the more conscious a wish is, the more it is accepted and becomes in itself a satisfaction. Thus, unconscious sexuality is experienced as isolation, loneliness, frustration, whereas conscious and accepted sexuality is a pleasurable experience of enhanced vitality. Unconscious rage may be experienced as unpleasant irritation or guilt, whereas accepted rage may be welcomed as a powerful striving for an end.

The following serves as one more instance of the bringing out of an unconscious desire and will show a way of dealing with visual distortions:[5]

Dr. N. now looked to me like a hidden wolf, an animal that is used to hunt for its prey in caves. He invited me to address the monster (that I saw him as), to relate directly to it, forgetting it was he, that I knew him, that he wouldn't harm me, and so on. I spoke with all the courage I had: "Why are you so ugly?" "What do you care about my being ugly?" he answered. "That is my problem, not yours." "But I wonder how you get along with that face. Who can love you like that?" And then I began to laugh as I thought that perhaps in his country everyone had a sinister face and maybe he was regarded as handsome. I told him of this thought, and his face began to clear up until Dr. N.'s face emerged with no distortion. He said that in his experience such distortions indicated repressed anger, and even though he did not see this in me it would be profitable to explore the question of possible resentment. I said that I could not imagine any resentment toward him since I had such good feeling toward him; he had helped me so much and been so kind to me. As I finished saying this, I went on almost unconsciously, as if somebody were using my voice to say, "Why should I resent you except for not having loved me." I was surprised. Dr. N. commented that this was an excellent reason for resentment. The experience ceased to be so burning and became more sweet, with that sad sweet sadness that remains after a good weep.

The importance of this session lay in the fact that not only could the patient's wish to be loved by the therapist be expressed, but even this appeared to be a substitute for the expression of her own loving. Some days later, she was able to accept her feeling as a richness rather than as a

[5] Exceptional with MMDA (5 per cent of subjects).

shortcoming, as she wrote a poem that was the first after ten years of interruption in her creative production.

In the examples cited above, the patients were in a conflict where a given urge (to love, to cry) was opposed by a resistance, and the outcome was the expression of the urge. This need not always be the case, and one of the foremost contributions of Gestalt therapy has been that of showing how the defense, too, is an urge that can be redirected to more satisfactory expressions than self-controlling and self-squeezing. To this end, the patient is encouraged to take sides with the voice of the super-ego ("top dog"), and to experience this as his own judgment rather than an external command by voluntarily "becoming" it.

WORKING THROUGH A PSYCHOSOMATIC SYMPTOM

The following excerpt from a tape recording deals with the conflict between the need to rest and self-squeezing in the most literal sense, relaxation and dysfunctional contracture. In fact, this is an example of working through a psychosomatic manifestation, since for the patient in it, the "squeezing of the soul" by her defensive system was embodied in a parallel physical symptom which caused her abdominal pain, and for which she had sought medical advice.

So, in dealing with this idea, we are also turning to the question of how to deal with MMDA syndromes of type 3 in our proposed classification: those in which the positive or negative feelings of the foregoing types are replaced by physical symptoms.[6] Naturally, an enhancement of physical sensations may be part of type 1 experiences, but the

---

[6] The aim will here be one of decoding the individual's attitudes toward self and others which lie encoded and expressed in body language.

substitution of bodily symptoms for feelings understandably occurs in the measure that the subject will not give in
to experiencing the emotional discomfort of the type 2
state. This may reflect the chronic tendency of the individual, as in the case of this patient, who at the time of
the session may have been described as a hypomanic hypo-
chondriac—happy with herself and unhappy about pains
that she tended to regard as the consequence of physical
illness.

This time I am quoting only my side of the dialogue
for a period that may have extended over twenty or thirty
minutes and eventually led to a figure-ground reversal in
the patient's experience. More than a dialogue, in fact, this
session might be regarded as comparable to that between
a movement therapist or a chiropractor and his patient, the
verbal part of it consisting mostly in therapeutic manipulations and the patient's reactions to them, often in the form
of postural changes, moans, yells, and sobs.

> Doctor. I can help you then, but I think there is only one
> way in which you can stop squeezing, and that is to
> learn *how* you are squeezing, become aware how *you*
> do the squeezing, and you can only really become
> aware by *becoming* that part of you that is really
> squeezing. . . .
>
> Did you become the squeezer or just the victim of
> it? . . .
>
> Yes . . . Is that something you can decide to do
> again? . . .
>
> I would like you to tell me what you are feeling.
> Just be aware how it is squeezing. . . .
>
> Preventing what? . . . Don't interpret, don't make
> theories, just go with your feelings. Do you feel
> squeezed? . . .
>
> Only there? . . .
>
> Does your voice sound squeezed? . . .

Now do you hear it? . . .

Are you aware *how* you are squeezing your own voice, *how* you squeeze your throat? . . .

You are aware of the squeeze in your chest? . . .

OK, there is a squeeze in the chest and down in the belly, both places.

You feel squeezed in your movements, your arms, your neck, your fingers? . . .

What about your hands now, and your arms now? You are squeezed now? . . .

Can you squeeze now, deliberately? . . .

No, I don't expect it to be the same thing. Just experience it. . . .

What does it want from you? . . .

What does it respond? . . .

Can you be it squeezing you so that you know what it wants, what you want when you are squeezing yourself? What is it you are wanting when you squeeze yourself like now? What do you want to do to you? And what is the satisfaction you are getting from this squeeze? . . .

Yes, the squeezer is getting a satisfaction. It wants to squeeze; it gets pleasure from squeezing. . . .

Don't struggle. Let it happen, let yourself be squeezed. Don't try to back out, be the victim now, let the torture end. . . .

You don't have to have the strength to suffer. To resist, you must, but if you . . .

Try not resisting now. . . .

Let go. Don't stop it. . . .

Let go, let go. Don't resist it. Let everything be. . . .

Don't resist it, you are resisting it, experience it. Be as open as you can and experience it. . . .

What are you experiencing? . . .

I saw a lot of activity coming through you for the first time. Can you feel . . . ? . . .

Can't you feel any desire for that activity, as if you wanted to go back to it? Any enjoyment of that movement? . . .

Just despair? . . .

This being tired is like a deadness, a grey deadness, lack of energy, and all this energy is contained behind it. . . .

And I feel that in the squeeze you have this energy, this force. . . .

So you have to become that other side, if you want to have strength. . . .

Maybe, while the squeezing is taking place, while you are being open to the squeezer, maybe you can experience yourself as wanting to squeeze. . . .

I want you to talk about it, the squeeze wanting sex. Can you elaborate on this, say more how it feels? But try to be the squeezer while you are talking about it. Say what you want as squeezer. . . .

Can you experience the squeeze as your urge, your satisfaction? . . . Your sex urge, your anger, your desperation? . . . Your longing? . . .

You still haven't been able to identify with the squeezer. . . .

Well, do it without taking pleasure, just let it come as it comes. "I am the one squeezing you," you can begin, even if you don't feel it. Just play the game.

Speak of what you want, you the squeezer, how you are, what kind of a person you are. . . .

At this point the patient had the insight that turned the session into a success. Being able now to switch from the position of victim to that of "squeezer," she could see that the force causing her pains was none other than greed for all and everything, a rapacious, clutching infant that could never be satisfied. Immediately after this, she spontaneously understood and was exhilarated at the discovery of the perversion involved in the turning back of desire upon herself in a relentless squeeze. Meister Eckhardt says that all our desires are ultimately the desire for God. Many woud perhaps choose another word and speak of a life urge, the absolute, Good, a longing for the ideal state, Eros; yet all these conceptions imply the recognition of a unity beyond the apparent multiplicity of human wants. A given desire can be understood as the expression of an implicit belief that the attainment of such specific goals will bring about happiness. Of course, this is not the way it works, but implicit or unconscious beliefs cannot be altered by reasoning (or even experience). Thus most thieves get little satisfaction from their stealing, moneymakers from their riches, or compulsive scholars from their learning. Whenever the therapeutic process leads to an understanding of the urge, the subject attains some freedom from that particular need, since it is now understood as merely a means to an end—and often a roundabout or inadequate one. So when the thief understands, not with the mind but with his feelings, his need to have something from others, he may begin to ask for love, and when the neurotic intellectual acknowledges his need for recognition, he may become less attached to the prestige game, since its value now does not appear to him as something intrinsic to the accumulation of knowledge.

I believe that an experience such as the one quoted above, leading to the realization of a "life force," is one step beyond all this, in that it leads to a realization of unity beyond rather limited needs, such as sex, ambition, greed, and protection. This is the domain of experience which interests the mystic, even though in the present quotation there is no usage of religious or mystical terms. And it is the domain that Jung regards as archetypal, beyond personal differentiation, even though its presentation in the case report is not essentially mediated by images.

ACTIVE PARTICIPATION AT NEUTRAL POINTS

One might understand the different types of reaction to MMDA as different points on a gradient of awareness and openness. An increase in awareness may transform the psychosomatic type of experience into one of the feeling type; and the latter, through understanding of resistances, may give way to the integrative peak experience. If we go to the other extreme, we find reactions in which the patient has less and less to report. Even physical sensations seem to be blurred in a state of restricted awareness, most probably of a defensive nature, which may culminate in drowsiness or sleep. It would seem that this state of calm constitutes a manifestation at another level of that calm or serenity which is characteristic of the peak experience with MMDA. One is a calm in richness, a stillness in the midst of inner movement, the other, a state of calm where little happens, a placid bluntness.

As we approach the unconscious end of the scale, where passivity takes the form of somnolence, the subject even becomes unaware of his dreamlike imagery. When questioned, he may be able to report an isolated scene that he is visualizing at the moment, but he is unable to remember the previous one. Or possibly he knows that his mind is active but cannot grasp the content of his thought or imagination. Fortunately, this is the case in only about 25 per cent of all instances.

Whenever the effect of MMDA is not remarkably productive in terms of either positive or negative feelings, a very active participation by the therapist may be required in order to deal with the patient's somatic sensations, imagery, or actual behavior.

Feelings may thus be brought into conscious focus by attending to the outer symbolic or physical expressions and the unfolding of experience or behavior, as is the practice in Gestalt therapy.

Take, for instance, the following illustration:

Doctor. Are you aware of your tight jaw?
(*Patient nods affirmatively and intensifies the contraction of her chewing muscles.*)
Doctor. Intensify that.
(*Patient begins to grind her teeth.*)
Doctor. (*after a few minutes*) Intensify that.
(*The grinding of teeth now gradually becomes a locked jaw once more while the patient, who is sitting, raises her head, opens her eyes in a fierce stare, and breathes deeply.*)
Patient. I feel strong. Not tense anymore, but severe, masterful.
Doctor. "Stay with it."
Patient. (*She gradually relaxes and begins to swallow saliva.*) My chewing has become swallowing. Now that I have found my strength, I don't have to knock angrily at the door to get satisfaction, but I can simply give it to myself.

Another patient felt very sleepy and relaxed, but tended to stretch his toes. He was encouraged to attempt to give in alternately to his desire to rest and his desire to stretch, and soon he realized the bearing of these opposed tendencies on his whole present life. He perceived the tension in his toes as an urge for excitement, an expression of boredom and dissatisfaction with his passivity, whereas the latter he understood as a resigned withdrawal from conflict. With this awareness, his need for excitement became stronger than his need for withdrawal, and this is what led him to engage in additional psychotherapy after his MMDA treatment.

Whenever not only feeling but physical sensations or the desire to communicate is slight, this may be an appropriate occasion to deal with a dream. As mentioned earlier, because of the increased faculty for creating imagery under MMDA, it may be easy to re-experience dreams, whereas an increased insight into symbolic or metaphoric forms is favorable to the unfolding of their meanings.

IMAGERY AND DREAMS

When imagery, rather than psychosomatic manifestations, dominates in the picture of symptoms elicited by MMDA, it is the content of such images which may be regarded as "the royal road to the unconscious." Indeed, such cues, like fertile seeds, may develop from within and reveal some of their meaning, if only attention is given to them. The first task of the therapist will usually be that of helping the patient to direct his attention to the unfolding sequence of scenes, so he can become aware of and remember their detail. The following example is from the session of a forty-seven-year-old man who lay most of the time with his eyes closed, feeling pleasantly relaxed, and who probably retained very little of what he saw. When questioned at one point, he described a scene that is one of three that he could remember after the session was over. This is how he described the image on the following day:

> One picture that came to me was about a camel being led by a lean, angular, Sherlock Holmes type of Englishman. They were on a tour. I don't know why the Englishman was leading the camel. It had no pack on its back. Possibly the Englishman was too impatient and felt he had to drag the camel in order to get there at all. My body goes slowly, has to, and much of the work I do seems to

have to be done in spells, with much resting in between times.

What the patient said nine days later, writing about the session, shows how the number and significance of associations between the symbol and his personality were increased after a period of spontaneous elaboration:

> What I originally mentioned hardly expresses what I have later come to feel about this picture. The Englishman who is taking a world tour is not riding; he is so foolish as to pull the camel along because he is impatient. The Englishman is me. He is very "hawk-nosed," and this is much emphasized. Actually I think of Englishmen as being fools who would go on playing cricket while their world falls apart and who play games with no one but themselves. The camel is the part of me that can carry me there. It represents all the wisdom of the East. The idea of the self, the kingdom of God within, is familiar to me. In my daily life, I do not seem to believe this; I do not feel it within or project it without . . . As for my thoughts about the camel, I feel that in this lifetime I am not going to allow myself to ride him and take me on the journey. I do not act as though there were a self to carry; evidence of inner spontaneity is very faint. Depending on others to run things, however, is becoming more intolerable to me.

The therapeutic implication of such readiness to read into the symbolism of the reverie is obvious. And since this is frequently of spontaneous occurrence, it may be mentioned as a cognitive aspect in the description of the MMDA experience. It might be suspected that it is precisely this proximity between visual and conceptual understanding that accounts for the tendency of some individuals to prevent aspects of their inner life from becoming expressed in conscious images.

In dealing with imagery at the time of the session proper, the aim should be, as with psychosomatic symptoms, that of contacting the *experience* which is dormant in the visual symbols. Mere contemplation of the latter

may not be sufficient to this end; on the other hand, identification with the characters or objects in the fantasy may
lead the patient to undo a projection and recognize a hitherto unacknowledged part of himself. This was the case of
a woman, for instance, who felt disgust at the sight of a
ridiculous clown, but who, when attempting to identify
with such a character, suddenly yelled in panic, for she
felt like a little baby tossed in the air. Then she realized
that she had been played with like a doll; she had actually
adopted this role and played the clown all her life to
please others. Yet all along, in the process of this "show,"
she was suffering from postponement of her real urges and
feeling the loneliness implied in the assumption that nobody would want her except as an object of amusement.

This sequence of events shows that the facilitating effect of MMDA on the therapeutic procedure lies not only
in the presentation of a significant clue (image of the
clown) to the patient's conflict ("playing" the clown vs.
wanting to be loved as she is). Once the button of the
significant symbol was pressed, her experience changed in
quality: The patient's emotion was released, and she
switched from a visual type of reaction to one of the feeling-enhancement type (being tossed in the air, treated as
an object). As a consequence of attending to the unpleasant feeling of being treated as an object, insight ensued:
She was treating *herself* as an object, in presenting herself
to others as such. Lastly, a new feeling came to the fore:
She did not *want* to treat herself like this; what she
wanted was love. It is significant that, for several days
after the session, she felt an intense desire for food, which
ended abruptly at a later appointment, during which she
came to accept her desire for love more fully. The entire
process may be seen like a rising from the feelingless type
3 MMDA reaction, though the latter was achieved after
the end of the session.

The condensed illustration above may give an over-
simplified view of what form the therapist's intervention

can take in the process of leading the patient to the de-symbolization of the experience embodied in visual terms. An image may have to be brought to mind again and again, its transformations followed, and attention directed to the patient's feelings, while watching or identifying with objects or persons in the scene, interpretations given at this or that point, and so on. The following passage, from the transcript of a tape recording, never led to the expected explosion of feelings, but illustrates in detail the exploration of an image and shows how much interpretation can be achieved by means of a non-interpretive approach:

Doctor. Let us work on this image. Could you *be* this place into which you enter?

Patient. *Be* that place?

Doctor. Yes, speak out of the experience of being that place.

Patient. I have a problem here, because I don't know what is in the center of it until I open it, so to find this place I have to be aware of what is inside of babies. Is that all right? Which one shall I do?

Doctor. Either.

Patient. OK. I'm this place, and there is this baby inside, and I'm waiting for someone to come and open the door and take it out. And somehow I'm trying to watch. I want to know what is inside, somehow. I'm being curious about it.

Doctor. Can you say how you are? Could you describe yourself?

Patient. I can't do it too well, but there is a part of me that is looking outside. Outside of me there is light, a bright light, a beautiful outside world, and I am kind of a shield that doesn't let this outside penetrate to the inside. The inside is amorphous, black, neuter, nothing about sense, but the sense of being shut off, kind of stopped, waiting for someone to pick up this baby and bring it out, and in a way my task seems to be to shield the baby from the outside, keep it in cold storage, almost.

Doctor. Keep it in cold storage. Can you sense this part
of yourself, this protective function?

Patient. You mean in my normal self, or right now?

Doctor. No, in your life, in your everyday self. Do you
see yourself as shielding a very precious part?

Patient. That's very interesting. My tendency—oh, I'm
getting quite a bit, I think—my conscious tendency as
soon as I realize how to get it will be to go in and pick
it up and get it out real fast, probably faster than I
should.

Doctor. The same thing! "Probably faster than I should"
. . . the fear of . . .

Patient. I want it to be that I get it out right away. I
force it.

Doctor. So there seems to be a conflict here for you between the tendency to overshield and really remove
this core of life from life, keep it in storage, and the
opposite tendency and over-tendency to take it out
fast into life.

Patient. Now I think what's happening is that, consciously,
I'm doing it much too fast, so it's blocked to my conscious mind so I can't get to it any faster than I'm
supposed to. So, unconsciously, I have to go to the
other extreme, to keep it shut. There is one interesting
thing which may help. In meditation and other experiences, whenever anything interesting starts happening,
I have to grab it spontaneously and put it down. So
I don't let myself. I pull myself out of it, as soon as an
image . . . I had this experience before, so this may
just indicate that.

Doctor. Which is, in a way, shielding the experience, and
in another way it is taking it out.

Patient. I try to take it out, so I lose it. Yes, wow!

Wife. (*As spectator*): I don't know if it's the MMDA
or Dr. N.

Doctor. It's the dream; all it takes is to start with a good
seed. So I think you can get more out of this, if you
go on being this room. Say all you can about yourself,
as a room, not disregarding the obvious—anything
about color, temperature, the dimensions, whatever.

Patient. I get the impression it was painted white, almost like an apparatus you'd see, like a machine in a hospital. It was obviously man-made.

Doctor. But say it in the first person.

Patient. I am painted white-yellow, kind of a warm white, and I'm obviously man-made, with handles and knobs and things, and the significance I get is that I am the part of intellect, not of emotion. That's very much like my conscious mind really is. Consciously, I'm usually very intellectual; the emotions are inside.

Doctor. So you are an artificial room, designed to protect this baby.

Patient. It's interesting that I wouldn't call it artificial at all. In a way, "artificial" is true, but to me it has a connotation of not being real. To me a machine is just as real as a human being. It's just created in a different way, so it kind of bothered me to use that connotation "artificial." It's here, but it's something else. It's just as real, though.

Doctor. Yes. You are controls, man-made . . .

Patient. . . . More a matter of well-defined, with boundaries and laws, that are clear-cut, that aren't fringes. Either it's here or it isn't here, like I can have it exactly, and that's what it is.

Doctor. What else can you see as a room in you? Could you give a description of your feelings regarding yourself as a room?

Patient. My main purpose, that I can see, is to take care of what's inside, which is this baby, and I can't get to it, for I feel that I have all around these devices and apparatuses, to maintain the right environment for the inside, like temperature, atmosphere, etcetera. So my main function, as I see it now, is to just keep the optimum environment for the baby.

Doctor. You said something about being sanitized?

Patient. Yes, the way it was in the dream . . . Now I am almost an incubator.

Doctor. Would you concentrate a bit more on that—how it feels to be an incubator.

Patient. How it feels to be an incubator? Somehow it

doesn't seem to be enough. I'm having trouble identifying with it, because what I was doing before was half looking at it. Now I'm trying to be it completely, and the action of being this incubator just isn't enough. I'd like to do other things, somehow, but I can't, because I'm an incubator, and an incubator isn't supposed to, and this baby is the most important thing, so I can't really be concerned with anything else.

Doctor. Does it make sense in your life to say, "I am an incubator for the baby to be born, but this is not enough—to be an incubator"?

Patient. In my life I have never been aware of being this incubator. What I have been trying to do is have the incubator do what the baby is supposed to do, if anything. I'm trying to get the baby out of here. Well, in the dream, the way I do it is to wait until somebody . . . No . . . OK, the way it is in the dream, I go to the incubator and pick up the baby. Now, as the incubator, I'm trying to do what the baby is supposed to do, rather than waiting for someone to come and pick it out, and it's interesting that there is no feeling that at some point the baby is going to wake up and open the door. It has to be an action from the outside.

Doctor. Isn't there anything in being an incubator that suggests an action from the outside?

Patient. I am an action from the outside, you say?

Doctor. The incubator is an action from the outside, a lot of action, a lot of manipulation of machinery, in that room, that sanitized room, which is all action from the outside, which converges on the baby, as if there were not enough faith that the baby will survive without so much incubation.

Patient. Well, it feels like this: I have been set up to do something specific, which is to keep everything normal and constant and all that. I should be doing that, and if I'm not, I'm failing. And I don't have any free will of my own as an incubator, so I have to wait until somebody from outside tries to do something through me, whether it's open the door or change any of the constants. Now, whether the baby needs it or not I don't know, because I don't really know anything about the baby.

The tape goes on for a long time and shows an impasse that could not be resolved in the session: The "baby" in the patient wants to get out, to be born, but will not cry for help or *feel* the despair of being locked in. Yet only feeling could free him, for it is the patient's feelings that are being locked in and replaced by thinking and self-manipulation (incubator). After this situation was exposed, the problem was tackled more directly in an encounter between the patient and his wife. The rule was that they could voice nothing but the feelings of the moment (i.e., withholding opinions, judgments, interpretations, thoughts). This was not only useful to the patient, but a rewarding experience in communication for the couple.

Whenever not only feelings and physical symptoms but imagery and the desire to communicate are slight, a previous dream of the patient may be taken as a starting point for therapy. The increased faculty of creating imagery under MMDA makes it easy for the patient to re-create dreams and deal with them as an ongoing process, whereas an enhancement of the ability to read into metaphoric or symbolic forms is favorable to the unfolding of their meaning.

The following instance, from the session of a young scientist, will complement previous examples of the handling of imagery, since it shows the process of "encountering" between the patient's different sub-selves as portrayed in multiple dream elements. This is a common resource of Gestalt therapy, but little has been described of this procedure, and it can be so useful with MMDA (and ibogaine) that it deserves detailed illustration.

The dream that was examined in this session consisted

of a single image, which the patient described before the drug had begun to take effect. In this scene—part of a dream that he could not remember—there was a shrimp stapled to the inside of a plastic bag full of water.

He was first instructed to look at the dream scene as a picture of his existence, regarding himself as the shrimp. He said, "This is my existence. I am a shrimp in a plastic bag. I am stapled. I can't move. And I have no head."

This made sense to him, since there was a sense of being immobilized in his life. At the suggestion that he describe the experience of being a shrimp, he now realizes that not only is he enclosed by the bag but by the shell that covers his body. He reacts to this by wanting to be free and have direct contact with the environment, and realizes that this is a true though unexpressed urge in him.

But then, when asked to enact the shell, he realizes that this is also part of himself, since he wants to protect himself. As he pursues the enactment of the dream elements, it turns out that all these are engaged in mutual antagonism, but after the various "voices" talk with one another, a sense of unity develops.

Thus the subject as shrimp does not feel encased in his shell, but endowed with it for his own purposes; the shell does not insist any more on protecting the shrimp beyond its interest, but wants to serve as his instrument; shrimp and water enjoy each other, and they all feel protected in the bag.

A new element of the dream is now recalled by the patient. It is from his mother's hand that the plastic bag is hanging, with all that there is in it. Shell, bag, and mother appear now as progressively explicit presentations of a function of himself, which both protects him and restrains him. I now ask him to enact the shrimp talking to his mother. At first, he wants to say, "Let me out, let me free," but cannot be heard from inside the bag. He cannot reach her, feels too distant and isolated, in the same manner that he does in real life. He now realizes he cannot communicate intimately with his mother.

I then ask him to take a step out of the dream and imagine his mother sitting in front of him and tell her of his feelings of constraint or imprisonment. The outcome of the encounter is a long episode which he retrospectively summed up as follows:

> I couldn't, I couldn't. I knew I had to really get angry at her, to hit her. I remember now the first time I saw her. I had set her up on the floor. She was just about two feet tall, and I felt like smashing her to pieces with a club. I really wanted to so much, but again I couldn't. Finally, she just sort of fell to pieces. I hoped for a second that this meant that she was gone for good, but I soon found out that she was still with me. I guess she won't ever go away until I knock her away, get really angry, cry, etcetera. When that day comes, I believe I will be totally free from her.

He was not able to go beyond the impasse, but he could now understand how his unfulfilled feeling was not mere inertia, but a silent struggle between rage and guilt.

We worked on the dream scene for about four more hours, in the course of which he was able to understand the image of the staple. It represented biting, childishly vindictive rage turned against himself. But after a period of contemplating this "Baby-me" attitude, his closed-off, clinging, biting hardness gave way—now he just wanted to be tucked up (folded and put away) and dropped in the corner of the bag. In other words, the hostility of the staple, which was initially directed to a possessive and hardheaded "biting" at the shrimp, came to be felt by the patient as a misdirected desire to hold on, to have contact, to be not alone. And he now saw that the baby in him that wanted to be loved did not need to go about it aggressively, but that, on the contrary, he could achieve much more by just enjoying his surroundings.

As to the bag, it was she "who is in charge," who wanted the status quo. Everyone else has other things he (or she) wants to do. Shrimp wants to go back to the sea and live free, with his head back on; water wants to evaporate; and staple wants to find his place, too. Only the bag wants to keep things the way they are—"she feels full and warm with water, shrimp and shell and staple all inside her." The end result of the session for this young man was insight into his inner world to an unknown and surprising degree.

He started out his report on the following day with the assertion, "I now *really* know how I see myself." And now, after eight months, he still explains that he is different from before, "in that now I see myself, understand myself." He values this understanding to such an extent that he has decided to study psychology.

The reading of the case illustrations presented on the foregoing pages may well seem, on the whole, not very different from a collection of accounts taken from ordinary psychotherapeutic sessions not involving the use of a drug. Most of the reactions to MMDA may be understood as an *intensification* of feelings, symptoms, and visual imagination rather than a qualitative change thereof. The value of such an intensification in the psychotherapeutic process lies mainly, perhaps, in that clues to the significant issues take more frequently the therapist's or patient's attention than they otherwise would, whereas, in the normal situation, much of the time and effort in a therapeutic process may go into cutting through a veil of verbiage and automatisms that form part of the habitual social role. With MMDA, there is a more prompt access to the patient's underlying *experience*, or symptoms resulting from its denial and distortion.

Another aspect of the effects of MMDA that contributes to the greater density of the therapeutic interaction, if not to its qualitative change, is that, without loss of the reflective disposition, thinking takes on a more experiential quality than it ordinarily would. Instead of being purely conceptual and verbal, the thinking that characterizes the

MMDA-elicited state seems linked to visual images, sensory data, and emotional experience, so that an abstract statement tends to bring about in the person's mind concrete instances of its application, and insight tends to be a complete, feeling-intellectual process rather than conceptual realization.

The value of visual fantasy in psychotherapy is another instance of this experiential thinking, bound to images and not divorced from feelings. Though some persons have a natural facility for summoning up visual images, and others may acquire it through training, the facilitation that MMDA can effect in active imagination must be listed in this final summary of its usefulness as an adjunct to psychotherapy.

Last but not least, the value of MMDA lies in its potential to bring about peak experiences which may occur either spontaneously or as a consequence of therapeutic work, and which may last seconds or hours. In such moments of serenity and love, a person may experience his reality from a different point of view and thus learn to let go of his habitual attitudes. The bearing of such peak experiences on the doctor-patient encounter may be that of a step toward learning to relate in the Now, a present free from transferential bondage to past conditions and stereotyped mechanisms.

CHAPTER IV

HARMALINE AND
THE COLLECTIVE
UNCONSCIOUS

H ARMALINE IS THE MAIN AL-
kaloid in the seeds of *Peganum harmala*, a plant native to
Central Asia and Syria, and which now grows wild along
the Mediterranean coasts of Africa, Europe, and the Near
East, in Persia, Afghanistan, and northeast Tibet. These
seeds have been used for centuries and appear in the Spanish
and Italian pharmacopoeia as *"semen Harmalae sive rutae
sylvestris."* They constitute an article of commerce from
Persia to India, where medical tradition recognizes them as
an emmenagogue, lactogogue, emetic, anthelmintic, and dis-
infectant, and they are known for their psychoactive effects.

Aside from *Peganum harmala*, harmaline is also found
in the South American rain-forest climbers of the genus
Banisteriopsis, which provide the main ingredients of the
drink variously called *yage, ayahuasca,* and *caapi*, employed by the cultures settled along the headwaters of the
Amazon and the Orinoco systems. This drink has been
employed in the initiation of shamans, in puberty rites,
and, in some cultures, for healing various ailments, and
more generally, to induce a state of clairvoyance; hence
the name *telepathine* once given to its active principle.

Although in this chapter I shall be dealing with the
effects of harmaline only from the angle of psychotherapy,

I want to mention that this alkaloid is of special interest because of its close resemblance to substances derived from the pineal gland of mammals. In particular, 10-methoxy-harmaline, which may be obtained in vitro from the incubation of seratonin in pineal tissue, resembles harmaline in its subjective effects and is of greater activity than the latter. This suggests that harmaline (differing from 10-methoxy-harmaline only in the position of the methoxy group) may derive its activity from the mimicry of a metabolite normally involved in the control of states of consciousness.

The effects of harmaline in the dosage range of 4 to 5 mg. per kilogram of body weight by mouth (or a total dose of 70–100 mg. intravenously) are a state of physical relaxation, a tendency to withdraw from the environment, keeping eyes closed and wanting noises and sounds to be kept to a minimum, a certain numbness in the extremities, and above all, very vivid visual images, which may take the form of meaningful dreamlike sequences. In addition to this, about 50 per cent of the subjects experience nausea or vomiting at some point in the session. On account of the symptoms described, it follows that the ideal setting for the use of this drug is a comfortable couch in a quiet, dark environment.

In a study carried out in 1964 of the subjective effects of harmaline, using volunteers who knew nothing about the drug's effects, one of the most surprising findings was that of the similarity of the content of their visions, which in turn resembled those of the Indians. Some of the more frequent items in the content analysis of the thirty sessions that composed that study were tigers and animals in general, birds or flying, dark-skinned men, death, and circular patterns conveying the idea of a center, source, or axis.

The recurrent expression of themes such as those enumerated and the mythical quality of many of the images reported by subjects leaves little doubt that harmaline characteristically evokes the presentation into consciousness of such transpersonal experiences (and the symbols thereof) as Jung contemplated in speaking of archetypes.

For one sharing the Jungian point of view, it would be natural to think of the artificial elicitation of archetypal experience as something that could facilitate personality integration, and therefore psychological healing. Yet the observation of the psychotherapeutic results of the harmaline experience was not the outcome of any deliberate attempt to test the Jungian hypothesis. These results came as a dramatic surprise in the above-mentioned study, even before the recurrence of images became apparent. Of the group of thirty subjects who were our volunteers, fifteen experienced some therapeutic benefit from their harmaline session, and ten showed remarkable improvement or symptomatic change comparable only to that which might be expected from intensive psychotherapy. Eight of the ten were psychoneurotic patients, and another had a character neurosis of which he was slightly aware. These nine amounted to 60 per cent of the subjects with obvious neurotic symptoms (N=15) among the volunteers.

My lack of further experience with pure harmaline derives from my having been engaged, since the time of the above research, in the study of harmaline combinations: harmaline-MDA, harmaline-TMA,[1] harmaline-mescaline and others. Since my intention in the present chapter is to present a view of the effects and use of harmaline when employed by itself, I shall mention only that these combinations can be useful in the cases of individuals who, for psychological or physiological reasons, do not respond well to the pure drug.

It would be hard to offer a simple explanation for the instances of improvement brought about by the harmaline experience. Such improvement usually occurred spontane-

[1] TMA: trimethoxyamphetamine.

ously, without necessarily entailing insight into the particulars of the patient's life and conflicts. As in all cases of successful deep therapy, it did involve greater acceptance by the patients of their feelings and impulses and a sense of proximity to their real self. Statements like these, however, are not very explicit, and only case histories can adequately illustrate the nature of the process.

One of the first subjects to experience the effects of the alkaloid was a young man who had spent five years in rather unsuccessful psychoanalytic treatment for an anxiety neurosis. His reaction after five or ten minutes, soon after I had finished injecting the drug into his vein,[2] was an exclamation of wonder: "It is unbelievable! Everything I do, everything I say, is a distortion! I have been living for years without suspecting *what I really am*. I must have forgotten as a child, and only now can I feel myself again, my *real* self!"

This realization was the most important of the day and one of the most important in his life. It was not arrived at through reasoning, or analyzing a life situation, nor was it the outcome of any therapeutic intervention on my part. The following is a description of the subject's experiences during these moments:

His first sensation upon receiving the injection he describes as "an internal buzzing and physical anxiety, as if I were to burst out through my nose, or my blood were to explode out of my arteries; it also had a tranquillity, like that of feeling a strong sun for the first time in my life, or at the last instant, something like seeing peace and life in the moment of death. It was physical despair, as if my faculties would not respond—neither my voice, nor my movements, nor my thoughts."

After this initial stage, which may have lasted only five minutes, he lost the fear and gave in to a rapid flow of

[2] Harmaline may be used in intravenous injection if an immediate onset and somewhat shorter duration of effects are desired.

imagery which he scarcely reported, since his effort to talk only interfered with the experience, (and he did not feel like interfering with it). Very soon, while he was having imagery related to his childhood, he achieved the insight that accounted for the therapeutic benefit of the day: "I see myself as I am, and this has no relation to the way I am living. I behave in contradiction to myself, because I don't acknowledge myself."

Here is more of his report written on the following day: "I felt like I had another person inside or was being another person—something I have never experienced before. I felt free from my everyday 'I.' I saw myself in a world of certainty, surprised at the ignorance in which I have lived with regard to what lies in the depth of my being. It was a being connected to my real self, like living in a different world in which nothing was hidden and in which I went along with great serenity."

Three months later, he wrote:

"There remains with me the image of a self of which I had no notion and had never even imagined, with more of those attributes which I considered desirable and perfect, a tranquil self with its eyes turned toward the world, with not the least worry about itself. And with an old taste in me, not new, but deeply united with my past and my true being.

"At this very moment, in which I am away from myself again, I can see as I walk along the street or ride the bus how I am contained in a sort of shell, blind to what is important, and yet I cannot escape the feeling of my true being inside."

I had known this patient for only two weeks prior to this day. His therapist had told me of the dead end to which his treatment had apparently come during the past month and suggested him as a possible volunteer for our research project. My knowledge of him was not exceptional as compared to that of other candidates whom I interviewed and tested during the days preceding their sessions. My rapport with the patient was less than average. The patient was rather withdrawn and seemed more interested in the exotic prospects of a mind-changing drug than in a therapeutic exchange. The outcome was only moderate in terms of immediate improvement, for, as the patient describes, his novel feeling of his true self was still no remedy for his estrangement from himself, but only a standard of comparison between his actual state and his potential or ideal. The main result of this experience was a change that was brought about in this patient's psychoanalytic treatment, which was never interrupted. His sense of authenticity and his enhanced awareness of "distortion" or "lying" or "being contained in a shell" now led to the establishment of a more productive relationship with his therapist and provided both with a goal to achieve in the treatment and a challenge that gave meaning to the analytical process. In other words, a "deficiency motivation" (becoming free from his symptoms) became a self-actualization motive. In psychotherapy, as in alchemy, "one must have gold to make gold," and in this case the session gave the patient the initial "capital" required for the work.

The episode described in the foregoing pages took place during a lapse of no more than thirty minutes and ended when I started questioning him. Soon after he stated that everything in his life was a lie or a distortion, I thought that it would be useful to him to look more closely into the particulars of this distortion, so that he could have something to remember after the session, something upon which he might anchor the otherwise vague sense of his reality. To my question as to *what* in his life was a distortion, he answered, "Everything. Everything that I say or do. Every gesture, the way I talk, the way I climb onto a bus." And now he suddenly felt nauseated and restless. As I continued to invite him to look into the concrete instances of the lie, the distortion that he had discovered, he felt increasing malaise, resented my speaking to him, and said that my questions made him feel more nauseated. Soon he started vomiting and spent the next four to five hours alternating between periods of vomiting and periods of sleeping. During this time, he said that he was thinking or contemplating images, but there was little that he could report, partly because of his inertia and his desire to withdraw from contact and partly because he could not remember anything that he did not mention as soon as he had experienced it. When he did speak, though, either in answer to a question or taking the initiative to talk, his physical discomfort increased. The clearest of the images that he did capture was very expressive of the world of harmaline on its "hellish" side—he was having a picnic with his family and was sitting in a circle around the fire where they were roasting . . . his father.

This session displays both a fragmentary sample of the harmaline peak experience and a view of the drug's unpleasant effects. The former is quite characteristic of the drug and consists of a state in which anxiety and destructive forces are assimilated into a peculiar type of ectasy marked by a sense of energy, even power and freedom ("as if I were to burst out through my nose, or my blood were to explode out of my arteries") and at the same time, tranquillity ("like feeling a strong sun for the first time in my life or . . . peace . . . in the moment of death"). Frequent symbols of this power are, aside from the sun and the process of dying, fire, tigers or lions, dragons, all of them typical of the psychic domain tapped by harmaline. Yet, to *be* fire or to *be* a lion in actual life is something that not many can even conceive, and this may account for the fact that either symbolic visualization or an experience of pure feeling (as in the quotations in the earlier parentheses) is the most that the average person can allow himself without meeting psychological obstacles. I think that this patient's discovery of his sense of self and freedom for his everyday "I" was a step toward practical realization, but this was all that he could afford to see without threatening the structure of his present personality.

The state of physical discomfort, fatigue, and half-sleep (with unclear dreams), present throughout most of the session just described, constitute the typical "adverse reaction" to harmaline. Though little in it would suggest its being more than a physical toxic syndrome, the time of onset, the persons who are prone to it, and the contexts in which I have seen such a reaction occur leave me with little doubt as to its being in the nature of a psychosomatic reaction. In this particular instance, illustrative of many others, the lethargic state seemed to be an active evasion of the discomfort accompanying the alternative state of attention to the ongoing process (a rich flow of imagery, memories, thoughts, and feelings) and communication. Why this experience turned into one of discomfort is probably not the right question to ask. The pain of self-confrontation may well be an individual constant, reflecting the person's present state. If this is so, the question to ask in the case under discussion is, How was the peak experience of the first minutes possible at all? The reason, I believe, is the same as that which accounts for the possibility of peak experiences in disturbed personalities in general: a realization is made possible by the temporary ignoring of its ultimate consequences; a state of being is grasped in abstraction (not as a conceptual abstraction, but more like a feeling abstraction), like the perfume of a rose without the sight of it, or like a feeling state conveyed by a work of art which may be identified with and enjoyed by many who would not carry that feeling state into embodied expression as a style of life.

It may be a matter of speculation whether the patient's initial state of well-being might have persisted had I not pressed him with questions. Apparently, my question posed to him a challenge of consciousness that he could not meet, but it is conceivable that he might have arrived at the corresponding answers himself if left to his spontaneous rhythm. The natural tendency of most persons to withdraw from contact under the influence of harmaline (the opposite of the typical MDA experience) may well be a constructive avoidance, a fencing of the seedling while it attains maturity, as discussed in more general terms in our introductory chapter. The metaphor used by Ramakrishna to speak of meditation and the way of detachment may be relevant to this point: Once butter has been separated by churning the milk, it can be put into the serum again or into water, and it will not dissolve.

Whether I was adding water prematurely or not, I do not know, but I am bringing up the issue because it illustrates what I see as a permanent dilemma in the guidance of harmaline sessions: the balance between stimulation and non-interference.

Little intervention may well leave a patient to his own inertia and result in an unproductive session; on the other hand, uncalled-for intervention may disrupt the organic development which is characteristic of the more successful harmaline experiences. As a consequence, more tact is needed in conducting these sessions than with any other.

The more successful experiences with harmaline have a characteristic spontaneity, and these pose little problem to the therapist. In contrast to experiences of self-exploration at the interpersonal level, it is probably in the nature of an archetypal experience to develop naturally from within, so that the most a person's ego can do is stand by watchfully. Yet such experiences of easy and spontaneous unfoldment of images and psychological events occur only in about every other person, so that it is the business of the psychotherapist to induce them when they will not naturally occur. To illustrate this, I am quoting some notes taken from one of the less interesting sessions, which is representative of many others in which the subjects were left to follow their own course. In this case, the subject was a rather conventional thirty-year-old woman suffering from anxiety neurosis. The following fragment adequately represents the whole transcript, which is that of a mono-

logue in which she reports images succeeding each other
with no clear logic of transition:

> I see a white bird.
> A cross.
> A lamp with violet teardrops—glass.
> I feel a ringing in the ears.
> I see two crystal balls, like glittering lamps.
> I see sand on a beach being tossed with shovels.
> I see a red rag.
> I see the image of an old and ugly man making globes
> with his mouth.
> Many lights are reflected, and then light and dark fol-
> low. Lights go on moving by in turquoise shades, green in
> the middle and turquoise all around.
> A black teardrop of a turning lamp.
> I see a radiant sun.
> I see the face of the beast in *Beauty and the Beast.*
> A large black blot.
> A map. I first see America and then Europe—Italy.
> I see some stained glass windows.
> I only see lights. I see glittering lights, many lanterns in
> red-green-yellow colors.
> A Persian carpet with a red background and shapes.

Anyone acquainted with the world of harmaline would
recognize here the typical themes: the bird, as the very
first image; then the archetype of the cross, with its religious connotation and its implied significance of intersec-
tion, center, and outward extension from it; the turning
lamp, again conveying centrality; the radiant sun, with its
significance of source once more, and stressing the element
of light; the colors, expressing light once again. Yet, in
spite of their potential or hidden significance, the images
followed each other in this inward display, without revealing their treasure, while the onlooker watched them go by
with little emotional participation other than curiosity.

It is in cases like these that the therapist can sometimes step in and help the patient unlock the experience
hidden in the visual symbol, not so much through inter-

pretations, which would interfere with the more important primary process, but through an encouragement of attention. Merely by more attention being given to these fleeting images, it may be discovered that they might start to unfold in a meaningful way; if only they are "listened to," they may begin to "talk."

The following excerpt is a literal transcript from part of a session, the first part of which had proceeded much like the one reported above. The passage quoted here is taken from a moment when the therapist chose to guide the process, and the fleeting and disjointed images then took the form of a continuous and coherent sequence. The episode transcribed took place after the first thirty minutes of the session.

> Patient. I see a woman dressed in white with a bandana on her head. She's leaning against an ivy-covered wall, and she is looking at a statue, a golden statue of a lion. Well, the statue is very close to her, on top of a tall white granite obelisk, as phallic as the Washington Monument.
>
> Doctor. What is the statue?
>
> Patient. What does it tell me?
>
> Doctor. No, what does it represent?
>
> Patient. The monument? Well, now I'm standing at the base of the monument and looking up at it. It's become a rocket.
>
> Doctor. A rocket. Did you mention a golden lion?
>
> Patient. Yes, a golden lion. It may have been on one of the friezes on a public building nearby. It looks like the lion on a European royal coat of arms. It is an almost Oriental or Siamese lion. The features on the face of the lion, the mouth in particular, suggest this. It is standing on its hind legs, with its forepaws in the air, its mouth open, half-lunging forward, as if it were attacking.
>
> Doctor. Do you have any feeling about the color? This golden color?

Patient. It's a very yellow gold.

Doctor. Do you like the color?

Patient. Yes.

Doctor. How does it feel? . . . (*Rest of question inaudible.*)

Patient. Well, I can feel myself touching the lion. When I touch it, though, it tends to become a real lion. It loses its cold metallic cover and becomes warm fur.

Doctor. Can you talk to the lion?

Patient. He's turned into a real lion now, an African lion. He has a tremendous tawny mane that is very stiff and bristly. His eyes are yellow.

Doctor. How do you feel about this lion?

Patient. I feel he is my friend. He is like a dog I might have for a pet. But he is nonetheless, in his own domain, a fierce and wild animal.

Doctor. Is this a good feeling, being a friend of an animal in its natural state?

Patient. Yes.

Doctor. Maybe that's what the image conveys, this pleasantness of joining the wild animal, being accepted by the wild animals.

Patient. I'm curious to know what things he could tell me if he could speak. The lion is turning and walking away toward the jungle.

Doctor. Can you follow him?

Patient. Yes. He's trotting now, and I have to trot, too, to keep up with him. Now he's loping. He's chasing an automobile. (*Sounds of outside traffic on tape at this time.*) There's a trainer, a man, running along behind the automobile. He jumps onto the rear bumper and hangs onto the back window. The car pulls away from the lion, the man riding on the back of it. The lion slows down and stops, looking after the car. Now he's turning around to talk to me. He says, "It's too bad that one got away," or something like that.

Doctor. What did it want to do?

Patient. I'm not sure. He may have been going to attack the man. Or he may have been just curious. But he is hungry. It doesn't make any difference to him whether his meat be human or some other animal.

Doctor. What does the lion do now?

Patient. He is standing there licking his chops. You know, licking his mouth with his tongue.

Doctor. What would you like from a lion?

Patient. What would I like from a lion?

Doctor. Or in a lion.

Patient. Warmth is the first thought that comes to mind. Strength, I suppose. And I see children climbing on the lion's back and sliding down on his sides and rolling under him and climbing up again and sliding over his back—having a wonderful time. And he is standing there enjoying it all.

Doctor. Can you imagine yourself as the lion?

Patient. No.

Doctor. Assume you have a lion in yourself. You would like to play with the children as they are playing with the lion. You have a wild animal as well . . . (Rest of sentence inaudible.)

Patient. I can do it better if I see the lion as a lioness. But somehow I don't see the lioness being as . . .

Doctor. . . . as lion-like.

Patient. I guess I see the lion as a dog, a playmate, whereas the lioness is strictly a mother of the children.

Doctor. For some purpose, it is a lion and not a lioness.

Patient. All right, we'll go back to the lion. (Long silence.) I'm having a lot of trouble becoming the lion. I guess I know why. It's because I don't much feel like taking on the job that he is performing.

Doctor. Suppose you have the lion talk to you.

Patient. Talk to me? And those are my children? (Long silence.) It isn't going anywhere.

Doctor. Let's see if some commentary leads anywhere. I see some themes in what you have been saying. There's a theme of nobility: the lion insignia, the chateau, the political figures. Not only nobility, but authority, let's say. Then there's the theme of the movement around a center—galaxies, drum, merry-go-round. Then there's a theme of animal life, impulse—the horses on the merry-go-round that became a stampede, wildness; then the cowboys, with revolvers . . . impulse, aggression. Then the lion. And the lion, I think, contains the three: the central role, the authority, the vitality, the aggression, and the nobility. I feel there's a place in your life for these feelings. It's something of your self-image that is being expressed, your ideal self. It should be very easy to enact the lion.

Patient. If he were doing something. But he is just standing. Very tired, and probably after hunting all day, he's come to rest in the park. And by accident some children come to climb on his back, and he's just too tired to do anything about it.

Doctor. Try saying, as if you were the lion, "I'm tired. I've been hunting all day . . ."

Patient. I'm tired. It feels good to have the children scratching my back, but they're getting heavy. He's a little afraid to start walking because one of the children might fall off. And yet he also has the desire to slip out from under them and be gone before they realize he's gone.

Doctor. Don't shift to the third person. "I'd like to slip out . . ."

Patient. Now the children have left.

Doctor. What do you feel like doing, lion?

Patient. Well, he urinated. It's getting dark. He is walking slowly but very softly. He is walking down a road with cars and trucks coming toward him with headlights on. (*Sound of traffic on tape in background.*) He stays over to the side of the road, and they don't see him. Now it's a lioness. She is looking at the trucks, and the truck drivers aren't aware of her, but she is thinking that if they weren't in the trucks, they would make a good dinner for her. And that although lions know what trucks are, she's wondering if the truck drivers know anything about lions. She is starting to hunt. She is walking down a dusty path trying not to stir up any dust. There's a log by the side of the path. A beggar in a tattered leather coat hobbles around behind the log, puts his hand on the shoulder of a man who was sitting there before he came along, and starts talking to him. The beggar has gray hair and . . . I don't know. The log has become a log cabin. The lioness sees a little snake crossing the path in front of her. She has no interest in eating it. Its taste would not be very good. Now the lioness is walking along an exquisitely designed walkway which is made up of inlaid tiles. It's a picture. The center of the figure depicts the rising sun. The light from the sun is drenching the sky in very rich yellow and orange glittering rays. And there are three women standing in the center in white Grecian robes with myrtle on their heads and with their arms uplifted, singing. (*Long silence.*)

Doctor. Do you hear the song?

Patient. Do I hear what?

Doctor. The song from the women.

Patient. It seems to be one note that is sustained throughout eternity. It's a great choral voice that they are singing with, although there are only three of them.

Doctor. Do you feel what that song wants to say throughout eternity?

Patient. I'm listening to it. It has a familiar sound. It's the sound of high power wire vibrating with electrical impulses. A high, humming sound.

Doctor. I would suggest that you pay as much attention to the sound as you can. Enter the sound, become the sound. It may contain something very important.

Patient. I think part of its function is to carry telephone messages. I almost heard some voices I could understand.

Doctor. You are hearing some voices?

Patient. I heard very indistinct voices.

Doctor. In the sound?

Patient. No, the sound continued. It is as if it had connected its circuit to a telephone switchboard so that an occasional call would come into it.

Doctor. There's always a hum?

Patient. It's a pulsating hum.

Doctor. (*Inaudible on tape.*)

Patient. It's much too high. (*Choral music on record player in background.*) (*Long silence.*) I see the heavens opening up. The clouds pull back and form a wide ring. And from the ground, floating upward, are women with one hand upraised, like somebody would

hold up their hand to be helped up a ladder. And they
are floating slowly up toward the peak of the dome.
Two of them are elderly, but they like the feeling of
floating upward in space to the point that they forget
the reason for this phenomenon, and they start doing
somersaults and laughing and giggling and playing,
enjoying themselves instead of assuming a pose. There
are other people waving goodbye. I still haven't heard
the music. (*Long silence.*) I heard one of the voices,
but I couldn't catch the complete sentence. The
woman who was talking on the phone was a farmer's
wife with an unpleasant voice.

Doctor. There's still a hum? Like an electric wire?

Patient. Or high speed.

Doctor. High-speed what?

Patient. I guess I am associating it with jet airliners.

Doctor. So it seems to suggest energy. Can you say anything else about the energy? How it feels? Aside from
speed, are there any other associations?

Patient. Power.

Doctor. Contained power?

Patient. Yes, very definitely contained.

Doctor. Inward? Like the essence of something? Something very essential, latent, potential?

Patient. I can't say I am the power, because it is a limited
power; it is only a utility.

Doctor. How do you know?

Patient. Well, the setting it appears in . . . telephone poles
with wires strung between them.

Doctor. But it originally was a song of the three women.

Patient. Yes, it was.

Doctor. The lion led you to a very beautiful place. While
listening to it . . .

Patient. It's a hymn, really, that they are singing.

Doctor. What words would you give to it to convey the
feeling of this hymn?

Patient. Praise God on the highest, or to the highest.

I would probably not have picked the image of a sculp-
tured lion as a starting point for a fantasy exploration had

I not become aware before this particular session of the prominence of big cats in harmaline experiences, in the lore of South American shamanism, and in mythology in general. The role of the lion as a guide to a domain of sacredness is not peculiar to the episode quoted above, but is similar to the role that the jaguar plays in the Indians' visions and that tigers and snakes play in the visions of other subjects. Even the association between the lion and the sun, indicated in this sequence by its walking on the sun's picture and also by its golden color, is a replica of South American mythology, in which the jaguar is regarded as the incarnation of solar energy.

The development of the sequence and the discussion may be seen as a gradual unfolding of an experience of power, first petrified in a sculpture, then emanating from the image as color and the expression of the lion as ready to attack, later meeting the observer as a live animal, then a *hungry* animal, and finally perhaps, speaking to the subject through the ear rather than the eye in the form of vibrating electrical impulses.

Still, we are left with the feeling of a certain lack. Rich as the episode may be in meanings or mythical overtones, the subject remains a detached observer, unrelated to the events in the dreamlike sequence by feelings that go beyond the aesthetic. The image of the lion, like a seed developing into a tree, has displayed its contents, but this is still bound up in visual symbols, much like a work of art which lies open to us but which, according to our state of mind, may either shake the foundations of our being or leave us cold.

It may have been noticed that many of my interventions were made to draw the subject's attention to her own feelings—of which the vision may be assumed to be the external indication and substitute. Yet the response to these questions usually came through the medium of a symbol. Asked, for instance, how she felt about the lion's color, she felt that she was touching the warm fur of a live animal. Asked about her feelings about being in the company of such an animal, she tried to understand its feelings and saw it engage in movement (walking toward the jungle). Asked what she wanted from a lion, she saw the children climbing on its back. Her experience was projected onto the screen of her fantasy, leaving her as a detached and rather indifferent observer, and she had difficulty in stepping into the action as a character. A way to re-own the experience of her unacknowledged lion nature might have been to enact the lion, stepping into its skin to feel how it felt. But she was reluctant to do this and would not even go through the moves of pretending to be the lion or speaking in the first person *as* it (him) rather than *of* it. The subject's tendency to project her experience into the medium of symbolic forms was expressed in a trait of her fantasy which also exemplified a typical defense mechanism in harmaline sessions—the abundance of art forms, which made her fantasy the *representation of representations*. The suggestive obelisk is merely granite, though when she attended to it, it became a rocket; the lion was a sculpture, a frieze in heraldic style; the sun, a mosaic. The opposite of this would naturally be an experience of interacting with beings perceived as fully alive; one where aesthetic distance gives way to some degree of forgetfulness of one's self as a person lying on a couch and contemplating an illusion.

The following is an example of this type of experience, which I have always seen to be followed by positive therapeutic results:

> We were face to face, the serpent with its open mouth, menacing, trying to devour me, and myself, full of curiosity, trying to enter it without being bitten. The solution to the problem was instantaneous: I had to get in very fast— so fast that the serpent wouldn't be able to get me with its fangs. Idea and action were simultaneous. In a leap, I found myself inside the serpent. Of course, this was a black tunnel with elastic walls, and I saw nothing. (It

seems the serpent had closed its mouth.) I felt a horrible
fear of never being able to get out of it. But then I remembered that this was a dream and that I could at any time go
through the walls—open my eyes—and find myself in bed.
Next, I considered that since I was already there, I should
find out what the serpent contained, for I was absolutely
sure that something was in it. I was still afraid, so I decided
to proceed as quickly as possible. I walked for a while
toward the tail, and suddenly there was light. There was a
grotto at the rear. It was a subterranean grotto, inside of
which was a lake. The water proceeded from a fountain
and was very pure and fresh. I felt an imperative need to
go into the water. I was very tired, and the water was
going to enliven me and especially purify me. It also
seemed that it was very hot inside the snake, so the fresh-
ness of the water left me with an exquisite sensation. I
entered the little lake wearing a white robe; I saw myself,
for I was at the same time bathing and on the shore, looking at myself while I bathed. The "I" that watched had no
body, but the one bathing felt very cold after the initial
pleasant sensation. I therefore left the water; both of my
"I"s became one, and I returned through the tunnel to the
snake's mouth. I was afraid of not being able to get out,
but as I reached the spot the serpent opened its mouth, and
with incredible speed—to avoid being bitten—I found myself in my bed.

This sequence is one of many in a session of great therapeutic value, and it illustrates a trait common to both. In
every episode, the patient is the main character of the
story, and as things happen to her, she is affected by them.
Not only does she visualize herself entering the serpent,
but she identifies with her visualized self and experiences
her experiences to the extent of forgetting that she is in
her own bedroom having a fantasy. She, the dreamer, feels
curiosity, fear, and delight, and finally feels that *she* has
taken decisions, surmounted obstacles, added something
to her own life. If we accept imagery as symbolic of
unconscious feelings and urges, we may regard experiences like the one quoted above as interactions of a person

with his unconscious, and find in this the reason for their therapeutic value. Moreover, it appears from the sessions that every time confrontation with the unconscious "other" takes place, some integrative experience ensues which is expressed in visual symbolism at the time (i.e., light and water of purification after facing the danger of being destroyed).

Several factors seem to be involved in making this type of experience possible. Some individuals appear to be naturally more prone to it than others, and the personality factors involved in this remain to be elucidated. I think that mental health is one of them, but definitely not the only one. I also have the impression that mesomorphic somatotonics are more likely to have a rich experience than cerebrotonic ectomorphs.

But beyond the question of individual differences, training can prepare the ground for a fruitful harmaline experience—training in the observation of mental events, as is provided by most forms of psychotherapy, and particularly training in active imagination. This particular patient had both, having been prepared for the session by a period of analysis and several guided daydreams.

In spite of the spontaneous unfolding of many harmaline experiences, such spontaneity most certainly needs favorable conditions. This was evidenced by the unpleasant and unproductive sessions of two subjects during the recording of electroencephalograms, as contrasted with productive and pleasant ones which they had in the standard setting. Rapport with, and trust in, the therapist also seem to play an important role, since the persons with less meaningful experiences were, on the whole, those who had communicated less during the preparatory interviews.

I believe that one of the most important functions of a therapist in a harmaline session is that of listening. Persons who volunteered for experimentation with harmaline, regardless of their personal interest in this venture, were instructed to report what they were experiencing, so that even when they kept quiet, they tried to keep a mental record of their reactions in view of making a report. I did some unsystematic experimentation on the bearing of this attitude of intentional watchfulness by not questioning the subjects at some periods in their sessions, by walking into the next room and telling them to spend the following half-hour as they wished and not care about reporting this episode. Also later, after the first thirty cases, I administered harmaline to other subjects without the standard instruction stressing watchfulness, alertness, and the prospect of a report. It is my impression that, under these circumstances, less was remembered or less actually took place in the person's mind—except in the cases of persons who were left to themselves after having arrived at what seemed to be a peak experience.

Conversely, when a highly productive level has not been reached, it seems that watchfulness will lead to it more easily than passive surrender. This watchfulness may be sustained through communication. I especially ask the subjects not to overlook reporting their physical sensations, since their doing so stresses a state of alertness, which counters the natural tendency to be carried along lethargically and forget the harmaline "dream," much as happens with nocturnal dreams. It appears that the usefulness of harmaline is that of bringing about an integration of the conscious and unconscious spheres by a facilitation of symbolic oneiric processes in the wakeful state. If alertness slackens, unconscious life proceeds unconsciously as in natural sleep or habitual "wakefulness."

There are instances in which imagery or feelings flow so meaningfully and spontaneously that little or no "coaching" is needed. Other cases illustrate how some guidance can lead the person to the point where such productiveness is reached. In the following example it was the guided daydream which channeled the subject's creativity into the visual sequence. This procedure proved most fruitful in several instances as a framework in which the person's feelings could be translated, manipulated, and eventually interpreted. I have generally adhered to Desoille's basic scheme of ascent, flight, and descent into the ocean, since this lends itself well to the expression of some basic attitudes (effort and search, freedom, plunging into the unknown) and, like the standard pictures of a projective test, it can give the psychotherapist some orientation on the person's individuality as contrasted with that of others in developing the common theme.

The following is an account of a complete sequence. The patient is a thirty-four-year-old man with marital problems and an anxiety state of short duration.

Dr. N. tells me to imagine a mountain, which I do easily . . . but I do not *see* it. The mountain is not there, like the previous images, but I only have the "idea" of a mountain in front of me. And not in *front* of me, really, but *in* me.

I describe the mountain. It is a truncated cone, very high, and of a blue-gray color. Strangely, if I were to see it, it would be different from all the mountains that I know.

I am asked to climb this mountain, and I see (from here onward I shall speak of "seeing" things, though the comment above continues to hold true) a very high ladder and innumerable men climbing it in a row, like ants.

I start climbing, and I do not go about it in the normal way, but on the side of the ladder, with one of the side rails between my legs, placing one foot in front and the other behind the rungs. I feel the rung between my thighs, and this suggests bicycle riding. Without any choice, there I am, on a bicycle. Gone are the mountain, ladder, and men. I am riding a bicycle in a street with a lot of traffic. I feel that I am intermingling with people and vehicles traveling at high speed. There is great disorder. A train going at high speed appears, and heads toward a tunnel. In passing through it, it tears off its concrete coating. Now it is a train covered with concrete, like a giant beetle, which goes on and on, penetrating everything that is in its way, and going under the bridges instead of over them. I would say that the crazy engineer wants to go through every hole that he finds.

But we must return to our mountain. Time now proceeds at a normal tempo, the mad rush of the previous scene being over. There are no other men now, and I am getting to the top of the mountain. The ladder is just as tall as the mountain, so that, on grasping the last rung, I am touching the very edge of the mountain top. This edge is very fragile and breakable, so I find no other solution then to enter with my whole body, like a reptile. I say "enter," for the mountain is hollow.

I am deciding on the best way of descending when strange beings appear, climbing the walls. They are like giant rats with bulging eyes and spider feet. They look at me and follow their way to the top where they wander along the edge.

I am on my belly like a worm and I crawl along. I have come down a considerable distance. I cannot resist looking up at the place through which I entered. It is almost a luminous spot, but—looking downward from the opening —I see myself! The descent goes on, and there is a Dantesque sight. There is, at the bottom, a sea of fire surrounded by a beach of white sand, which encloses the fire like a ring. The ground on which I find myself is dry and rough. I do not know how I came to be on the beach and on my feet.

I look at the sight. It is marvelous—a fiery sea. What a strange mixture of water and fire in which water does not extinguish the fire and fire does not evaporate the water. The fiery waves, breaking close to the beach and caressing it, turn to crystalline fresh water.

I slowly draw closer. I can see the foam. I touch it and enter the water. It is fresh, refreshing, very refreshing.

I am instructed to approach the fire. I am afraid of getting burned, though something tells me that I will not be burned. I question my reasons for being in that mountain. Why am I here? What am I here for? And I feel like returning. Dr. N. then insists: "Try to enter the fire. After all, if you happen to die that will be only an illusion, and it may prove to be worthwhile."

I then continue to advance, and the water now reaches my calves. It is now that I contact the fire. Before breaking, one of the waves touches my leg, and, far from burning me, it tickles me. Soon I am swimming in the midst of the sea of flames. I swim like a frog.

I was expecting it—Dr. N. asks me to dive into this sea of fire and see what is beneath. I do it, and I feel myself swimming vigorously, head down. I do not feel fire any longer, only water. I do not need to breathe, and I could go on swimming indefinitely. I try to reach the bottom, but without success. I think of returning. The excuse is the same: lack of incentive. But I am well into all this, and it is not the time to worry. I must get to the bottom.

The water gets clear, and now I dimly see the bottom of the fiery sea. It is of white sand. I touch it with my hands. It is coarse. I am with my feet on the sand, now, and I walk, half-floating. I see, to the left, giant pearls (sixty centimeters in diameter, approximately) which look wet, like they were perspiring. There is no plant life. The sea bottom is sterile.

To my right I see three naked woman. Two are white and the other black. Only black in color, for their bodies are identical, and they are like one woman. The three have exceedingly beautiful breasts. I feel instantly attracted and would like to make love to her (or them?).

Once more, I am struck by the absence of humidity on this sea bed, in spite of the fact that it's all under the water. There is nothing that I feel as wetness, that wetness that gives warmth to things, which enhances their odor, and is to me an expression of life. Though the pearls are wet, I am not satisfied with them. I look for plant life, green color, smell of earth or sand or wet grass, and I do not find it.

To my right there is a young couple. He is leaning on a gigantic slice of melon, which supports his back or on which he half-sits. She is firmly attached to his chest. Their mouths are united in a tight kiss. He caresses her breasts and sex at the same time with his hands. Their faces look complacent. She enjoys his hands, and he enjoys her pleasure.

At once I imagine making love on a great slice of melon.

No doubt I have found the wetness I was looking for. The wetness of a melon, of a mouth, of a gigantic vagina. Why not enter? After swimming in fire I think that there are many things that I could do.

I enter into a dark cavity and touch its soft, wet walls with my hands. I would say that the enclosure *caresses* with an enveloping caress. I am naked and feel the contact with my body.

At the end, there is a spiral stairway which leads through tubes to the ovaries. I start climbing, and feel tremendous excitement at being on the verge of knowing the place where life begins! I have arrived, and I find myself in a spacious hall where the color white predominates. Behind a table there is a young lady in a white cloak and wearing eyeglasses. She looks very serious. I dislike her. She is cold.

I ask her what she does, why she is there. I am surprised to hear that she and a companion in a similar hall are in charge of determining conceptions. I am aware of my own astounded expression, but she does not notice. At my request, she explains that people believe that conception is the outcome of sexual intercourse. But such intercourse is just an act of love, she says, and she is in charge of controlling conception.

I inquire about the criterion or policy in such decision-making, and she tells me that all conceptions are registered in a big book, which is something like a book of life.

I draw close to see it. It is extremely old, somewhat like an old Bible, with a peculiar binding. The book indicates all births, with nine-month waiting period. It is not complete, but ends in 1892. The rest is blank pages. The last sentence is: "And the day will come when man, with the help of science and technology, will become his own creator."

The place displeases me, and I decide to leave. I try to descend the way I came up, by the spiral staircase, but I do it through a narrow tube, falling at last in a giant womb. I bounce against its walls, which look like rubber.

As my sight gets used to the dark I see big erosions in the walls, half-healed gouges that have been left by a huge curette. I feel that I am witnessing the register of all the children who were not born.

One thing that can be noticed in this fantasy—as in most —is that many events in it would not have taken place were it not for a specific direction to this effect. Furthermore, the most significant episodes generally unfold only after meeting some resistance. Where the dreamer would, left to himself, interrupt a sequence, follow the most pleasant aspect of his imagination, or be distracted, the therapist can press him to enter the burning sea, to dive in spite of his initial lack of interest, to meet the monsters, to knock at the door, all of which involves increased interaction between his everyday "I" and his other self, between his usual center of consciousness and the symbolic presentation of his unconscious processes. In the case of this man, the dream leads to an increasing expression of an urge for all that he symbolizes as "wetness": sensuousness, sex, earthiness, woman, love. A peak is reached in the expression of this theme with the fantasy of entering the womb, after which a sudden change takes place from "wetness" to frustrating "dryness."

I would advance the hypothesis that fantasies of the wish-fulfillment type express the fact that a person is accepting his own impulses, whereas self-defeating fantasies are the expression of self-rejection in the form of repression. In other words, the pleasure which generally accompanies a fantasy is not so much that which arises from the imaginary fulfillment of a wish, as it would appear, but that of self-acceptance, involved in the *acceptance of fulfillment.*

In the present instance, the final episodes of the patient's dream faithfully depicted his chronic state of being and feelings and may be rightly regarded as a regression from the previously experienced state of inner freedom and fluency. Such a chronic state of being, nevertheless, was unconscious to the patient, in that only unconsciously did he experience dissatisfaction (i.e., as symptoms), while consciously developing much resignation and even idealizing the *postponement* of his spontaneity. Only after the episode in his harmaline session described above in which he felt all-spontaneous and all-himself was he able to sense the contrast between such openness and the sterility of his neat and clean but artificial and self-rejecting way of going about his ordinary life. Thus, he associated the abortion scars, dryness, and texture of the womb in the last part of his fantasy with the idea that his mother had undergone abortions and with the thought that she had considered an abortion at the time when she was pregnant with him. Even this thought, stemming from a comment heard as a child, may have been no more than a symbol itself for the final experience of not feeling loved by his mother, which he had denied, but could now no longer avoid acknowledging.

The conception-controlling nurses in the patient's "dream" are like an echo of his mother's attitude during his childhood, during which time she continually guarded him from imagined illness and dangers, subjected him to restrictive diets and schedules. Her overprotectiveness may further be indicated by the fact that when she was told that her thirty-five-year-old son would be undergoing the above-described session, she sent me (a stranger to her) a detailed account of his medical history since the time of his birth—a history no different from that of an average child.

The patient had found himself a wife with many of his mother's traits: intellectual, moralistic, responsible, polite, and sexually inhibited. He admired her and felt guilty for not loving her more than he did. Yet he did not find with her the depth of communication or intimacy which he later knew with another woman. For four years, he felt unable to decide between his home and his new love, and he felt continually more aware of these alternatives as entailing a choice between different sets of values. At a time when a choice had become critical, he volunteered for the experiment involving the cited harmaline session, in the hope that this might give him a better understanding of himself and thus help him in his decision.

After the session, the patient sensed that his marriage had been to him a choice of "dryness," to which he had been adhering out of a sense of duty but not love. His wants now became more pressing, and his demands on himself diminished. Indeed, five days after the session he indulged in impulsive behavior which had no precedent in him. He got drunk in the company of friends and became violent, and then forgot the whole incident.

One might speculate as to the effect that this exceptional reaction to an already exceptional state for the patient (alcoholic intoxication) constituted an intuitively sought continuation of his harmaline session. For the latter had set up the scenery, so to speak, of his psychological state of affairs, but it still remained for the patient to experience the violence of his smothered self in face of the "antiseptic" nurses implanted in his soul as a chronic anti-life force. Comparable episodes did not occur after this explosion of anger, and the patient continued to feel more like himself than he did before the session. Now he has been living for four years with his second wife in what he feels is his own style.

Some of the experiences undergone by persons during their single exposure to the effects of harmaline (as has been seen so far in both the illustrations and commentary) constitute a plunging of the mind into an area of myth, transpersonal symbols, and archetypes, and thus constitute an analogue to what is the essence of initiation in many cultures. Typically, for instance, the puberty ordeals are occasions when the young are brought into contact (with or without drugs) with the symbols, myths, or art works which summarize the spiritual legacy of their culture's collective experience. The attitude toward the world that is expressed by such symbols is regarded as important to maturity and to the order of life in the community, and for this reason its transmission is reverently perpetuated, made the object of initiations and of other rituals or feasts in which the people renew their contact with, or awareness of, this domain of existence, irrelevant to practical life but central to the question of life's meaning. The harmala-alkaloid-containing drinks of South American Indians are not only employed in puberty rituals but also in the initiation of the shamans, primitive psychiatrists whose expertise in psychological phenomena is revealed, for instance, in the fact that they are frequently expected to understand the meaning of dreams.

Aside from the apparently therapeutic implications of an initiatory process (understood as one of establishing a connection between everyday consciousness and the archetypal domain), we may be left, after considering the sessions reported so far, with a feeling of incompleteness. A process has been initiated, but then what? A person has undergone a novel experience and emerges from it with an enriched sense of selfhood, the intimation of a connection with a deeper region of himself, a more clear awareness of the noble and archaic animal within, and the taste of a greater spontaneity than he has heretofore known. All this is an asset and may suffice to bring about changes in feelings or symptomatic relief, to awaken new interests or orient the individual in a decision, as shown above. Yet most of the sessions that I have seen leave me with the impression of my having witnessed no more than the first act of a drama. Symbols may remain undeciphered, conflicts unresolved, events in the visual display interrupted at crucial points. In the case of the subject in our last illustration, the ending of the dreamlike sequence itself suggests the subject's defeat and the incompleteness of his soul's journey, and we can imagine his unacknowledged frustration as the motive behind his alcoholic intoxication and his unexplained outburst of anger.

All this suggests the desirability of an appropriate context for the assimilation of the harmaline experience, which implies time for reflection in the days following a session, a certain freedom from excessive environmental constraints, and particularly the continuity of the thera-peutic contact. The question also naturally arises as to the effect of a series of harmaline experiences on the develop-ment of the themes, insights, or feelings encountered in the first one. I have only occasionally given harmaline more than once, but the following case history, comprising a series of four sessions, may illustrate both the nature of such an evolution and the bearing of the sessions on clini-cal manifestations in the course of time.

This is the case of a twenty-five-year-old woman who had undergone psychoanalytic therapy for a year and a half with great gains in terms of her personality, but with no improvement noted in the symptoms which consti-tuted her main reason for undergoing treatment. These consisted of intense anxiety, fear of dying or fainting, and physical symptoms like suffocation and paresthesia. These symptoms occurred especially in gray city streets, less so in curved, irregular streets, or those bordered by trees. She also experienced anxiety in movie houses and would usu-ally close her eyes whenever something unpleasant was to be expected in a film. The phobia was preceded by a pe-riod of absent-mindedness in the streets, during which she would often go beyond her destination, either walking or by bus. The closest associations to the feared situation in analysis were episodes of danger during the war, when she had actually been (with her parents) in open spaces under aircraft fire and in areas under attack by bombing. Yet the symptoms developed many years later, during her father's fatal illness. The exact relationship between these two incidents had never become clear. She had been very attached to her father, and also shared his extreme vio-lence. When she was a child, he used to take her to the shore, and now that she was grown up, the sight of a beach would put an end to all her anxiety and depression.

Much of the patient's first session with harmaline took the form of a series of dreamlike sequences rich in archetypal content. The image of a tiger was prominent in these visions and constituted the very first of them. "Floating spots like a tiger's eyes" were the first symptom of the drug's effect and then many tiger faces. Panthers followed and all sorts of cats, black and yellow, and then *the* tiger. This was a very large Siberian tiger, and she knew (for she could read its mind) that she must follow it. This she did several times, but none of the scenes seemed complete. Still, a "longing for the tiger" persisted in her. After an episode (to be described) in which she met her father, she intuitively knew that she was now ready to follow the tiger, and this proved to be the case. Here is the description of the last episode, in her own words. The quotation begins at a point after she has followed the animal to the edge of a plateau and is looking down toward the abyss, which is hell. It is round and filled with liquid fire or fluid gold. People swim in it.

> The tiger wants me to go there. I don't know how to descend. I grasp the tiger's tail, and he jumps. Because of his musculature, the jump is graceful and slow. The tiger swims in the liquid fire as I sit on his back. I then suddenly see my tiger eating up a woman. But no! It is not the tiger. It is an animal with a crocodile's head and the body of a fatter, larger animal with four feet (though these weren't visible). All kinds of lizards and frogs begin to appear now. And the pond gradually turns into a greenish swamp of stagnant water, though full of life: primitive forms of life such as algae, anenomes, microorganisms, etcetera. It is a prehistoric pond. A shore appears, not sandy but covered with vegetation. Some dinosaurs are seen in the distance. I ride on the tiger on the shore. The serpent follows us. It catches up with us. I stand aside and let the tiger take care of her. But the serpent is strong and my tiger is in danger. I decide to take part in the fight. The serpent notices my intention, lets go of the tiger, and prepares to attack us. I hold its head and press on its sides so that it will open its

mouth. It has an iron piece inside, like the bit of a horse. I press on the ends of this bit, and the serpent dies or disintegrates; it falls to pieces as if it were a mechanical serpent. I go onward with the tiger. I walk next to him, my arm over his neck. We climb the high mountain. There is a zigzag path between high bushes. We arrive. There is a crater. We wait for some time, and there begins an enormous eruption. The tiger tells me I must throw myself into the crater. I am sad to leave my companion, but I know that this last journey I must travel. I throw myself into the fire that comes out of the crater. I ascend with the flames toward the sky and fly onward.

As I mentioned earlier, the journey related in the foregoing paragraphs was insinuated on many occasions early in the session, but could not be completed before she confronted her father, and as soon as she did this, she at once knew that she was ready to follow the tigers. Yet it took some insistence on the therapist's part to lead the patient to the point of finding her father—the first personal image in an otherwise anonymous array of dream characters.

I saw many faces, one after another, faces of elderly, gray-haired gentlemen. But none resembled my father. I finally set out to *rebuild* my father's face, feature by feature. I first saw his hair and forehead, then his nose, the mouth, and finally the eyes and shape of the face. But still he had no ears. In spite of my efforts, I was not able to put them on. I finally decided that this was unimportant.

Then her father came alive and smiled, and she could see his whole body. They embraced and kissed on the mouth. The meeting took place in a tunnel which was a place of communication between the living and the dead. She told him she was in love and introduced her fiancé to him, with some fear. He approved, as he was more affectionate than in real life. As he finally withdrew toward the dark side of the tunnel, she wept.

On two occasions during this patient's session, I suggested an exploration into her phobia of streets by confronting such scenes in fantasy. The following description (prior to the one just quoted) tells, in her own words, of the first attempt to cross the main avenue in Santiago at a familiar and threatening spot:

> I am standing on the Alameda at the corner of Victoria-Subercaseaux. All is gray as on a foggy day. I look toward the hill, and this is vaguely green, but I do not discern colors very well. I approach a little tree that is there on the corner. It is as if I wanted its protection. I reflect that I may support myself on it if I don't feel well, and I may thus avoid falling into the street. I get ready to cross the Alameda. I look at the cars. There is much traffic, and the cars go faster and faster. Suddenly, this becomes a continuous row of cars that looks like a train going at high speed. There are faces in all the windows—men, women, and children—and all of them look in my direction. Then this fades away, and the traffic becomes normal again. I wait for the green light, and I cross, feeling very afraid. Because I feel afraid, I feel that I don't quite touch the ground but float in the air. A man approaches. He is short and wears a brown overcoat and hat; his complexion is dark and he has a mustache. A typical Chilean face that can be seen in any street. He says, "Good afternoon." I answer his greeting. I vaguely sense that he is the man who assaulted me in the elevator, even though I don't remember my assailant's face. I walk on toward Portugal Avenue, but with effort, trying to avoid the tendency to float. I stay close to the University walls so that they can hold me in case I fall. I look toward the palm trees and I see in the sky a procession of bishops—bishops in a line, all in ceremonial dress, miters, and robes of white and gold, all identical, with the face of Nehru.

Here the first dream fades away. The second attempt took place toward the end of the session, after the vision of hell. As she attempts to cross the Alameda at the same spot, a crocodile falls from the sky.

It is a gray crocodile with a green design on its back, and I believe it is plastic, since real ones are not like this. I cross as far as the middle of the street. Then traffic becomes very thick so that a continuous line of cars passes at great speed on each side going in opposite directions. I panic to see myself running up the street together with the cars and at the same speed. I think, "What a crazy woman!" Only then do I realize that this crazy woman is myself. This cannot be, so I force myself back to the place where I was before I ran. The lights soon change, traffic stops, and I walk with deliberate calm to the other side of the Alameda. There I walk toward the University. People pass— ugly people, fat women, badly dressed—and I feel that I have to look at all these faces, ugly as they may be. I relate these to the ones I saw in a previous dream. These were here for me to look straight at, without fear and perhaps without compassion. They were all ugly, unpleasant. I have always sought after beauty, light, and harmony. But I realized that the beautiful and the ugly were different aspects of a whole: that I could not appreciate nor even know a part without looking at the whole. That is, beauty without ugliness loses its quality as such, its specific hue which makes it unique and distinct, beautiful. Again I looked at the faces of the persons crossing. There was a man with a scar on his face as if the flesh had been bitten out of his cheek or his face burnt with an acid. I felt that I had to look at those faces as I had had to look at the ones in the previous dream.

I have cited both sequences in spite of their similarity, precisely because of the consistency that this resemblance indicates, whereas a single piece of fantasy might appear as a rather chaotic or arbitrary array of images. In both, she experiences the familiar fear of falling and the search for support (on the tree or the walls). Yet her confrontation of fear in both leads to unsuspected embodiments of danger—the commonplace man resembling an assailant and the crocodile falling from the sky. A crocodile became part of the patient's fantasy in the later episode (already quoted), which underlines its significance in spite of its present appearance as a lifeless plastic object. This appearance, like the transformation of animals into toys or cartoons, is a common process by which the mind protects itself from the feelings potentially conveyed by some images. Interestingly, the colors of this crocodile are very relevant to her phobia: the gray of the avoided streets (like the color of the sky from which it falls in this fantasy) and the green of trees that make them tolerable.

Like the crocodile and the human "aggressor," the mad traffic in both episodes conveys violence which the patient was not aware of fearing in the streets on the occasions when she experienced anxiety and the accompanying physical symptoms. The dreams now confront her with faces she would normally avoid looking at (and this session actually marked the end of her avoidance of looking at the screen in the movies). Such faces were later associated with war memories, and precisely one—that of the man with a wounded cheek—evoked the repressed memory of a wounded soldier running in the street that had impressed her deeply as a child.

The overall effect of this session was positive to the patient in many ways, but her phobia persisted. There was a change in the quality of her fear, though. Whereas it had always been that of fainting or falling in the street, it now took the form of a fear of aggression. The wheels of trolley buses and truck noises seemed menacing to her now, and for the first time she had fantasies of being attacked by a man with a knife. Associations to the symptom in subsequent psychoanalytic sessions were richer and included consideration of the assailant mentioned above, which took place when she was fourteen, and which she remembered, but had never mentioned or seen as important in any respect.

Two months after the session quoted above and the change in her symptoms, she was administered harmaline for a second time, following which she wrote an account from which I am quoting at length because of its manifold interest.

I have great difficulty reliving the experience. I don't remember anything. I have only disconnected images: the girl—myself—in front of the church on a dusty road, myself at Communion, receiving the Host from an invisible hand at a grandiose altar.

I feel that I am going crazy. Something inside. Indescribable. It is not anxiety. Not depression. Yet something of both. Irritation, disorientation. *I am dead.* I still have to come back to life. *Sex. I cannot accept it. It is bad. I like it. I am bad. I strongly feel that God and sex cannot go together. I need God, and I am all sex.* It is horrible. I suspect that there must be some way of fitting things together, but outside myself, not inside. I am facing a reality of mine that I cannot accept. I believe this makes me feel as I do.

I also knew yesterday why I couldn't go out in the street. Not now. It escapes me. Now I remember. I could cross the Alameda; I could do it at the same spot at which I failed to do it in the previous session. This was after the doctor left. *I crossed with all ease, dancing. The music was inside myself.* The dress I wore was red, very tight, glittering, with brilliant golden ornaments. *But this dress was my own skin.* I crossed the Alameda dancing, passing between the automobiles without caring about anything. I enjoyed moving my feet, happy to dance and be in the street. I felt great pleasure in effecting every movement, in being able to follow my own music. As I crossed, there was a wreck in the middle of the street. Several cars collided head-on and formed a rising bouquet. I passed on without caring much. I knew that there were probably dead people in the accident, but I didn't care. Their time had come, and things were just as they were. I knew that I would die, too, some day, but this didn't matter either, since that was the way it was. I carried my skeleton inside since the time of my conception. This is what I was: dance and death, but all together. I was my death and my skeleton alive, and danced with joy in crossing the street.

But I knew why I couldn't cross the streets, why I couldn't walk in the streets, and this I have forgotten now. It had to do with my being bad, with death, with the wish to die, because I am bad.

I want to die. Or I wanted to die. I was seeking this instant—a point, infinitely small, or a fraction of time imperceptible in its brevity, the moment of death, this extremely short bridge where life and death touch, where the opposed, contradictory, and disunited cease to exist. This was the only way of uniting all my pieces. This is the only way of finding, for an instant, harmony. The moment when one is neither alive nor dead: in this moment one KNOWS. I don't know of what knowing consists. It is not just knowing, but knowing and understanding at the same time . . . It is the essence of life that matters, and the only way of grasping it is in the moment of dying. Moreover, here the opposites disappear; God and sex come together; they blend. All things are one, the good and evil, beauty and ugliness.

The thing is that I *had* to die. Unknowingly, I was seeking death. But without joy, with consciousness. And something in me held me back. Streets are death. It is so easy to die. Not that I would deliberately throw myself under the wheels of a car, or that I would step down from the curb on purpose to do it. But it is as if the protective mechanism would suddenly not work. I wouldn't realize anything. This happened to me several times before the onset of my phobia. I would walk in the streets and suddenly realize that I had walked for several blocks without knowing how I had done so. And I would also, on occasion, "wake up" in the middle of the street, surrounded by terrible traffic. At least once, I remember, I was awakened by the cursing of a driver who had to jam on his brakes to avoid running me over.

But there was a part of me that did not want to die. It knew what was happening. This part of me fought the skeleton, did not want to go out into the street, didn't want to risk. But this was the bad part. Sex, perhaps? But was it really the bad part? For it seems that one of the reasons I had for dying was that of killing what was bad in me. What is bad is sex, but sex is the only force that can reunite my parts, give me unity, stick the flesh onto the skeleton. Dancing is also sex. It doesn't seem to be bad; it is what gives me life. But it lacks an essential factor and an indispensable catalyst—God. How can God be brought into this mess? Where has God been all this time?

The same happened with God as with the skeleton. He was originally within me, grew with me, moved with me. The skeleton then disappeared, and I had an external, metallic skeleton, with the wings of a jeweled butterfly. I had to find support somewhere, and I got dry inside. I became encysted in the butterfly. Its wings were like those of a bat, and its joints made an unpleasant and unharmonious metallic crack-crack. It is the same with God. He came out of me. He became a remote god, killed by the sadism of a maid, who told me in fine detail how He was crucified, crowned with thorns. I cried as she told me, and as she was stimulated by my crying, she made even more vivid the descriptions of the perforation of His side and the tearing of the skin in the mouth of the Christ Child. (I don't know whether it was due to my confusion or to the way in which I heard this story that I thought that it was Jesus as a child that had been crucified.) Perhaps my believing Him a small boy made crying and feeling sorry for Him easier. Then came school. And God now sat on a cloud, in a distant sky, and wore a beard. And the eye within the triangle. The eye that persecuted Cain. We were told about this bearded God on the cloud, that this is not how He really was, and we weren't told anything else about Him. But much was said about the eye in the triangle. It was the eye of God, the most important, alive and active part, which was always present, seeing us, watching us, the part that told each of us how wicked we were and repeated it second after second. And God, with His eye, was a menace.

Then my mother's God. It had much of Allah and a lot of class consciousness. Everything that happened was God's will. Whatever one did would not affect the way God had set things up. Therefore, there was no reason to be affected, or annoyed, and no reason to seek. There was no way of changing anything or doing anything. All was predetermined by God, and destiny reigned over everything. To rebel was a waste of time. Moreover, Jesus was not God. This was something to satisfy the imagination of the people. But a "cultivated" person didn't have to believe in Jesus' divinity. Christ was not for the aristocrats, who were born mystics, who believed in God and felt God from the time of their birth. Christ was a means of explaining God to the people, the vulgar and stupid ones who needed religious precepts to behave like human beings, or would otherwise lose control and be in constant revolution. Yet my mother, who did not believe in Christ, did believe in about a half-dozen virgins and a long list of saints.

Then came the processions in southern Italy. We also had processions at home, but ours were beautiful, with many flowers and were followed by fireworks. They were grand parties, when everybody rejoiced; delicious food was cooked in all the houses, and special pastry was made which was eaten only on the occasion of certain feasts. Not in southern Italy. Nobody was gay there. Those in the procession suffered and the onlookers, too. They wore hoods. Hooded old men dressed in black sang sad songs out of tune. And the people looked, tightly pressed against each other, and cried. Women knelt down on the street, others screamed hysterically, and not a few of them fainted. This was a vindictive God, who demanded blood for the blood He had shed. He received all that shouting and theatrical suffering. These events fascinated me and caused me repugnance at the same time. God, my God, was not in them. He was outside myself. Not a God of love any more, but a butcher-God wanting victims, and I didn't want to be one of them.

Then came the Swiss-clock God. I had to study, had to eat apples, had to go to Mass. Children's Mass, at eight-fifteen in the morning. Not in the afternoon, for this was laziness. Nobody asked me whether I *wanted* to go to Mass. After my First Communion, I had to ask for Communion every Sunday. I was asked, "Are you going to church?" and this was an order more than a question, the way I was asked, "Did you brush your teeth?" (I hated it at this time.)

Then, distance.

An indefinite discomfort.

Doubts. Preoccupation, always. But God was very far away. God, lost. A wish to return. Now and then, Communion. But then doubt again, indifference, and search. At last, God was buried. It doesn't interest me. I don't see why I should have to. And then came the symptoms. I cannot enter a church. In the church is the eye. Really, the eye is everywhere, watches and accuses the children who don't behave.

All this was written on the day following that of the harmaline experience, and the text shows the importance of this effort. This is not the only instance in which the process of expressing in written form the content of a drug session is almost as significant as the session itself. What is repressed is so repressed that associations and feelings, if not images, may be "forgotten" if they are not told. In this instance, it is particularly understandable that this might tend to happen, as the session involved the discovery of almost intolerable guilt. It is this which made her feel at the beginning of her writing that she was going crazy or that she was dead. Yet this feeling changed as she became aware of guilt as such, of the eye of God that had persecuted her all through her life and now lay buried in her unconscious. Yet this is a very fragmentary report, she says, and it took her about a month before she attempted to recapture more of the experience. Some of this is contained in the following paragraphs, which constitute a valuable document for the psychology of religion:

After the first ingestion of harmaline, I decidedly felt the need of God to justify death. Useless death, unnecessary death of those who die in the wars, of those whose lives are left incomplete. I believe that I can now see more clearly. I needed to justify *death* in general and not just that of those who died in war. And I think that, as I had to justify death, what I finally had to justify is the absurdity of a limited, finite life, where death is implied.

I shall try to remember my thoughts after the second harmaline experience. The only death which could be justified was that of Christ. Each one of us was responsible for making His death something justifiable and not just one more useless death. That is, the sacrifice of God's son was not justified in itself. Every one of us could kill Christ once more or resurrect Him. And hence Communion. This was a conscious, voluntary act showing one's readiness to justify the death of Christ—justify it through profound respect and love toward everything that lives, for in every living being there lies a divine essence. This was a way of partaking of a universal harmony. It was also a way of resurrecting the Christ in the depths of each one of us. But there was also a more human side in my longing for Communion. This was a longing to be united in brotherhood to other beings who professed this same love of Christ toward living beings. It was a way of feeling less alone, a way to belong in a group without any loss of individuality.

As these lines show, a basic concern of the patient after the second drug experience is that of accepting the inevitability of *her own death.* Only at one point during the session proper was she accepting it, as she felt herself that red sensuous woman who danced across the dangerous street. She "doesn't care" about the dead and allows her own death, in an attitude of seeing that "that's the way it is." She doesn't oppose death as she doesn't oppose life— she is definitely sexual and takes delight in every movement of her dance. In not opposing life or death, in allowing them to be, beyond good and evil, she transcends life and death. By letting them be, she becomes their embodiment, as her dance is the embodiment of her inner music. Yet aside from this moment, she is the battleground of Eros and Thanatos. Her death wish answers the demand of a God for whom sex is evil, that revengeful God, thirsty for blood, at the processions in southern Italy, whom she had buried in her mind and avoided in churches. Yet she needs him, and she must suffer his condemnation: "I need

God, and I am all sex." Not only did she feel guilty after the session, but she became frigid and on occasion experienced during sexual intercourse the same anxiety that she used to feel in the street.

The patient's oneiric life became very rich in the months that followed the session, and her dreams presented symbols first contemplated with harmaline or their equivalents. One of the dreams reiterates the ideas of dance, dark skin, and dissociation into two persons that were part of the previous two experiences and which reflects her present sexual guilt: "I was two persons at the same time. One, naked, was a Negro woman dancing, while the other watched in horror."

The following dream shows a connection between the sexual impulse and the tiger theme: "I was by a swimming pool, letting myself be tanned by the sun. My friend Alfredo appeared. Then I saw myself covered by a sort of tiger skin. Under that I wore a bikini. He uncovered me. I said, 'No, Alfredo, cover me.' 'Why?' 'Because this way I look more naked.'"

The patient's free association also underwent a marked change during this period. Not only did she display a greater prominence of sexual matter in her thoughts, as in her dreams, but sexuality extended into her memories, too, and for the first time she became aware of a sexual aspect in her relationship with her father. The scene in her first harmaline session when she kissed her father on the mouth was a clue, which, like a magnet, attracted unexamined memories. "I loved my mother, and more than that," she once said, "but my father *was mine*. He used to tell me that when I was older we would go to Paris all by ourselves. He kept his promise. I have the feeling that we were a couple. We had a world of our own that we shared." Yet the attachment and unconditional acceptance that she expressed with regard to her father were in poignant contrast with the facts she remembered, which presented the father as a very violent, arbitrary man and suggested him as the source of her own unconscious (now half-conscious) persecutor. The hostility which she did not consciously experience or express did speak through her dreams of that time, as is portrayed in the following scene:

"I dreamt about my father. It was in a basement full of corpses. They were deformed, mutilated, killed at war. This was something related to Warsaw. The resistance of the ghetto. I walked over them, stepping on them. I felt pleasure in their tortured condition. I picked up a severed head and knew that it was my father's. I felt that it was all right that he was dead."

Shortly after the time of this dream (four months after her second harmaline experience), the patient underwent another session,[3] and now, for the first time, her feeling of guilt turned into resentment, frustration, and sadness in confronting her father. The following is one of the more expressive passages in my notes:

Doctor. What makes you cry?
Patient. I don't know. Everything. I could cry for days and days. I am not wicked. I have been very lonely. I would have liked to have a little brother or sister. I was never allowed to play with anybody. My mother used to take me to my granny's to play with my cousins, but always on the quiet and for a short time, because my father would hit me and raise hell with her if he knew. He didn't dare hit her, though. He knew she was like a wild animal that could literally kill him. I don't blame her at all. I loved my granny so much! But this brute of an old man did not let me visit her. I had to lie, and lying was bad. And later he was surprised that I couldn't stand other children. They were strange creatures; they knew games whose existence I didn't even suspect. Perhaps I didn't even conceive that there were games for children! I hate this old man! He made her suffer so, so much! And how good

[3] On this occasion, 100 mg. of mescaline were added to 500 mg. of harmaline.

my mother was to me! She was not born to be caged, and this old man fussed and fussed and fussed! About stupid details. Why couldn't I visit my granny? It was not that he didn't like them. I think he felt jealous. He wanted me all for himself.

Doctor. And you gave him that exclusiveness?

Patient. Later, yes. But I don't think I did. I had no choice. War was at its peak, and I had no choice but to be with them. But it was he who took me everywhere My mother didn't any more. Perhaps she preferred not to, to avoid fights. And these were always my fault. He wouldn't let me drink water. Once he knew I had drunk some, and he got angry with her. It was my fault, but I had to drink water! He shouted so much that I wanted to leave the house . . .

He had so much life, so much energy, and all of it went into idiocies. He didn't pursue what he liked most, which was mathematics. He is like a great absurdity. He has caused me much harm, without being evil—that is what's sad.

It would not be possible to give a complete picture of the patient's inner life and evolution without taking considerably more space, but what has been presented shows the progressive unfolding of insight brought about by successive sessions and the nature of the process that would eventually lead to a cure. The action of harmaline here could very aptly be regarded as "mind-manifesting" in that, like a developer on photographic film, it successively made the patient aware of her fear of destruction, her death wish behind that fear, and the reasons for which she was hating herself. One of these was sexual guilt deriving from incestuous fantasies, but this, too, revealed itself as a by-product of a very frustrating relationship with her father, her need to win his love by all means, and her unconscious surrender in the face of his jealousy and possessiveness. More deeply lay her own hostility, unsuspected by her but projected on crocodilian aggressors and sustaining a basic feeling of personal evilness.

A month after the last session, I left the country, but the patient continued a self-analytic process which led her to ever-increasing clarity. A year later. I received a letter from which I quote the following paragraphs:

> Four days ago I went out and walked in the streets. Why? I don't know. What happened? A beautiful day, and it was silly to stay at home. I wanted to go out and I did. That is all. Simple, wonderful, and absurd; after all the searching, suffering, theories, and associations. A beautiful day, and no more. I went out with my daughter. This helped a lot. Holding the carriage gives me some security. Furthermore, I am concerned with her and not with phantoms. I am happy and afraid at the same time. I feel that I have acquired something precious and fragile that can be spoiled or evaporate at any moment. It is like having a new tool and not knowing what to do with it. I have gone out every day, each time a bit farther. But the world already seems to me very small. And furthermore, it is not a matter of walking, walking, and walking. I need some place to go. And now as I write, I don't know what that place might be.
>
> I have fulfilled all my projects. (Do you remember? teaching, earning money to pay for my own study.) My marriage is still a wonder of non-communication. At this moment, John looks at me as one might look at a time bomb. When I told him that I was going out by myself, he congratulated me dryly and then warned me to be very careful, because I would develop other symptoms. In truth, I have had another symptom for some time—a severe headache in half of my head. But this is very clear: I have it only when I suppress my anger. And I prefer the headaches to the phobia. I don't dare express my annoyances because I feel my temper is too violent.
>
> In spite of my symptom being over, I feel as needful of therapy as ever. Not only do I fear a relapse, but I am afraid of being normal (if anybody can ever be called that). Now I know that I can achieve what I want, for the barriers that I placed in my way have vanished. But I don't know what I want, and I am afraid of knowing. I suspect that it is something *bad*. How exciting! (I notice that I am

writing to myself.) I thought that I did want to do something bad, but as soon as I had the thought, the "bad" thing turned into something funny, childish.

This is turning into a written analytic session. A frustrating one, too. I would like to tell you other things: How happy I am in spite of my doubts and fears, how well I feel in spite of occasional depressions, headaches, and stupid problems, how close I felt to you when I went out the first time—I almost phoned you to tell you.

Four more years have elapsed now, showing that the patient's symptomatic improvement was not a transient state. Her problems at the time of this letter are still those evidenced in her harmaline sessions—a difficulty in expressing her anger and a doubt of the goodness of her spontaneity—but these seem but a shadow of her repression of hostility and her guilt feelings at earlier stages in her treatment. She eventually experienced further improvement as she realized that her inability to express anger was related to an idealized image of herself as a "good," loving person, and she had been enslaved to this image instead of daring to be herself, whatever her present limitations. The process of healing cannot be considered complete, but she is now much closer to the nature of that tiger which served her as a guide in the first harmaline experience, spontaneous and powerful, graceful and knowing in the mysteries of life. Her evolution shows the distance and effort that can mediate between the presentation of any archetype in fantasy and its embodiment, between the harmony and beauty conceived and experienced as a projection in a dreamlike sequence and that experienced in everyday life. Some elaboration seems to lie between the two, in order that a given abstract insight obtained in the symbolic domain may be recognized in the particulars of action, so that the "heaven" of a harmaline session may be eventually translated into earthly terms.

The panorama of session reports in this chapter should, I feel, give a fair idea of the specific domain of experiences that harmaline is instrumental in opening up. To speak of archetypes is relevant, but this does not cover the complete range of reactions to the drug. Some of them, as case reports show, may be quite "personal." But something links these "personal" experiences of reminiscence, fantasy, or insight with those of the "mythical" type: instinct. The most frequent themes appearing in the content of harmaline visions—tigers and Negroes—are highly expressive images of the instinctual, basic, and natural level of our existence, in both its aggressive and its sexual connotations. The mythical type of vision is one in which the instinctual forces are in order, and flow, we might say, in accordance with the cosmic design. The resulting picture is one of beauty, for each element finds its place in the whole, which is only enriched by conflict and destruction.

In the non-mythical types of visions, aggression and sex appear as questionable or disruptive, and this, understandably, is more likely to happen the more the individual brings himself and his personal life into the scenario of visions. Only a person who is free from fear and guilt can see in his own life and circumstances the same glow of the myth or fairy tale, in which every object suggests a hidden significance and stands in its own right like a jewel. To this end, the abstract myth of a remote hero is like a blueprint, a map; or it is like a medium that conveys a certain attitude that can be carried over into the contemplation of all events. Needless to say, none of the patients cited in this chapter has fully attained such a goal.

I want to end this chapter by pointing out that, useful as pure harmaline can be in psychotherapy, the therapist employing the drug should always keep in mind the fact that some individuals are rather unsusceptible to its psychological effects. As was mentioned earlier, some of them may have no more than a physical reaction to the drug, an unpleasant state of malaise, somnolence, and vomiting that is most probably the result of a conversion reaction.

Early in our work with harmaline, we formed the impression that these "untoward reactions" (consisting of a lack of psychological effects and the presence of physical distress) were most likely to occur in individuals who feel comparatively ill-at-ease in their animal level of existence, which it is the drug's virtue to lay bare. If it were true that a poor or unpleasant reaction was the consequence of a desperate though unconscious attempt to inhibit that which harmaline stimulates, it would be conceivable that this might be obviated by another drug.

First I thought of mescaline, both in view of the condition of self-acceptance which it can bring about and the fact that one of the admixtures in the native Amazonian *ayahuasca* drink has been proved to contain DMT.[4] Small doses of mescaline indeed proved to increase productivity and diminish the unpleasantness that the experience has for some subjects. Yet mescaline has effects of its own, which may not be desirable in a given case. MDA, on the other hand, proved to have the properties of an ideal admixture. The feeling-enhancing quality of MDA facilitates the decoding of visual imagery into direct experience; its amphetamine-like quality serves to counteract the somnolence induced by pure harmaline, and its stimulation of the drive toward interpersonal contact and communication opposes the tendency to withdraw that leads some subjects into a dreamlike state, the content of which they cannot recapture.

The effects of the drug combination seem to be more than a summation of their properties in isolation, however. In the first place, the duration of the harmaline-MDA experience is much longer, averaging twelve hours. Qualitatively, there can be differences that I will not go into, since their clinical importance is slight. Yet there is one particular type of reaction which, uncommon as it is, deserves

---

[4] F. A. Hochstein and A. M. Paradies, "Alkaloids of Banisteria Caapi and Prestonia Amazonicum," *Journal of the American Chemical Society* 79: 5735 (1957). DMT: N,N-dimethyl tryptamine.

special mention, both as a warning and a reassurance. This is a state of confusion and great excitement in which a person may talk to dream companions and thrash around —even risking getting bruised against the walls or furniture. It would seem that the aggression that usually emerges in harmaline experiences in the symbolic guise of animals or other fantasies is here released in a physical way, though still in a fantasy world of delirium. I have seen this occur twice (in about thirty sessions), the reaction being followed in both instances by amnesia. Alarming as these sessions were at the time, however, they proved to be extremely beneficial to the patients for reasons which can only be a matter of speculation.

In one instance, the patient was a shy and inhibited young woman who, early in her session, started screaming at her absent mother all that she had withheld from expressing and from feeling toward her. Soon her speech became confused, and interaction with her was almost impossible. She kept playing the parts of some dialogue, which was increasingly hard to follow because of her mumbling. Still, it was obvious that the direct, energetic person that she became at that moment was the opposite of her shy and depressed ordinary self. When she recovered, she was somewhat bruised from rolling on the floor, but her voice and style of movement had changed, retaining some of the assertiveness that she lacked in life, but had displayed in her intoxicated state. Not only was this change enduring, but it carried over into her feelings and decisions. In this particular case, the patient had experienced moments of exceptional freedom under the effects of LSD in a non-therapeutic setting, and this freedom had not carried over into her life. On this occasion, though, when she did not even remember what she had felt and said, her temporary loss of control proved to be a life-changing catharsis.

The other case was similar in essence: that of a frigid woman with mildly compulsive character style, who rolled about and talked for hours without remembering her experience, but who came out of her session greatly refreshed and with a capacity for sensuous enjoyment unknown to her before.

In mentioning these two experiences, I want to share a sense of trust with which I have been left after the initial worry—a trust which, I believe, may be beneficial for other patients to be surrounded with in similar situations. We psychiatrists are prone to put great faith in the value of verbal expression and tend to underrate the value of motoric expression as displayed by these patients, calling it *just* psychomotor excitement. Though pure instances of this, like the above, are rare, I think they are important to know of, because of the light they shed on the non-verbal dimension of every drug experience, if not every therapeutic session.

CHAPTER V

IBOGAINE:
FANTASY AND REALITY

Ibogaine is one of the twelve alkaloids obtained from the root of the plant *Tabernanthe iboga* found in West Africa. From vague reports as to its local use in the Congo, it was believed to be mainly a stimulant, and it is as such that it is mentioned in De Ropp's *Drugs and the Mind*. It is as a stimulant, too, that iboga extract was introduced into French medicine several decades ago.[1]

In July 1966 I presented, at the conference on psychedelic substances organized in San Francisco by Richard Baker (Roshi) for the University of California, a report on my initial work with the alkaloid as an adjunct to psychotherapy, which described the hallucinogenic effects of the higher doses of ibogaine. Since then, it has been used in a similar context by an increasing number of psychiatrists, mostly in South America.

For the writing of the present account, I have examined notes from forty therapeutic sessions with thirty patients, in which I used either ibogaine or total iboga ex-

---

[1] Gershon's finding that ibogaine is an inhibitor of MAO (monoamine oxidase) explains its classic use and shows that it was the first antidepressant of this kind in official medicine, much before the advent of iproniazide, Tofranil, and so on.

tract, plus ten sessions with a different group, in which I used iboga extract in conjunction with one or another amphetamine. In my general statements, I am also drawing upon a wider experience not documented by notes which I could use for statistics. This is partly direct experience with additional patients and partly information amassed in clinical meetings with my colleagues at the University of Chile. I estimate the total number of treatments which I have either witnessed or known indirectly to be approximately one hundred.

As to physical effects, neither ibogaine nor the harmala alkaloids cause dilation of the pupils or a rise in blood pressure, as is the case with the LSD-like hallucinogens or the amphetamine derivatives MDA and MMDA. Ibogaine also resembles harmaline in that it elicits a disturbance in body balance and vomiting more often than any other mind-affecting chemical aside from alcohol.

In view of the high incidence of these symptoms, it is advisable to administer the drug when the patient has an empty stomach, and not to use more than 4 mg. per kilogram of body weight on a first session. I find that the optimal dosage may range from 3 to 5 mg. per kilogram, depending on the individual's sensitivity to the drug.[2] Dramamine may also be used as a preventive for vomiting, either in a first session or thereafter, if the subject is already known to react with vomiting.

A comfortable couch or bed must be considered part of the setting for the treatment, for most patients want to

---

[2] With such dosages taken orally in a gelatin capsule, the symptoms become manifest about forty-five to sixty minutes after ingestion. These may extend from eight to twelve hours, and some patients have reported subjective after-effects even twenty-four (20 per cent), thirty-six (15 per cent), or more (5 per cent) hours later. Yet even in such instances, the patient is usually able to function normally after six to eight hours from the beginning of the effects. In the majority of instances, I have ended the therapeutic session in seven hours or less, leaving the patient in congenial company.

lie down during the first few hours, or even throughout most of their session, and feel nauseated when they get up or move. However, others feel the desire to move or even dance at some point in the session (35 per cent in my data), and this may prove a very significant aspect of their experience—as will be elaborated upon later. For this reason, some degree of space to move about is desirable.

Proceeding to the subjective domain, one finds some similarity between the *content* of experiences elicited with ibogaine and those typical of harmaline, although it is in this sphere, too, that the specificity of each becomes most noticeable. In broad terms, it can be said that archetypal contents and animals are prominent among the visions produced by both, and the actions involved in the plot of dreamlike sequences frequently involve destruction or sexuality.

In spite of the similarity pointed out between ibogaine and harmaline, there are specificities of the former that give it a place of its own in psychotherapy. Ibogaine elicits a less purely visual-symbolic experience than harmaline. With no drug have I witnessed such frequent explosions of rage as with this particular one. Aggression is a frequent theme in harmaline experiences, but there it is portrayed only in visual symbols. TMA, which has been reported to release hostility, is in my experience characterized by a delusional state where hostility is expressed more as paranoid thoughts than as actual feeling. With ibogaine, anger is not directed (I would say *transferred*, in the psychoanalytic sense) to the present situation but, rather, to persons or situations in the patient's past, toward whom and by which it was originally aroused. This is in accord with the general tendency for the person under ibogaine to become concerned with childhood reminiscences and fantasies.

The salience of animals, primitives, sexual themes, and aggression in ibogaine and harmaline experiences would justify regarding them as drugs that bring out the instinctual side of the psyche. This stressing of man-the-animal contrasts with the effect of the airy or ethereal "psychedelics," which bring out man-the-god or man-the-devil, and with man-centered drugs like MDA or MMDA, which lead the person to focus on his individuality and relationship with others.

Aside from differences in the quality of the ibogaine experience, there are differences in content: a less purely archetypal content, more childhood imagery, and certain themes that appear to be specific to the mental state evoked by the alkaloid—notably fantasies of fountains, tubes, and marshy creatures. The reader will appreciate this specificity throughout the clinical illustrations on the following pages.

The first case report that I am presenting consists of the description of a complete session. The variety of episodes in it may serve as a condensed panorama of the drug's possible types of effects and lead us to a consideration of how these may be pertinent to psychotherapy.

The subject of this illustration is a physician in psychiatric training whose interest in a therapeutic encounter arose out of a sense of lack of contact with others and of not giving his whole being to his love life, his work, or his doings in general. "I feel that much in me is automatic and that what I do is worthless," he said. "I would like my contact with others to be more from center to center."

In preparation for the session with ibogaine, he had undergone four Gestalt therapy sessions and complied with the request for a written autobiography. Forty-five minutes after the ingestion, he reported a great relaxation and a desire to lie down. He did so, folding his arms and legs and closing his eyes, while he listened to a record that he had brought with him. Every note in the music was clear and forceful in a way he had never heard before.

When he opened his eyes, he was surprised by the beauty and richness in detail of objects in the room, which he had not noticed before. Looking at photographs in the *Family of Man* book, which lay next to the couch, he had insights both into the significance of the scenes and into his own attitudes. After this, he felt like lying down again, and when he closed his eyes he had a fantasy of his father making faces as if in a game, with a contented smile. He commented that this is how the expression of his father must have appeared to him as a small boy. But then the expression turned into a contortion of great rage. He visualized a naked woman with round hips hiding her face with her arms, and then his father, also naked, falling upon her to penetrate her. He sensed controlled rage in the woman, whom he now identified as his mother.

I chose this sequence as a starting point for a therapeutic procedure and asked the subject to have these characters talks to each other. This is a means of bringing out the latent content of the images, so that it becomes conscious and explicit. "What does she say?"—"Go away."—"What does he feel?" He could not imagine that. "Maybe perplexity," he suggested. This was an appropriate moment to take another step in the same direction, that is, to unfold and bring into the spheres of feeling and action the meaning that is packed in the fantasy. "Be your father, now," I said. "Become him to the best of your dramatic ability and hear what she has said to you." He now found himself able to impersonate his father and felt, not perplexity, but great sorrow, suffering, and anger in the face of rejection. He wrote down on the following day: "I see my mother as hard, with no affection and afraid, and I no longer regard my father as that insensitive being who hurts her with his love affairs, but as somebody who wants to open the gate of her love without succeeding. Yet I feel compassion toward my mother."

There followed a fantasy of being licked by a lion, and then a lioness bit his genitals off, leaving him as a lifeless doll. At this point, he left the couch, walked around, went into the garden, where everything looked to him "as if it existed for the first time." He went back to the room, put Stravinsky's *The Rite of Spring* on the record player, and with the very first notes felt drawn to move, specifically his hands.

This is how he later describes the experience: "I gradually surrendered to the rhythm so that I soon found myself dancing like someone possessed. I felt balanced, expressive, and above all, *myself*. At one point, I saw myself in the mirror and noticed a conventional movement of the hands which did not stem from the music. I rejected it at once. When one side of the record was over, I turned it over and went on dancing. I felt no fatigue, and movement gave me great pleasure."

After the dancing, I proposed that we work on a dream, which I shall not describe, though it was important in giving him a greater sense of his own worth. Following the dream, he looked at family photographs that he had brought along with him and which helped to clarify more of his relationship to his father and mother. Four hours after the initial symptoms occurred, he felt that much of the effect of the ibogaine had worn off. He talked to some friends who came over. "Some faces I saw as very beautiful and expressive," he reported later. "Others I saw as distant, fearful, and these did not show their beauty, but hid it behind the fear." This perceptiveness of the masks people wear, as he puts it, went on through the next day.

After the session, the subject felt that the experience had been valuable to him in several ways. After a month, he pointed out different aspects of his life in which he sensed improvement. To one of these he refers in the following terms:

A fineness of perception, a revelation of the true or genuine—a knowledge that there are false and incomplete things in the world, human attitudes that are not whole, experiences that are watered down, works that are half-works. I now feel the need to go beyond this. And I acknowledge aggression as a means of going beyond.

This may be the place to mention that, in spite of the subject's wish to undergo the experience, he could have

been described as a contented, easygoing, passive viscerotonic, but now presents himself as more striving, active,
and firm.

Another benefit of the session he reports is a clarification of his family relationships. He now felt that he could
see his parents as they really are; he became aware of how
"castrating" the relationship with his mother had been.

As a third gain from the experience, he cites the knowledge or awareness of the body as a means of expression, as
it became apparent to him in the dancing. "It was important for me to know," he says, "that there are movements
of mine that are not mine but borrowed, used in view of
ends, but not emanating from an inner being." This awareness of a distinction between that which stems from his
"inner being" and that which is not really his seems to be
the same as that of the difference between what is genuine
or not in other domains, and which is the source of his new
longing for greater depth in experience, action, and relationships. It is also related to what he regards as another
area of progress, which is an enduring awareness of
"masks"—"an awareness of how faces are manipulated,
and how behind the masks there is fear."

Finally, the subject has discovered both a lack in his
experience of the religious and the fact that what he used
to regard as his religious problems were only imaginary.

To this it must be added that the subject had been a
devout and rather proselytizing Catholic, raised in a religious school, and a member of several religious organizations. To persons who knew him well, and to myself, much
of his religiosity seemed conventional, and some problems
which he labeled "religious" involved the decision of accepting or rejecting a dogmatic religious authority. It is
noteworthy that his insight into the distinction between
such concepts of religion and religious experience proper
was not brought about by the discussion of his life and
problems, but spontaneously elicited while looking at the
photographs in the *Family of Man* collection, where he

found one of a Buddhist monk praying with true devotion and another of a man kneeling out of idolatrous respect for the religious authority.

The session that I have briefly recounted shows a variety of situations which have been sources of insight and therapeutic benefit: relaxing, dancing, looking at objects and people, looking at photographs, acting out fantasies, working on a dream, a guided reverie. All these are possible domains for self-unfolding and discovery or for more elaborate psychotherapeutic procedures. In the case of this particular person, we find that it is of his contact with the external world that we can more appropriately speak in terms of *self*-unfolding, *self*-expression, *self*-discovery. In fact, his basic experience was, in dancing, that of *his own* style and his own movements; looking at external objects or persons led him to a discovery of the truth of things by means of the use of his own eyes, whose functioning he had, in a way, been holding in abeyance. The fantasy, however, had a different experiential quality. The sexual scene where his mother rejects his father, or that of the castrating lioness, or the dream sequence, which I have omitted for the sake of brevity, express his psychopathology rather than his sanity and his fragmented personality rather than his "self." Whereas life may be the best psychotherapist in the moments when it is flowing at its natural, undistorted rhythm, this is not the case in those moments when the person's sub-selves are in conflict. It is here that the psychotherapist finds his proper element. Here, his function—like that of the Eskimo shaman—is that of finding lost souls. Accordingly, it is with the darker sides of the ibogaine experiences that most of this chapter will deal.

Yet before moving into that domain, we must consider the most typical form of the ibogaine peak experience, which is precisely the kind that the subject in the illustration above did not display. Whereas in his case—probably due to his being an extrovert—it was his contact with the external world that was permeated with peak-experience characteristics, for others it is the symbolic medium of imagery that reflects such a quality, assuming forms of great beauty and significance or the half-veiled meaningfulness of myth. This is the realm of archetypal experience, if we take the expression in its more common meaning, which stresses the visual medium of representation. Particularly from my experience in working with ibogaine, though, I think that the essence of an archetype is not the visual symbol but the experience that the latter conveys, and this experience may just as well find a motoric form of expression (dance, rituals) as be projected upon the perception of the external world. This was the case in our patient's perception of things, "as if they had just been created," his feeling of communication with the selfhood of other persons beyond their masks, and, in looking at photographs, his proneness to see each gesture as a symbol and embodiment of a transcendent intention or, on the contrary, as remarkable for its meaninglessness. Whatever the validity of speaking of archetypal perception, movement, thinking, or relating, as well as archetypal imagining, the latter is a distinct psychological event which has been part of the experience, either fleetingly or throughout much of the session, of about half the persons that took ibogaine. The following are quotations from a retrospective account given by one such subject:

> I see BLUE, blue, blue. I am on the floor, but with the body upright. I can rotate easily all the way round in a sitting position. All is blue . . . blue . . . Everything is beautiful. I extend my arm and as I turn I draw a circle around me. I am sitting on the floor, and I draw a *white* circle around me in this turquoise-blue atmosphere in which I float. I then draw with my hand a smaller *white* circle while I look upward. I am entirely surrounded by this blue atmosphere in which I see a *white* circle around me and a smaller circle above . . . *White*, too. This atmosphere is dense. I try to look through my upper circle . . .

a periscope? What is there? A ray of clear light is being formed in this dense blue atmosphere. It is becoming a shaft of light. I look, look through my white circle, look, and more light is coming into this tube, more white light, more and *more*, with blinding and filling force, and always more. And more, and more. I look through that ray of *white light* and *I know that He is there*, He, and . . . and that light, that tube, that immense white ray beyond is blue, blue, BLUE! (And this is a different blue from that of the first time.) This is a pure, clean blue, transparent, eternal, infinite, serene, that goes upward, that is the ALL! White-blue that is distance with no physics, enormity with no measure, Universe devoid of laws. It was God. It was God. God. God.

This was unexpected. I wept. I weep now and every time I remember. I withdraw to remember and weep.

Nothingness again. I feel fullness in relaxation as after a great pain. I am on the floor again and I hear the music from the radio with fast rhythms. Now it is my body that responds, not my mind or spirit. I feel I am a puppy. I am surrounded by other puppies and play with them. I hear their sweet barking. Then I believe I am a cat . . . no! I am a pony! I gallop. Now I am something like a tiger . . . like . . . I am a panther! A black panther! I defend myself, I back up. I breathe forcefully with a panther's breathing, feline's breathing! I move as a panther, my eyes are a panther's, and I can see my whiskers. I growl, and I bite. I react as a panther that defends itself and attacks.

Now I hear drums. I dance. My joints are gears, hinges, nuts. I can be a knee, a bolt, I can be anything, almost everything. And get lost again in that chaos of nothingness and sensations that relate to abstract ideas with vague and changing forms, where there is the intuition of the truth of everything and an Order which one is about to discover.

And toward the end of the session, four hours later:

Again into nothingness. Tiredness. I am on my knees on the floor, my hands on the rug, my head hanging. I feel the wave coming again, the dizziness taking possession of

me. I press into the floor . . . I am on a lid . . . a great wheel
that is also a lid, and I must open it! I strain to the limit to
make it turn, grabbing the spokes. The lid turns, gyrates.
Suddenly I find myself under it, on a big wheel with
spokes and spaces between. There is a thick axle at the
center which seems to unite it to the lid, and also goes
further under the wheel I am on. How have I fallen in
here? I cannot explain. I did not realize when I fell . . . I
must get out of here. . . . I must get out! Going up is
impossible. It must be down. Through the bars I see a deep
darkness. Perhaps I will fall through that tube of emptiness
. . . It doesn't matter . . . I must get out of here, away from
this wheel that is suspended in this tunnel with no walls.
Perhaps through the mechanism of the axle . . . I know
that this wheel can go up and down. Desperately, I seek
among the parts of the mechanism. I hear the doctor's
voice telling me: "*You* be the axle." Surprise. I begin to
feel like the axle. Steely, hard, turning, turning, turning,
with a noise. I am the axle for hours, hours . . . There is no
time, being the axle. I turn and make a noise. I turn, I turn,
I turn . . . I feel that I am lifting my right-hand axle, which
turns. I rise slowly to the limit of stretching—always an
axle. My hand then moves forward. I have a dagger in my
hand, and I am going to kill! I am going to kill! I step
forward to kill. I am going to kill a . . . a . . . a . . . a
mummy! How horrible it is! It is a mummified corpse of a
woman, dry, with a brown leather-like skin, and she has a
bandage over her eyes! And she has a smile that is grue-
some and sweet, as if she were having sweet dreams or
listening ironically to what is going on. I sink my dagger
into her twice. I feel that she rips like leather. I feel dirty,
absurd . . .

These excerpts are enough to show several of the mo-
tifs that are characteristic of ibogaine imagery: light (and
particularly its white and blue colors), animals (and more
specifically the feline ones), rotating motion and circular
shapes, and the tube. The latter, in the present context,
appears to be linked to the image of darkness, downward
movement and enclosure, constituting a complex that is

the polar opposite of that of the beam of white light from above, and the sense of freedom implicit in the beginning scenes. Later on in this chapter, I shall explain in greater detail how the image of the tube may play an important role in ibogaine sessions, and had I had more experience in this matter at the time, I would have waited for the completion of the descent which the patient was already envisaging, and probably encouraged him to fall into the darkness. Yet the outcome of this particular episode—the sudden outburst of aggression taking place at the end—also illustrates a frequent trait of ibogaine experiences, and I suspect a partial therapeutic breakthrough. Such hostility might be understood as the polar opposite to the feeling of enclosure in the previous image, which I have often seen as its antecedent in other instances—either in the form of imagery, as a feeling of restraint, lack of freedom, heavy apathy, or as a physical sensation of being held in and limited in the body. I feel drawn to interpret such experiences as an inward-turning and paralysis of the aggressive potential in the personality, which, once directed toward its natural target outside, leads to feelings of relief, freedom, and power. In this instance, however, the patient's guilt after stabbing the mummy with his knife is far from such relief and tells us that he has withdrawn again, still not feeling free vis-à-vis this female presence in his inner world.

One might wonder what relevance an experience as impersonal as this one may have to the therapeutic endeavor, and more generally to a person's feelings or behavior "in the world." In the present instance, the subject feels no doubt:

> In my daily life, I kept discovering such important little details. Everything that I said had a transcendence, a simple and true reality, an importance in terms of sincerity that it has even today and will continue to have tomorrow. I did not react in the normal way to things, but in a way that was . . . emotional? No—*sensitive*. I did not talk

vaguely, but directly to the point, and made wise decisions.

This first repercussion of the session might be understood as a carry-over of an archetypal mode of perception into everyday life—not in the literal sense of hallucinating, but in the sense of seeing ordinary words and actions as instances of more universal meanings. Even five months later, he thought that his judgments of personal situations, aesthetic matters, and everyday issues felt to him "more whole" than before.

Another effect of the session was on his mood. His description of it was "spiritual tranquillity." He had been prone to feeling rushed most of the time, anxious about the expending of time and effort; now he speaks of "a peacefulness at the certainty that the whole world, of which I am a spectator and a part, is experientially within *myself*, and is not something remote or mysterious."

In his relation to others, the after-effect was one of increased empathy, resulting from his own enhanced introspection. Four months after the session he says: "I saw that I had so many parts, and to each there was a little whole. And I saw that the rest of the people were the same. There was such intensity of human contact in those days! I saw myself in every attitude of others toward what interested them. I did not identify with them as a whole, but I understood them from within."

I have not seen that an experience of archetypal content necessarily brings about the consequences that this particular one did. Both ibogaine and harmaline may elicit mythical, dreamlike sequences that are contemplated with little emotional involvement, the outcome of such sessions being no different from what we might expect from exposure to a film of similar content. The experience described above, though, differed from the passive contemplation of a film in the definite participation of the subject in each of the scenes. He was the recipient of the light, it was he who turned into animals or mechanical parts, and while he saw himself on the circular lid and tried to open it he actually pressed with his hands on the floor. Not only was he experiencing himself as an actor in his fantasy, but reacting to the events with intense feelings and engaged in continuous motion with his body.

Just as the impact of a work of art will depend on more than our sense perceptions, requiring some measure of empathy, just as a novel would be meaningless to us unless we could identify with its characters, by stepping into their shoes or implicitly recognizing them as parts of our inner theater, the same may be said of fantasy productions. Whether these appear to the person as uninteresting and meaningless productions of his brain, interesting hieroglyphs, or revelations will probably depend on the degree of his contact with his unconscious life in general, and with the handling of a session. But I think that this can also be subjected to some pharmacological regulation, and I shall discuss later the association of ibogaine with feeling-enhancing drugs.

In commenting on his session, the patient later said that it was a surprise to him in view of his romantic expectations. Instead of an experience of integration into the "cosmic order or the race," "the simple and primordial, elemental and telluric," and, in short, the mysterious, he found "a world of my own, personal, sincere, simple, which perhaps coincides to some extent with all *my life experiences*, which are not as numerous as I would have liked, but *are mine*. Yes. It was a mixture of disenchantment and wonder. Wonder! The bluebird is in your home."

On the whole, I think that this is a significant report in that it informs us of the importance of *an experience with virtually no personal content*. This may seem a statement in contradiction to that of the patient, who claims to have discovered the richness of his own world. We may put it differently and say that the only personal element in the subject's experience is *that of himself* as the container of all his feelings, the source of all his images and actions.

But these feelings, images, and actions are not those of his previous conscious life. To anybody watching his movements, they would have appeared more like those of a ritual than those of practicality, just as his feelings are in the domain of the religious or aesthetic, and his imaginings in that of the mythical rather than the personal. And just as his experience was of intrinsic value to him at the time, its consequence appears to be in the nature of an enhancement of those aesthetic, religious, and mythical overtones in everyday reality, and a heightening of inspiration which carries for him a sense of intrinsic satisfaction.

Only toward the end of the session, in the last sequence quoted, do we see conflict, and we may sense a personal reality behind the veil of the symbolic murder scene. The fact that this was the last fantasy episode in the session suggests that more personal and psychopathological material might have followed but was repressed, and this we cannot know. I do know from other instances, though, that a peak experience does not necessarily imply the transcendence of chronic personal conflicts. It may merely indicate that these are not aroused by the real or imaginary situation which is the subject's focus of attention.

I think that it may be useful in this connection to consider a peak experience in terms of its completeness, and not just its quality. Just as I have spoken of archetypal visual experiences which are incomplete in that the subject does not feel involved in the symbolic action, so there are others where the motor element may predominate, with slight ideational concomitants, or—with other drugs more than with ibogaine—feelings may be dissociated from either action or understanding. In the present instance, I think that the incompleteness of the session is to be seen in the domain of relating. Just as the extroverted patient of our previous illustration experienced moments of fulfillment in the contact with others (even photographs of others) and objects, the introverted subject in this session expressed himself best in imagery and movement, not in the perception of the external world or in contact. Even in his imagery there is a predominance of elements, objects, and animals over human beings. When other persons appear (omitted from the quotation), they are vague, unknown, semi-mythical and practically unrelated to him in the plot of his fantasy, except at the very end, in the stabbing of the mummy with the dagger. Aside from the anger and subsequent feeling of dirtiness in this scene, interpersonal feelings are absent from his session, whereas in a complete peak experience I would expect feelings of love as well as those of beauty and holiness.

At the time of this session, I was still too unfamiliar with the use of ibogaine to take the initiative in presenting to the patient the challenge of relationship, bringing out the (presumably) avoided issues and his psychopathology. This is what I have since done in my practice, however, and I think that the exploration of conflict can not only lead to more enduring change but in no way detracts from the contribution of a peak experience.

The following instance shows how a state of subjective enjoyment and relative integration may be interrupted by a shift in attention toward a conflicting issue, as the patient confronts painful emotions, only to be resumed with greater fullness after a problem has been successfully lived out.

This illustration is from the account of a twenty-three-year-old woman of a seemingly mild, subdued, and dependent character, who consulted partly in compliance with her husband's wishes, and also in the hope of achieving a more fluent expression of her feelings and thoughts. Her difficulty in communicating had become apparent to her as a source of unhappiness in her marriage, and I could assume from interviews with her husband that her life with him must have been a source of intense frustration. She did say so during the two appointments prior to the session with iboga—not out of a lack of sincerity, it seemed to me, but a lack of awareness of her feelings.

In approximately the third hour of the patient's session, she entered a pleasurable state of absorption in a world of imagery:

> It was snowing. This was no ordinary snowfall. The snowflakes were larger, and one could see their component particles. These were very fine fibers with irregular edges, covered with innumerable little diamonds. The snowflakes danced and played. In the midst of this snow-feast I saw myself as a beautiful young woman, naked, with very white skin and long blond hair. I danced along with the snowflakes in what seemed a contest of agility. I ran after them laughing, trying to catch them, and when I did, I pressed them against my face. Everything was bathed in a golden light. It conveyed a feeling of freedom, beauty, and joy. A great peace enveloped me.

This may be enough as a sample of a peak experience being lived in the symbolic domain of visual imagery. The dominant feeling and impulse content (as is frequently the case in ibogaine peak experiences) is conveyed by the images of dance and light. It became clear to the patient that the woman dancing was herself, and she enjoyed feeling so full of life, beautiful, and free. Then she felt the urge to dance herself, rather than merely watching mental pictures, but, significantly, this she was not able to do. She felt weak and nauseated and went back to lying down.

From my experience of the drug, I have the impression that its effect is closely linked with the domain of action and, particularly, physical movement. Much of the imagery may suggest this (dancing, beating of drums), but the experiences that have impressed me as most fulfilling and complete have involved actual participation of the body. (It is worthy of note that the iboga root is eaten by dancers in Gabon.)

The purely visual quality of the experience described above, plus the sudden malaise that she felt when attempting to enact with her physical self the dance that she was enjoying in her imagination, suggest to me what could be an "encapsulated" peak experience—one that cannot be brought to bear in more than one field of experience, and which can be sustained only at the expense of avoiding certain feelings, issues, or areas of awareness. This is not to say that such an experience is of no value; on the contrary, such avoidances may be used as a strategy in the elicitation of peak experiences in meditation techniques, where immobility and even the stillness of thinking are sought. But once the higher feelings or understandings have been achieved, the issue becomes that of bringing them down to earth, translating them into the terms of action and living—and a crucial step in this process seems to me to be the simple awareness and functioning of the body. In several instances of ibogaine therapy, I have seen the transition into a higher state of integration accompanied by a "remembering" of the body and its sensations after a period of absorption in fantasy, or by a sudden opening up of the channels of movement. The present case was no exception. Suspecting that the incompleteness of the patient's experience was related to her holding back her feelings for her husband, I suggested working on a dream into which we had looked the previous day. Here is the patient's account of this episode:

> While I danced with a handsome and virile man, I saw my husband turned into a weak, fat man with hanging red cheeks, laughing in a feminine way. I went beyond the original dream and described how, seeing this horrible change, I turned away and walked with my partner into the next room. We danced, and later he took me home. We said goodbye at the door. As I walked into the living room, I met my husband, who still looked as ugly as before. At first I locked myself up in my room, but the doctor instructed me to face him, and I told him how ugly and weak I found him.
>
> I suddenly found myself beating up a cushion that rep-

resented Peter. My hand flew! With what pleasure I hit him! I screamed at him, too, scolding him and telling him that if he did not change I would rather not see him any more.

What relief I felt after having shouted! I felt so light afterward. I felt happy to know that I had the right to defend myself, for I had some worth of my own. I did not need to lean on somebody as I had done before. It had been horrible to crawl at the feet of the others. (I imitated this crawling with my hands.) I was no longer useless, I had such force, and life did not seem ridiculous to me any longer. It was a gift. (I thanked the doctor for having told me that before. He handed me a mirror.) I saw myself as very beautiful, so much of a child still. [She had earlier in the session seen herself as old and ugly.] I was a flower which had just opened to the world, with a radiant gaze and fresh skin. The disdainful line in my mouth had disappeared. My body was agile, full of life. *For the first time, I loved myself.*

It may be noticed that the terms in which she describes herself are very much the same as those she had previously used in describing her self-image: beautiful, young, fresh, full of life. But to see these qualities in her very flesh or in the mirror took more than contemplating them in her essential nature. This entailed "coming out" into her body, becoming present in her actions, and this meant having the courage to break the bondage of the submissive personality pattern which her body had been serving throughout her life.

The change in her was obvious to her husband and close acquaintances, and even after one year, a friend of hers described her much in her own words: "Since the treatment, she is like a flower open to the world." In her marriage, she was patient while there was a need for her to be so, until her husband's cure about a year later. But now this was not the self-denying and compulsive "patience" of non-communication, but one grounded on self-acceptance and understanding love.

The three sessions illustrated thus far have in common what can be understood as an unusual and spontaneous expression of the person's "self," which takes place in the form of actions, dance, feelings, perceptions, or judgments. In stating this, I am staying close to the persons' descriptions of their experiences and their own use of the word "self," rather than speculating on what this self (or the source of such an experience) might be. The subject of our first illustration stressed that *he* was looking at pictures or at other persons *with his own eyes*, and he realized that it was *not himself* that was present in his daily, automatic way of perceiving things or using his body. Our second subject, too, was left with a taste of his own world and "the certainty that the whole world, of which I am a spectator and a part, is experientially in myself, and is not something remote or mysterious." Lastly, the woman in the third illustration also felt, as she saw the beautiful girl dancing among the snowflakes, that she was the image of her real self; she wondered at "the richness of life that there is in myself" and ended up by loving herself—not with what we usually call self-love, which means no more than living for a mental audience—but with warm appreciation for herself.

In contrast to such experiences of relatively spontaneous unfolding of the self—that center of gravity in psychological functioning where the individual feels complete, and his impulses are not in contradiction with one another—there is a greater number of sessions in which the patient's self-expression needs coaxing, or in which self-expression is virtually impossible before conflicting aspects of the personality are reconciled.

Two devices which I find useful as openings for self-expression (as well as starting points for more elaborate procedures) are the presentation of potentially significant photographs and the evocation of dreams or creation of imaginary sequences. In both situations, the potential of ibogaine is somewhat different from that of other drugs.

Under the effect of LSD-like hallucinogens, photographs are either seen with distortions that may point to the individual's projections, or, in peak experiences, they permit the translation of the ongoing state of mind into a particular kind of relationship with the person contemplated (e.g., "I could see my mother's essence, for the first time, and love her beyond her difficult personality. Just as she was not responsible for her body, I saw that she was helpless against her own psychological make-up, which had harmed me so much. But this was not *herself*, really, that I was seeing now.")

With MMDA, there is little interest in looking at external objects in conflicting states, when physical sensations, images, or intense feelings dominate the picture, and where the *Now* is all-important. Yet in the peak experience of MMDA, all stimuli are welcomed as part of the Now, and in this case the experience of looking at photographs is also one of developing ways of relating to others that are in accordance with the ongoing state of mind. The difference with LSD here lies in the realistic perception of others with MMDA, both in terms of less projective elements (no distortions) and less bypassing of their circumstantial reality.

With ibogaine, the situation is more comparable to that of MMDA, where there is increased insight and emotional response, and occasional clues to the reliving of childhood events. I find directiveness to be more accepted with ibogaine, and this permits manipulation of the apperceptive phantoms whenever the experience is not that of an unmasked self seeing others behind their masks.

The potential of ibogaine in working with imagery and dreams may be seen from the following instance, where both this and the use of photographs are illustrated in detail.

I shall begin this account from the point at which I suggested to the patient (a thirty-six-year-old artist) that we might work on a dream he had reported to me the previous week. This was one in which he sat at the table in his parents' home while they seemed to be present in a distant corner of the room. He felt something between his teeth, which he started pulling out in the form of white threads, but gradually they became little greenish creatures. At this point, he woke up horrified.

In the session he sets out to re-experience the dream, and it turns out that, after pulling out fibrous and gelatinous threads and living things, nothing further happens. Yet he feels that there is more to come out. When instructed to become the threads and experience the dream from that point of view, he soon feels that he is turning into a white worm with dark hairs. The worm then turns into another thread, half white and half green, out of which grow feet and which develops into a small, rodent-like green animal.

At this point, he is again perceiving images in front of him as in the dream and feels that he cannot identify with them. The rodent now becomes a duck with a long beak, and then a heron. "Become that heron," I say at this point. "Feel what *it* is feeling."

"I enter the bird," he reports. "I see wings at the sides of that head that is becoming mine; I begin to fly over the wide and tranquil sea. The sky is of pure unclouded blue, and the sun sheds a white light along the line of the horizon."

This dreamlike sequence continues with his going through the sun and finding a huge white sphere on the other side of it. At this point, I suggest that we return to the original dream.

Again he pulls threads from his mouth. As he is pulling out green ones, a whitish fluid begins to gush out, brushing away the little animals. He feels surprised that there are so few of them and that they seem so harmless, so he thinks that there may be more of them left.

At this point, I see the subject open his mouth more and more as he gradually sits more erect and stretches his arms and hands as if to embrace something in front of him. This is how he later describes this episode: "The gushing fluid now wets the hand with which I was trying to pick the little creatures out of my mouth, and now I gradually extend the hand without avoiding the wetting. The fluid becomes whiter and more abundant. I stretch and I open my mouth further and further. The milky torrent has strength and pressure. I place my hands in it so that they may be washed." (Given something he said about this washing at the time of the experience, I associated the process to that expressed in Hercules' cleaning the Augean stables with the waters of the Alpheus and Peneus rivers.)

"Let us wash Jacob, now," I suggested. At this point, Jacob visualized a naked body whose head he did not see. He directed the flow of milky sap toward that body, and it went through it, washing the hollow of the chest and abdomen. When he directed the stream to the head, though, he was surprised to find, not his own head, but his mother's. (In brief, this face appeared to be a mask, which he removed to find his mother's real face.) As he continued the washing, the mother opened her eyes and began to rise. She left the earth and floated higher and higher into a luminous area above. "This was very strange to me," wrote the patient later, "since I did not believe there was a heaven to rise to." At this point in the experience, he noticed a diagonal discontinuity between the area where the mother was and where he stood, on the earth. This was a transparent brownish-yellow plane, which he perceived as endowed with visceral vitality and which gradually evolved into a sphere. On this sphere, a throne now appeared and on it sat the owner of the earth. He was a domineering character. The subject approached and became him. This seemed to us to be a logical ending, and the dream sequence did stop at this point. Yet there is no feeling that matches the explicit content of the fantasy. The subject later reported that he was, in fact, surprised at feeling neither happy nor sad.

As will be seen, the subject went through this fantasy once more about four hours later, and this time the outcome was different. The success of this second attempt was probably prepared by the insights and feelings stemming from the contemplation of family photographs.

After looking at a photograph of his parents in their youth, he was impressed by one in which they are seen together after several years of marriage. "What a remarkable change!" he wrote later in reference to this part of the session. "Mother had become an intensely suffering and tortured being. The looks of both of them are turned inward, and their expressions are very sad. Father is tense, his lips pressed together. His nose conveys violence. Hardheaded and irritable. What a difference between this and the brilliance of his glance in the 1910 photo!"

After he had described his parents' expressions, I suggested that he have them talk to each other. This was very hard for him, since, as he was now aware, he felt that he would be criticized by his mother for his sharing his view of her with a stranger. Yet "Mother" finally spoke:

"I know that this is a marriage of convenience, yet why are you so violent to me? Why do you shout and insult me?"

"I must do that because I am very weak," said "Father." The patient now realized how isolated his parents are from each other and how rigid they are. "This is not how I saw them in the LSD experience," he remarked. "They almost don't look human, but like statues."

"Maybe you do see them as monuments," I said.

"In the moment that I hear that," he wrote later, "I am filled with the characteristic glow of clarity. I have reached the bottom. I see to what extent I am still building monuments or funeral edifices to my parents."

We returned to the dialogue.

Mother said, "Why have you been so mean to me? Can't you give me some love?" Father answered, "I cannot love because I feel excluded from your world, your friends."

And now the subject had another insight. He realized that this was himself speaking to his lover. Stimulated to imagine her as present and to talk to her out of this feeling, he said, "You are a whore and a stranger. I don't want to love you, because you give yourself to anyone."

When I suggested that he was still speaking of her rather than to her, he realized that he was unable to do so. "She is going to eat me," he said, and as he did so, he imagined that he had dreamed of many little animals, because the real ones were beyond his visual field. These were huge monsters which ate children up, especially lonely children.

"According to this," he commented, "every woman who is different from one's mother (who is a 'heavenly being') must be a monster it would be better not to get too close to, since she can eat the 'boy.' I don't know how I escaped being impotent or homosexual."

Presumably, these insights became important when the patient turned back to the experiencing of his dream. The feeling was that there had been something incomplete in the previous contemplation of it.

Here is the new sequence, in the patient's own words:

> Things occurred as before in the first part: the threads, the greenish creatures, the rat, the bird, the washing of Jacob's body, and the washing of my mother's face with closed eyes in the milky stream. I am aware that this is a sexual act. I go on washing her face and stay with her until she rises into the heights. I now turn to the man in the shadows, who sits domineering and menacing on his throne. I fly toward him to see what he will do to me, since I realize that this man is not myself. As I approach that shadowy height, I see that the man puffs out his cheeks and contorts his face as if to frighten me away, moving his arms like a big gorilla. And then I suddenly realize that these are the contortions of old, toothless Fa-

ther. And suddenly, too, as I approach further, I see that there is no longer any flesh on that face, but only bone.

I fly closer and closer and finally reach the great monument. I fly through one of the eye sockets (the whole proves to be an artificial concrete structure) and come out on the other side. Looking back, I see that the great monument is nothing but a façade, ruined on the inside. Now the ruins disappear, and only the seat remains. I understand that this is the place that Dad left, and I take it. I am not the owner of the world, but I have taken my father's place. And I realize that to be a father is to own the world. A great wave of laughter and crying invades me. I laugh and cry for a long time. I was free from a great restlessness. I felt beatific. I later wondered: What place can my father leave me? Is there anything which I have admired in him? And I recalled that he was an authority on making fur coats. He was a master in his craft, and I had always respected him for that. I felt relieved and thought that I would pursue a similar perfection as a sculptor, and that sculpture itself was, at another level, like an inheritance from my father.

I could open my eyes now and rise from the bed. I have my place. I cannot be excluded by anybody, anywhere. I can conquer my fears, I can go through them.

I have my place.

It is not even necessary to go or come, forget or close ghettos. I have my place within, without, with whomever it may be.

I do not need to ask for anything because I *have* my place. I don't need to go or come, flee, escape, since I *have* my place.

Everything is part of ME. I AM. It is not that I *must* sculpt. I will do my work, whatever I care for, wherever, since, it being part of me, I am not bound to it in a symbiosis. Neither X nor Y will pull me toward them, since I am where I *really* am.

There is no need to escape from anything, pleasant, unpleasant, hateful or terrible, whatever it is, since it is always possible to go beyond, into the most definitive—that is, within.

I enjoy feeling how it resounds in me: I have my place,
I have my place, *I have my place.*

The therapeutic benefit of the session is clear enough from
the patient's words. I can only add that this state of mind
persisted.

We can recognize in this session several elements mentioned earlier in this chapter as frequent traits of ibogaine
experiences, and here they show their place in the therapeutic process: the animals (the devouring monsters or
the gorilla-like father), symbolizing the instinctive forces,
sexual imagery ("washing" the mother), the flight toward
the light (the bird approaching the white light of the sun
and the ascent of the mother to a luminous area), feelings
of resentment, loneliness, exclusion ("I feel excluded from
your world"; "You are a whore and a stranger"), and, particularly, the Oedipal situation in which the sexual and
aggressive urges are embedded.

If we compare the patient's first dream, resulting in a
feeling of incompleteness, with the second sequence,
which ended in the tears of "arrival," we see that the first
is the blueprint, the second the real building, a two-
dimensional event as compared to a three-dimensional
one. The first raises the issue of the subject's relating to his
mother and then taking the place of his father, but his life
is still not in it; the challenge is not accepted. In contrast
to these rather indifferent images, those of the second
dream are loaded with an instinctual charge, for which the
patient must take responsibility by making the unfolding
scene the result of a real decision. It is his doing. In particular, among the main differences between the two scenes
are the recognition of a sexual element in the washing of the
mother's face with the milky sap, and the menacing attitude of the father as the subject approaches (*in spite of
which*, he does).

I think that we may safely assume that the difference
between the first and second attempts was brought about

by the discussion of the photographs, since this was the point at which the feelings that dominate the dream entered the patient's awareness and became really *felt*. Here was his first intimation of his father's supposed brutality, experienced from both his mother's point of view (a victim) and from his father's (hostile because of a feeling of rejection).

With his own feeling of rejection now activated, with a recognition of his own want in his father's wanting his mother's love, and with his aggressivity somewhat released, he was ready for the symbolic action that signified and proved his acceptance of his instinctual reality. With this action, he literally undid the repressive process to which he had subjected himself since childhood in face of his "monumental" parents. Now he is not split into a "father" and a "mother," fragments of his personality which reject each other, but *he* accepts his striving to be a man and sees himself as a father with a wife and children in the external world.

It can be seen in retrospect that, in his previous position of self-rejection, he was identifying with a parasitic mother-image and *being* this mother who "excludes" the man (father and son) instead of living his life from inside out. Laying out the attitudes of "father" and "mother" was the starting point for the process of becoming one with his own feelings, regardless of the historical reality of his parents. For this reason, we might say that the former process was in the nature of an analytical phase which made the synthesis in the dream sequence possible.

I have stated elsewhere that therapy with ibogaine is most suited to the exploration of the past, in contrast with MMDA, which is most adequate for the clarification of the present. This is true to such an extent that one might even say that, in contrast with the dictum of "I and Thou, Here and Now"—that compressed description of Gestalt therapy that fits MMDA therapy so well—that of therapy with ibogaine is typically one of "He and She, There and Then."

The reason is easy to understand, for the effect of MMDA is predominantly on the feelings, whereas the reaction to ibogaine is noteworthy for its emphasis on symbols, and only by means of symbols—conceptual or visual—can we deal with a reality that is not present.

There is a great difference between the domain of past experience to which MDA facilitates the access and that which is exposed by means of ibogaine. Whereas with the former it is a matter of *events* being remembered, and perhaps reactions or feelings in the face of such events, with ibogaine it is a world of fantasies that the person meets. Parental images evoked by means of ibogaine probably correspond to the child's conception of his parents, which still lies in the unconscious of the adult—but these do not necessarily match the parents' reality. The therapeutic process with ibogaine may be depicted as that of seeing such constructions for what they are and being freed through confrontation of them. With MDA, on the other hand, it would seem that reminiscence of the true events is the confrontation that can implicitly counteract the power of distorted images, since these were based on the denial of a reality which the child could not face at the time.

This "seeing things as they are" rather than colored by the bias of imagination or prejudice, can also describe the view of things at the time of an LSD peak experience, but this usually applies to the present, and the sleeping dragon of fantasy resumes its post as guardian of the path. The patient in our last illustration had an LSD experience of this kind eight months before the one with ibogaine, and some of his reflections on the difference between the two drugs may be of interest, because of the clearer light they shed on the nature of the process described in the account above. Speaking of LSD, he says:

> I had the certainty of seeing the world as it is, for the first time; as it has been and will be, independent of myself. Everything became conspicuous in its finest details

and was a harmonious and intelligible part of a whole. I received it as if it were paradise and understood that I had lost it in the windings of my own non-being. I saw my parents for the first time as they were, beyond their own myths. I saw them as sad, defeated, abandoned to their separateness. The experience with LSD was of a visionary gazing with the eyes wide open, looking in wonder at the world for the first time, as it may be seen when free from the screen of fear.

I felt an urgent need to recover that world, for I intuitively perceived that my happiness was there. I understood that I could achieve this only by working on myself in all honesty, with no fear or playing at hide-and-seek. Ibogaine, on the other hand, led me to look at myself, inwards, with eyes closed. Through an incessant supply of mental pictures projected on a sort of three-dimensional screen, it compelled me to meet the monsters of my inner world face to face, to stay with my fears to the very end, without the interruptions that often occur in dreams, and to fight my way beyond the phony, illusory threats that I had erected in myself.

In contrast with LSD, ibogaine made me see my parents —the central characters of my phantasmagoric scene—in accordance with the image in which they were imprisoned in my inner world: imposing monuments that covered the whole field of vision. Ibogaine, making it possible for me to confront these legendary giants, also led me to an area where open combat with them was possible. I did fight, and realized that the path of freedom leads through the ruins of inner fears.

One aspect of the quotation is that the patient believes that the LSD experience, by showing him the goal, gave him the drive to fight his way through the ibogaine experience and achieve his aims. LSD is like a look out of a window into the open; ibogaine is more like an occasion to destroy the old building and make room for a new one. It is more of a "work drug" in the sense of facilitating an analytic process on the unconscious obstacles to life.

I think that this patient has made a good and important point in the distinction which he draws between the objectivity of "things as they are" and subjectively tainted experience. Naturally, we cannot perceive "things as they are," being restricted to the awareness of our experiences, but these terms point at the contraposition between two ways of experiencing: one in which the mind empties itself, so to speak, of preconceptions and grasps reality "as it is," and another in which the external world becomes a mirror for personal anticipations, expectations, and desires. Which of these we may want to regard as "reality"—that of things out there, as independent as possible of our being, or that of our own constructs—may be a matter of taste. The "objective" world may seem more substantial than a world of phantom-like mental images, but it is not ours. And our phantoms, while we house them, are *what we are*. And if this is non-being, so is the condition of having a receptive void inside.

A decisive step in the unfolding of this patient's experience was, we may assume, his implicit decision to "fly" toward the threatening father-figure, for it was this that led him to the discovery of his own "inner" father, his male component. The threat that the fantasy conveys bespeaks a barrier built into the subject's mental functioning, since he would have attained his psychological integration long before, if it had not been for a reluctance to open up to certain points of view or feelings. When the barrier is too great, not even direction can substitute for the person's incentive in taking the symbolic leap into the threatening domain. The images will fade away (as in the following illustration), or the feeling content will slip out of them. But an external push may at least show the impasse or result in the conquest of a limited portion of firm ground from the ocean of the unconscious. This push may consist in a given direction, reassurance, a call to pay attention at a point where the unpleasantness of a process could otherwise incite the subject to look away. To some extent, this push is provided by the mere presence of the therapist, which gives the patient enough security to let go and contact certain domains of his inner world. Sometimes an active interest on the part of the therapist in what the patient is experiencing supplements the latter's disinterest at a crucial point and may rescue him from a vicious circle of self-deprecation and psychological immobilization. While the patient in this case felt ready to meet the fantasied threat and was driven by the wisdom of his unconscious to do so before waiting for any instructions, the following is a case where persistent directions were needed to have the patient confront for increasing periods of time and familiarize herself with threatening imagery.

This session, involving a thirty-nine-year-old woman, started with an outburst of rage at her sister, who, she felt, had not trusted, loved, or understood her. In a similar rage, she then turned on the other members of her family and finally her husband (in her imagination), whom she reprimanded in a loud voice. At last, she exclaimed, "I am free! What a relief I feel!" Next came a "white light" phase followed by a scene of panic at being confronted by a tribe of Negroes beating drums. An over-controlled and over-"civilized" person, she saw herself with long hair and a primitive skirt, also beating a drum. Then this scene was interrupted, and the "light scene" began again:

> A beam of light comes toward me from above. It enters through the window of a great belfry. I see the sky beyond, intensely blue, with white clouds. Now another ray of light comes from a high mountain, and as this ray of golden light advances, the other one (from the belfry) disappears. It disappears completely, and a huge reddish-orange-colored sun advances. It illuminates the desert and the room in which I am. Everything is gradually flooded with reddish light. The room gets warmer and extremely beautiful. The sun embraces me and gives me its light and heat. I feel like walking, pacing about the room, and when I stand up I see that I am in a black place, like a pond of dark water. There is only a piece of land, where the doctor and myself are.

How terrifying! Next to us, as if emerging from the water, a horrible monster appears. It is like a crocodile split in half. Intensely green. Its eye, from the side, is that of a brilliant bluish parrot with a curved beak. And the crocodile's tail is not really a crocodile's, but black feathers. What terrifies me most are its eyes and the electric-like movement with which it jumps from one place to another. Scarcely have I taken refuge when it appears all of a sudden in a different place. I scream and hear the doctor's voice saying, "Face it. Don't be afraid. Let yourself be attacked." But my fear is greater than the wish to comply, and I cannot do so. I close my eyes and see it again appear and disappear, to reappear once more in a different spot—here—there—tac-tac-tac . . . and I cannot stand the fear.

Now I am at the crossing of two paths inside a huge cave. Two enormous animals appear, side by side. They are of an intense pale green color. They are plant-like. They seem to be formed of some kind of cactus. Their skin is granular. Disgusting. I am impressed, but not afraid. The doctor says, "Face them." I look at them attentively. One of them has a huge head like an elephant's—slightly funny—and from its chest hang twisted plantlike formations. When it moves, they quiver. I find it funny and disgusting.

"Imitate it. *Be* that animal," the doctor says. I can see that I will not be able to do so. I put my legs together and try, but I do not succeed. I resist it, I don't want it, I cannot. I tremble. That is impossible. *I feel that he wants me to dance.* Did he say so, or did I imagine that? I do *not* want to dance. I don't feel like it. He insists: "Be that trembling." I end up trying to obey. I lift my arms, surrendering to what may come. I start to tremble and I feel that my two arms are one flame, and they emit light. An energy that has come from above moves them, has put them together, and now they turn and turn as if electrified, beyond my power to stop them . . . My arms burn. They are fire and continue to turn. I fall to the floor with my arms still reaching up, and gradually they begin to slow down and descend, while an infinite peace starts to invade me. It is a sweet, silent peace . . .

I feel an understanding without words that I did not know before. It is consciousness. Great and deeper than ever before. I understand many ineffable things. I have not known how to love. I have lived without living. I see my little mind, when separate, as a fragment of my I AM. Understanding, consciousness—it is the same thing. There are no words, but understanding is infinite in that instant with no time.

Here we have a characteristic sample of the world of ibogaine, both in its luminous and its dark sides: the beam of white light and the cave with monsters, the sun and the black pond with the hidden crocodile. Furthermore, we see how the hellish and heavenly scenes follow one another: after her initial outburst of rage (which she describes as being like the eruption of a volcano) comes an episode of light. Feeling full of joy, she starts beating on the floor with her hands, and the Negroes appear. She cannot sustain for long the fear of the unknown and the primitive; the image fades, and while she prepares to rest, she sees the light coming through the belfry. Again, at the climax of this pleasant episode, she feels like moving about, standing up—and darkness supervenes. This time, the process does not stop by itself. She looks away; she cannot resist it. The incompleteness of the process probably leads her to another dark scene, as if there were something for her to assimilate in such darkness. Now the worst part seems to be over, or she has become somewhat desensitized to the fear through her repeated attempts to stay with it. Now she can at least look at the monsters and feel calm in spite of her disgust. *Movement* is again what seems to impress her most (as with the Negroes and the displacements of the crocodile).[3] Visual confrontation appears to have reached its end by now, since she can describe the monster in detail and bear the discomfort. The aim is now for her to see and give the "monster" its

[3] The brilliant colors in the images and the "electrical" feelings in her own body convey the same dynamic quality as the imagery of movement.

due place in herself, for it must be from her own reality that the image has proceeded. Interestingly, trembling means dancing to her. Obviously, the act of trembling or dancing meets with great resistance in her. She finally gives in to the trembling, and I speak of it as a "giving in" because at the moment she does not experience herself any more as purposefully *doing* it or enacting it, but as being moved by a real urge. And in the moment at which she begins to tremble, we witness the transition from the world of monsters to that of light, which now originates in her own body.

The feeling of rage at the beginning of the session, the primitive, sensuous drumming, the crocodile with electric-like movements, and the trembling monster all point to the same instinctual domain that the patient has held in abeyance at the cost of feeling complete. It is no wonder that only now that she has stopped resisting can she also see how her "little mind" has been only a part of her I AM. Dancing—the spontaneity of movement in which basic aggression and sensuousness are united and reconciled—has been at the same time her deepest wish and greatest taboo. Dancing, too, is what would give her freedom. But she has not danced, yet. She has only told herself to do so, believing that it was I who suggested it (i.e., projecting her unacknowledged urge into the outside world as an expectation). The unfinished situation occurs more than once. About half an hour later, for instance, I ask her to imitate the animal again, feeling that she has not succeeded in doing so, and this is how she describes the episode three days later:

> I am standing up. The doctor has asked me something. What was it? To dance? To tremble? To bring back the rhythm of the Negroes? Or that I imitate the cactus-animal? I don't know. Perhaps even then I didn't know. But I see myself standing in front of a giant drum. Beyond the drum I see many Negroes moving to a rhythm. They have thick lips, painted white, and skirts formed of

white strips that hang from a red belt. Their legs and chests are bare. I beat the drum forcefully with my right hand, and then with my left. I have something like wooden hammers in my hands, and I beat with them. I stop drumming to carry the rhythm with my body. I want to dance. It does not come out right. I try again, and I cannot. Then I see, among the Negroes, Maria's white, smiling face. Her expression changes as I look at her, and she laughs aloud. She mocks me because I cannot dance. I feel so angry that I throw the hammer and kill somebody, but I do not care. Something is interrupted. The doctor asks me to call the scene back to mind, but I find myself unable to do so. I sit down, and then I lie down. The doctor speaks, but I don't remember what he says. I only know that I cannot understand, I cannot understand. Something is going on.

Then I suddenly become aware of having been sexually aroused for a long time. I say this. The doctor tells me: "Give in to your desire. Feel it." And then I feel as if somebody took my legs and moved them in such a way that it became like a sexual act. There is no orgasm—or thousands—it is difficult to explain. But nothing ends. Arousal continues. Again I see beautiful landscapes, sunsets, vegetation, the sea, great expanses of desert, and the sun as a marvelous fireball in the background. I say, "How beautiful!" The doctor has asked me not to judge whether what I see is beautiful or ugly, but just describe it. But how can I not say it, if it is so beautiful? The sensation of being, the sensation of coarse vibrations that beat on and sink into my flesh. I feel like saying a thousand times, "I am I, I am I, I am." It is everything and too much.

Once more we see here the transition from the dark underworld of instinct to the beauty of the earth at large, the sun, being. But there are differences between these episodes and the previous ones. She participates more actively this time, as a drummer, being practically one with the crowd of dancing Negroes, actually beating (the floor) with her hands and, at last, *wanting* to dance rather than feeling under instruction to do so. And she feels murderous rage, too, though this moment puts an end to the scene. Another difference gives us a clue to understanding her rigidity and her difficulty in dancing in particular—her friend (Maria), who laughs at her for not doing well. It is her pride that will not unconditionally accept the spontaneity of her movements. These must, according to pre-established standards, be perfect, so that there is no room for improvisation, unpremeditated flow of action, animal intuition. Lastly, she becomes sexually aroused, and this is not a symbol any more, but an experience that she allows herself to have and express through her own body.

It is interesting to note that the imagery during the phase of resolution and integration is not otherworldly any more, but rather like a synthesis of the dark wet plant and animal world with the world of pure light, sky, and extension. Such synthesis is the ordinary world—though seen with no ordinary eyes. I am reminded of Blake's

> God appears, and God is Light,
> To those poor souls who dwell in Night;
> But does a Human Form display
> To those who dwell in realms of Day.

In a similar fashion, the cosmic "I am" has become a more earthly "I am I."

The patient has not danced, though, and this suggests that there still may be a barrier to her wish and that the process that we have been following may be incomplete. In fact, as sometimes happens with incomplete ibogaine experiences, she went on reminiscing the events of the session and visualizing occasional images for about twenty-four hours. At this point, impersonating a huge saurian with crocodile-like skin that she has seen, she berates the monster and screams at the top of her voice:

> I am horrible, black, gray, hard!
> I live in this horrible underground cave.

I want to be alone. I don't want life around me. I want
to be alone, alone.

A queen, powerful in this solitude.

I am the queen of the darkness.

I aaaam the beeeast!

I want to screech, roar, howl, destroy.

I want to kill, break, pierce, crush, scratch, smash, shat-
ter, tear, squash.

I am *implacable*!

I am *implacable*!!

I am *implacable*!!!

I am implacable with myself.

Wherever "monstrous" instinctive energies are being
controlled, an equally powerful monster must be there to
do such controlling, and it is just such a repressive operation that the person must recognize as her own doing before she can redirect its power. What in a previous moment had been mildly experienced by the patient as a
laugh of scorn from her "top dog" (Maria) has now
emerged as the implacable monster it is, and she has discovered the presence of the monster in her everyday self.

The results of this session were, as could be expected, a
significant gain in spontaneity and in freedom to express
anger. The change was visible in the patient's movements,
which became more supple, and in her facial expression,
now more tender and responsive to feelings. This was the
third session she had had with pharmacological agents,
the other two having been with LSD-25 and MDA. The
former, a year before, was an experience of discovering
beauty in the external world and yet seeing herself as ugly,
which dramatically displayed her self-rejection and
pointed to the work to be done in herself. MDA, six
months later, led her for the first time to the "I am I"
experience, where she realized the distinctness of her own
feelings and points of view in contrast to the stereotyped
attitudes she had picked up throughout her lifetime. The
session with ibogaine was the first in which her instinctive

life was touched, and it was after this that the most noticeable change occurred, according to both the patient's self-perception and the view of others.

Summing up, we can see the psychological process throughout the session above as one of a progressive recognition, acceptance, and expression of impulses. What had first reached consciousness as fleeting and threatening images (suffused with both aggression and sensuality) became more and more detailed and led to the idea of dancing, to actual movement, to sexual arousal, and to the patient's shouting at the top of her voice. More precisely, we can speak of an unfolding of repressed instincts side by side with an unfolding or expression of "phantoms"—the "introjects," the top-doggish monsters which constitute the clamp that holds down the impulses. Yet these phantoms are nourished by the blood of the repressed. It is precisely in these guardian-monsters that the patient's energy is imprisoned, and in giving the phantoms a voice, it is eventually the energies they have swallowed that speak—the patient's impulses—herself.

I think that we should not minimize the process of impulse expression depicted above in our usual concern—the legacy of psychoanalysis—with insight, interpretation, and the understanding of psychodynamics. I think that ibogaine can facilitate an openness to impulse that leads to learning, so that an avenue of expression remains open thereafter. This may be understood as a corrective experience in that the patient has the opportunity to discover that what he feared to let out is not really threatening or unacceptable.

One of the most clear-cut results that I have seen after an ibogaine treatment was that of a man with a homosexual history who had married, but who felt unrelated to his wife and physically uninterested in her. Although he expressed "castration feelings" in his session, these were left mostly unanalyzed, as was his hypothetical fear of women. Instead of this, when he felt sexually aroused at one point in the session, he went to the bathroom and thought that he would masturbate. But when he attempted to do so, he realized that this would only be a substitute for intercourse and that what he wanted was a woman. He then imagined that he had his wife in his arms and started moving as in intercourse—rigidly first, as in real life, but then with greater freedom and suppleness. He felt now that his legs and body were fashioned expressly to serve this function, and his movement became rhythmical and musical. As he felt closer to orgasm, he realized how perfectly bodies are conceived; he became aware of the exact anatomy of man and woman, and he felt that the woman was not merely the receptacle for his semen but for all his being. With his semen, his very being flowed and flowed into the feminine body that received him as he underwent the process of a terrible yet pleasurable disintegration.

This was not a physical orgasm, but what he called "psychological orgasm," without even an erection. Nevertheless, it was followed by a sensation of fulfillment.

I have described the event with all the detail in the patient's description, because only this detail conveys the quality of experience. This episode amounts to no more than about five minutes in a session of six hours, in which many issues were covered, but it is significant in that this was the first time that he had really let go in sexual intercourse with his wife, even though in imagination, and it proved not to be the last, for it was the beginning of their sexual and emotional closeness.

The patient's experience conveys much more than a simple episode of sexual arousal and "release of tension." What he described is much more in the nature of an archetypal experience of opening up to the archaic sexual pattern in the species and understanding from within the relationship between the sexes. In enacting to some extent the sexual scene—just as the patient in the previous example enacted her ritual movements—he lent reality to his inspirations and erased the fears to which he had been conditioned throughout his life history. The experience seems to have acted as an opening for further exploration and development rather than precipitating a drastic change. The patient, who had traveled a long way to consult me, returned to his country and wrote after six months: "I feel closer to my wife. Even the fact of having told her that I did not love her seems to have contributed to my feeling of closeness. Things that exasperated me to the limit don't bother me much now, and I feel desire for her more often. Our sexual relations are more complete and more like sharing. I feel freer in making love, and I am enjoying it more. I do not feel trapped in marriage as before, and I feel that we have more in common. I think that I know her better."

I have thus far dealt with processes of spontaneous self-expression in imagery, word, or action, with their elicitation by such means as the guided daydream, re-dreaming of past dreams, photographs, and with ways of handling different kinds of material through confrontation and impersonation; the latter may on occasion (with ibogaine as in the use of Gestalt therapy without drugs) lead to elaborate play-acting. There is still one situation that I want to discuss, not only because I have encountered it in about one out of every three sessions, but because of the particular quality and importance of these moments. This is the reminiscence or re-enactment of early life events, which may set in by association with the ongoing situation, with imagery, photographs, or interpretations of the patient's behavior.

I have already stated that what ibogaine typically does is to bring about the memory, not of external events (like MDA), but rather, of inner events or fantasies. These may be chronic fantasies, like the parental images, or may be more in the nature of events in time. This may be seen in the case of a middle-aged woman who at some point in her session remembered the following: Her father had come home with gifts for all the family, and gave her brothers and sisters what they had asked for beforehand. She had only said, wanting to be the favorite daughter, "Don't worry about me, Daddy; don't waste money on me." In fact, he brought her something less valuable than he had for her sisters—a little brooch in the shape of a dog. The story as told thus far was probably available to her conscious reminiscence, though she had not thought about the incident since her childhood days. What she discovered with surprise, though, was that, frustrated and disappointed with the small gift, she right then had a fantasy that the little dog (or she, she could not tell) bit off her father's penis and ate it. Moreover, she now realized that she felt guilty afterward, as if the imaginary event had actually taken place, and that this guilt had permeated her relationship with her father ever since. Those few seconds of inner life had magically affected her whole life, putting an end to the period of closeness to her father. Instructed to imagine that she could talk to her father now, she told him what had happened. "He" understood, and again she could feel clean and free. When she met her father in real life, she felt that she could love him well again.

This episode not only shows us how a mental event can influence life as much as, or more than, a fact, but is important in documenting that it is possible, after a lifetime, to remember a fantasy that was probably unconscious even at the time when it occurred. The nature of this particular fantasy seems to be very congruent with that of iboga imagery (the animal biting off and eating the genitals, the Oedipal situation) in general and the feelings (anger, resentment, frustration) that it tends to elicit, so that we even feel tempted to interpret this whole aspect of the "iboga world" as a regressive manifestation. But this I can only leave as a suggestion.

Whereas, in the last illustration, the patient recognized her fantasy as such, there are instances of apparent reminiscence of an external reality where one can suspect that a fantasy is being projected onto the past as pseudo-memory, just as a hallucination is a pseudo-perception of the present. Whenever I think that this may be taking place, I deal with the memory as if it were a piece of imagination, assuming that the characters in it are projections of the patient's personality. I therefore ask him to confront them or impersonate them until their psychological reality in the person's present state of mind can be discovered.

Consider the following fragment of a session. The patient (a young actress consulting because of marital difficulties) was telling me of a dream in which she was surprised to find that she had given birth to an elf. This was a strong and healthy miniature man. When I asked her to talk as he would, "he" said "You'll call me Shawn. I am very intelligent. I am going to sing and I am going to *dance*. I'll show you, I'll show you." On repeating this in the elf's voice and remembering him physically, she realized that she had always been wanting to show everyone that she was intelligent and could do things. Then she noticed that the elf had the body of her husband and that of a previous boyfriend, and that she had been trying to live their lives instead of her own. "I guess that I have always wanted to be a boy," she said. "I never loved myself very much."

I suggested at this point that, just as an elf conveys a feeling of strangeness and uniqueness, of not belonging to the ordinary human world, perhaps she had felt a comparable strangeness with regard to her parents. This was evident to her. Her mother had looked upon her as if she were a little monster and made her feel like a strange creature. Part of her own feeling of being from a different world she traced to the fact that her parents hardly ever seemed to pick her up in their arms, as if they were afraid of doing so or did not know how. So I now suggested that she might try to feel like a baby again and experience what she might have felt at that time. For her, this felt like a very realistic memory: "I went back to about one year, perhaps more, in my crib. The baby bed had a kind of railing around it, and I remembered my parents and re-lived the scene as if it were here and now, with all my emotions and movements, colors, light of day, everything. They were looking into the crib, waving their hands and playfully saying, 'Gailie, Gailie.' They didn't touch me, and I wanted them to. They looked at me like something strange. I found that the elf had really been born at that time—in that I was on exhibition and didn't feel like an-other human being. It seems that love was the thing that was lacking there. I was also in that baby bed, which was something like a cage."

Note the "imprisonment" theme in addition to the feel-ing of frustration. While she told of these memories, she suffered. She continually felt that she was very sick, not like other people, not loved. The most intense feeling of lack of love occurred while she was thinking of her mother. She remembered her coming into the room, shouting at her, and stamping her feet. While she, the baby, cried and needed her, she said, "Stop bothering me. Stop that crying and let me do the dishes!" I asked her to talk like her, and she did, imitating her voice and her inflections. This is how she later remembered the following episode and her feel-ings:

> The doctor asked me to answer her and tell her what she was doing to me, and how I felt. I answered just as she had screamed at me. He called my attention to that and asked that I try to answer her as Gail, looking for my own feelings and expression. I was crying and looking for my own voice, but it wasn't there. I couldn't find myself. He asked me to have my mother take me and love me. She took me, but I hated her for not having done it before. I hated her so much at that moment. I wanted to do her harm and to show her how I felt. The doctor suggested that I hit her. I began to pound on a pillow, but I couldn't do it with much force, because I loved her, too. I felt

guilty because she didn't let me love her. I realized that she had never taught me how to love. I realized, too, that it is not only important to be loved, but to be allowed to love back. The doctor then asked me to take her and love her. I took her and loved her and felt better. Still I felt sad. I asked him what to do with the guilt. He said, "Accept it." I still felt bad. I was alone in that room. I felt bad, bad, bad inside. It seemed that there was a great empty black hole inside of me. I didn't tell him of this, because I felt it to be so bad. While I was sitting in the baby bed, I continually felt the light, which cast a sharp shaft from the window into the room and on the floor. The light was warm and filled me in my loneliness. I played with the light. It was God. I loved that light and the green plants that I saw outside the window. The day outside was brilliant and warm, and Mother so cold and bad-tempered. Once or twice in talking with Mother, I found my voice. It was sad, the voice of a little girl asking for love. The only thing that kept me from suffering was the light.

Once more in this example we can see the peak experience quality drawing closer in the measure in which the patient is able to give in to her true feelings. It is in sorrow and the need for love that she finds herself (her own voice) and the consolation of the white light. The image of light as a beam, and the religious feeling associated with it are too much like other peak experiences with ibogaine to believe that this is a real memory. Yet we cannot discard the possibility that the child's experience of light may be a source of delight and support and constitute the original experience at the root of the notion of God as light-giver.

In spite of the positive element in the quotation above, it can be seen from it that the patient's situation was still not resolved. She was still torn by her ambivalence, not being able to love wholeheartedly. As in Jacob's case, though, these minutes of analysis laid the ground for a synthesis in the following hour, and their fruit was the most noticeable among the numerous changes that she reported during the following months. This may be appreciated in the following page of a diary, written by her two weeks later:

> I used to ask other people if they ever had feelings like I had. I was ashamed of feelings. I used to ask Mother whether I was a freak! "Doesn't anybody love me?" I said. Why don't they love me? I didn't love myself either. Where was Gail? Gail is inside of Gail, but sleeping. She is just waking up, and it is time. I am a person. I am like anybody else. I have been living the lives of others. Afraid to try my own. My mother destroyed my life until this time. She never saw herself. Maybe that is why she could not see me. She lived the lives of others. Envy, greed, and guilt. She is tortured. I am tortured, but I can do something about it. I must exercise myself, I must live in the world and use my energies. Only at certain moments have I realized myself, and only through other people. I cannot help looking into and living the lives of others. I have my own good one. I think I am freeing myself from my parents. I am not my mother, thank God. I must respect the lives of others. How can I take responsibility for others if I don't have any for myself? I am me. I must be me. I must be me from now on—whatever I may be. I have my own responsibility.

The patient's feeling of completeness and relief had its sudden onset in the session at a point where she saw herself climbing on the inside of a vertical tube. This tube was her own life, she knew, but was bottomless, and where she was born and downward there was a black, inky, hazy substance which continued downward without end. At the suggestion that she fall down into the tube, she let go of the handles and began to fall in the inky substance. As she fell, she saw a spiral in motion, but principally, she says, "*I became myself in falling.* The sensation was very pleasurable and *I began to like being me.* I felt that love was possible and that it was a way of living."[4]

[4] Italics mine.

This process of becoming herself and discovering love was the natural continuation of the contacting of her own feelings and the finding of her own voice in the earlier episode—her own reality buried under her identification with mother. As before, becoming herself was achieved by means of falling. In the earlier part of the session, it had been a falling into her sorrow, her despair, by letting go of her defensiveness. Now it was a total letting go of effort, paralleled and expressed in the image of falling. In the process of the falling and spiraling, the image ceased to be a purely visual one, so that her own body woke up and took part in the event.

The process of "entering" an image, becoming it, and in this manner reassimilating a quality that was being disowned, is familiar to us from Gestalt therapy and has a long tradition that antedates psychotherapy as we now know it. The classical Hindu sculptor, for instance, would meditate on the god to which he was to give form, by first summoning his image to mind and then *becoming* it. A similar practice, without its artistic end, is found in the Jewish Kabbalah and in magical traditions. Gods that are invoked in such practices are particular functions or processes of the mind, and so are the images most usually dealt with in psychotherapy. In the present instance, the tube stands for the whole of the patient's life—*her own* life—and yet is bottomless and goes beyond. It is certainly a great event to find such a door to knock at. The possibility of entering is already awaiting the person who sees the entrance, which is the synthetic view (if only a view) of his existence. I have been surprised by the frequency with which tubes are seen under the effects of ibogaine, and I want to share my impression that these generally constitute such an "entrance," so that they are valuable clues to act upon. We have seen the tube in two of the cases already reported, but further illustrations may serve to clarify its significance. The following is part of a session where the patient had been visualizing image after image without any strong feelings or interest in them. They appeared rather meaningless and disconnected from one another, and there seemed (to us) to be no definite pattern or development apparent in their progression.

At one point, the subject visualized a drum. This is very much an image of the ibogaine world, because of its association with impulse, power, movement, and perhaps primitiveness. It can also be seen as a variation on the tube theme, because of its cylindrical shape and its emptiness. I asked the patient to impersonate this instrument, and he described how he was becoming a large golden drum, only used to beat upon on great historical occasions. Then the drum rolled down a hill and ended up becoming a general's cap. It belonged to a very insignificant man, who put on airs by acting in a domineering manner. Such an insignificant man appears to be the opposite of the great golden drum, suggesting feelings of inadequacy that the patient is covering up behind a pompous self-image. It is interesting that the transition from one image to the other is mediated by a *rolling down* of the drum, reminiscent of the falling down through the tube in the previous example. Letting go of an inflated self-image will naturally feel like a falling into one's self, or, at least, a falling into an area of insignificance, darkness, and unpleasantness, in the midst of which the true self is to be encountered. I now asked the patient to be the general, and as he was in the process of becoming this character, he saw a tube with no ending, like a train. I ask him to enter the tube, and it became a jet, and then a little airplane that flew playfully. These are images of energy, and I feel inclined to understand the sequence as a process of the patient's contacting his drive-energy through the "falling" involved in becoming insignificant. The tube marks the point of transition, an endless hollow. But this immediately became full of dynamism, first by the superimposition of the idea of a train in motion, and then a jet. Jets, spurts (remember the gushing sap), and beams of light could all be understood as the tube coming to life, or as life flowing through its hollowness—just as in our first case, where the subject received the white light as he looked up the periscope-like tube he had created. In taking the form of an airplane, the "jet" energy became individualized, for it is obvious from the patient's description of its mischievous looping that he was speaking of his own style of being. In fact, he discovered this by himself. This flying reflected his *real* feelings. He flew like a playful little boy, small and eager to explore, wanting more and more, and enjoying the display of his own ability. He did not experience his smallness as insignificance, as the general did, nor did he have to struggle for competitive greatness. The energy locked up in his "drum personality" was now released to a more direct enjoyment of himself, and instead of the gold that, in the drum, conveyed greatness to others, he relished his own feeling in the golden light of the sun.

After some time of enjoying the feeling of freedom in an open world, he (the airplane) felt the need of a direction and flew toward the sun. He hesitated as he drew near, fearing a destruction like that of Icarus. Nevertheless, he proceeded, entered the sun, and found paradise behind it.

The airplane, after all, is only a transformation of the endless tube, which may be the channel for a force, but not the source itself. The little plane played in the light of the sun as the sun's child, and though it had an activity of its own, we might say that its movement toward the sun stemmed from the sun's attraction. The plane is a portion of energy that wants more of itself, and this it finds by returning to its source. It is literally a "vehicle," not the end, and it stands in face of the sun like the son in face of the father (see Jacob's case), or like the ego in face of the self.

We have seen two domains of energy as part of the world of ibogaine: one of light and playfulness, the other of darkness and greed; a world of the sun, of spirits and dancing, and another of dark ponds, devouring dragons, castrating dogs, threatening gorillas. Somewhere in between are images such as that of a golden lion or a dancing Negro. How do the tube and the sun relate to the "lower" domain of ibogaine experiences, that of animality, rage, and lonely separateness? I think that the consideration of one further case will serve to organize and understand better some of the clues which have been provided by the material presented thus far.

In brief, it may be said that, for the first four hours, the thoughts and fantasies of this patient (a thirty-eight-year-old politician) were predominantly sexual and aggressive. During this time, two images kept reappearing with some variations: one, the tube (which was at first a ring, or an eye), and the other a gorilla-like anthropoid. The gorilla was the first vision of all, and then it appeared to be completely an animal. Later, the patient recognized the animal's self-important and bombastic attitude as his own, and the more he did, the more the image changed into a more human one, that of a gigantic and monkey-like man that he called "the bully." At the end of the fourth hour, I anticipated that the effect of the drug would not last more than two hours or so and I saw little development, if any, in the nature of the patient's experience for the past hour. In view of this, I decided to interrupt what seemed to be a changeless merry-go-round of imagery by means of a brief administration of carbon dioxide. I hoped that the inhalation of the gas would bring about a transient weakening of the ego functions and a release of heretofore unconscious material. It happened that the patient could not tolerate more than ten inhalations, for he felt that he—the boastful giant—was being shoved up through a tube so that his head was pressing with tremendous force against the ceiling, and it would certainly break!

After this moment of impotence and fear of death, there was a change in the patient's feeling tone and in the content of his conversation. Not only did he see more of the bully in himself, wanting to threaten others in order to feel safe, but also the child under the bully—a greedy child wanting affection that he did not dare let others see. Now the giant appeared to him with a big chest but small legs, and wearing the short pants of a child. Many reminiscences followed, and these had a quality of confession, for the patient was expressing more and more of his weakness, guilt, and insecurity.

Fearing that the session would be over before reaching a definite goal, I used CO_2 once more, and this time with an even more dramatic consequence, for the result was a state of ecstasy, the taste of which remained as the patient's dominant feeling for the rest of the day: *The sun* was at the other end of the tube!

The patient spent the following hour in what I can best describe as an adoration of the sun. Not the physical sun, which had already set, nor a hallucinated sun, but whatever it is that is symbolized in it. As I remember that time, as we sat, silent at times, and at times talking, I picture the sun above our heads almost as another being in the room, for I, too, was drawn into the patient's exultation and gratefulness toward the fountain of life.

I have commented upon how, with both iboga and harmaline, a given theme can be either *experienced* or merely contemplated as a sequence of images with which the subject scarcely identifies. In this instance, I believe that we are witnessing the primordial experience—not in the sense of old, but eternal—from which have sprung both the solar myths and the conception of God as light that still reaches us through the meaning of the word "God" in most languages.

We looked back on his experience throughout the day —a compendium of his life. The gorilla in him, the bully, the one who wanted to be the big man, were hiding unacceptable weakness and much guilt. Much of the weakness was that of wanting, needing, and feeling afraid to expose his needfulness. And most of his guilt was about sex. Most of the life history that he had presented to me was the history of his sexual life, and the theme had run through the whole of his session. "How can I reconcile sex with the sun?" he said now, feeling in the presence of two incompatible worlds, one of pure spirit and the other of the flesh. But his doubt did not last very long, his change in view being reflected in the remark that followed: "But the penis in erection also points toward the sun!" This was not mere playing with words and ideas, but the expression of a change in feelings toward sex, which suddenly became clean and holy in the measure that it, too, was aiming at the sun—just like the airplane in the vision discussed before. The light was the ultimate end or beginning of the sexual urge, and, this being so, sex was itself luminous.

I find this session interesting because of how it shows a gradual transmutation of psychological energy, paralleled by the opening up of its tubelike channel. It may be said that, in the beginning, the patient *was* a closed tube and even wanted to be like that. At one point, he pictured a tube stretching beyond his field of vision and described it with a feeling of dissatisfaction or discomfort at its lack of beginning or end. "A tube, a tube, a tube, tube, tube . . . It never ends!" And then he commented that a tube with no limits is *nothing*. I find this rejection of the tube's "beyondness" noteworthy, because it is precisely a tube's endlessness and openness that seem characteristic of ibogaine peak experiences. But this openness to the rigid little ego is like death; it is "nothing." Therefore, the assertive bully kept pushing his head against the ceiling. The image tells us that the tube's closedness and the man's rigid defensiveness were the same. The tube's opening would be the smashing of the man's head, and that would amount to *his* death. In fact, *that* man eventually disappeared.

So what first wanted to go through the tube was gorilla-like assertiveness, and that could not go through. The tube cannot be permeable to a form of energy which, after all, seeks separateness. In identifying with this phony image of himself, the patient was preventing the flow of his life. But what is this life that wants to flow? On several occasions, he saw tubes coming from underground, or rising from a basement. At some point, water flowed out from it—not gushing, just barely leaking. "Now, now, now!" he exclaimed in great excitement. And then "Ouch, ouch, ouch!" The image changed to that of somebody being crucified, and then he could not remember any more. Not only the underground but the context in which these images are embedded suggest that it was "dark" instincts that wanted out, for the rest of the visions are of muddy ponds, crocodiles, Negroes. Then the transformation occurred by which the darkness and animal life became light —and not only light, for the sun heats, conveying great energy. In fact, it is the source of all energy and life. The sun is, quite literally, the father of plants, animals, and men, and the patient only had to become a child to know this.

The present example shows only an amplification of what we have seen in many others. When we consider, for instance, Gail's sight of the light coming in through the window while she lay in her crib ("It was God"), or how the experience of light followed each contact of another patient with the animal forces portrayed in her imagination, or how in Jacob's case the threads-worms-animals coming out of his mouth became the bird that flies toward the sun—in all of these instances it would seem that the drive that is "embodied" in the animals (or the greedy baby) is the same which, from a different point of view, comes to be experienced as a flight toward the light and light itself.

And the shift in point of view is very much that of "entering the tube": entering life and living it from inside rather than being an outside observer of its manifestations; experiencing it as closely as it may be experienced, identifying with its central axis, with its inner core; becoming life rather than *having* it; reaching a state where subject and object are the same, the thinker and his thoughts, the feeler and his feelings, body and mind. So the process of entering the tube is no other than that of *entering one's experience*, which is the object of so many traditional forms of meditation.

> Thus have I heard. At one time the Blessed One was living among the Kurus, at Kammasadamma, a market town of the Kuru people.
> There the Blessed One addressed the monks thus: "Monks," and they replied to him "Venerable Sir." And the Blessed One spoke as follows:
> "This is the sole way, monks, for the purification of beings, for the overcoming of sorrow and lamentation, for the destroying of pain and grief, for reaching the right path, for the realization of Nirvana, namely for four Foundations of Mindfulness.
> "What are the four? Herein (in this teaching) a monk dwells practising body-contemplation on the body, ardent, clearly comprehending, and mindful, having overcome covetousness and grief concerning the world; he dwells practising feeling-contemplation on feelings, ardent, clearly comprehending, and mindful, having overcome covetousness and grief concerning the world; he dwells practising mind-contemplation on the mind, ardent, clearly comprehending, and mindful, having overcome covetousness and grief concerning the world; he dwells practising mind-object-contemplation on mind-objects, ardent, clearly comprehending, and mindful, having overcome covetousness and grief concerning the world."[5]

The seeming paradox is that this process of attending to actuality (in body, feelings, or thoughts) appears as a *downward* movement, toward earthly existence, and yet within the earthliness of its forms is found a spiritual entity which beams *from above*. The more we go into the

[5] *Maha-Satipatthana-Sutta*: "Twenty-second text of the collection of Long Discourses of the Buddha," from Nyaponika Thera, *The Heart of Buddhist Meditation* (London: Rider & Co., n.d.).

same thing, the more it turns into something different. The more we go into reality, the more "unreal" it becomes. But this is no different from the process by which science finds a reality which is incomprehensible to our senses, and art transfigures the world of familiar appearances when it reaches for the essence of things.

INDEX

Abramson, Harold, 4
age regression, 27, 57, 60–2, 71,
  215; therapeutic value of, 28
aggression, 176, 179, 185, 205–8;
  and harmaline, 176; and ibogaine, 176, 185, 201, 205–8,
  212
alcohol, 20
alcoholic rehabilitation, 4
Alexander, F. Matthias, 91–2
Alles, G., 26
Allport, Gordon, xx
altered consciousness states, 3–5
amnesia, 42, 55, 61, 172
amphetamines, xviii, 3, 14, 175
amphetamine shock, 4
anxiety reactions, 10–11, 55, 63,
  79, 82, 100, 158, 165
Apuleius, 41
archetypal experience, 126, 132–
  3, 151–2, 154–6, 169–70, 174,
  182, 186–8, 213; and Jung,
  126; and personality integration, 126, 142–3
Aristotle, 17
art forms, frequent evocation of,
  141–5
autobiography, therapeutic use,
  29, 50–3, 81–4, 177
avoidance, 12–14, 22–3

ayahuasca, 124, 171
Ayur Veda, 26

Bach, Johann Sebastian, 9
Baker, Richard, 174
Banisteriopsis, 124
barbiturates, 3, 6
being, 9–10, 44
benzedrine, 4
Benoit, Hubert, 16
bioenergetics, x
Blake, William, 210
body awareness, importance of,
  31–2, 39, 42, 57–8, 180, 191

caapi, 124
Camus, Jean-Pierre, 92
case histories, 28; with harmaline, 127–31, 134–40, 141–2,
  145–51, 153–69; with ibogaine, 177–81, 182–9, 190–2,
  194–201, 205–12, 212–13,
  214–20, 221–2, 223–5; with
  MDA, 29–39, 44–54, 55–64,
  67–72; with MMDA, 82–94,
  95–7, 98–9, 101–2, 102–5,
  105–9, 112–14, 115–19, 120–
  22

catatonia, 10
centeredness, 21, 24, 84, 87, 90–4
Centro de Estudios de Antropología Médica (The Center for Studies in Medical Anthropology), xvi
cerebrotonic, 7
cerebrotonic ectomorphs, 143
childhood reminiscences, 27–8, 30–2, 42, 49, 176–7, 194, 202, 214, 216
Christianity, 17, 18, 24, 159–63
classical myths, 11, 98, 140
collective unconscious, 125–73
compulsive character structure, xvii
conditioned personality structure, xvii
conflict resolution, 11, 14, 17, 189
confrontation, value of, 14–15, 24, 74, 94–6, 98, 131, 189, 214
confrontation with unconscious, 11, 14–15, 142–3, 149; and body-type, 143; with harmaline, 142; and integration, 143
consciousness, importance in therapy, 12–13, 76, 90, 103, 143–4, 149, 152
consciousness expansion, 17
conversion manifestations, 10, 170
counteractive defenses, 55, 65

Dabrowski, Kazimierz, 3, 14
Dante Alighieri, 11–13, 17–19
death wish, 164, 167
defenses, operation of, 42, 55–7, 61, 65, 80, 88, 96, 105, 141, 225. See also denial; repression; substitutive symbolic expression
deficiency motivation, 129
dehumanization, xvi
Delay, Jean, 4

delusions, 10
denial, 14, 55, 59, 78
depersonalization, 5, 80
depression, 10, 40, 70, 82
De Ropp, Robert, 174
"desensitization," 14
desires, unconscious, 102–4, 209–11
Desoille, Robert, x, 145
desymbolization, 115
dianetics, 27
disinhibition, 20, 77
dissociation, 71–2, 165
dissolution, 80
Divine Comedy (Dante) 11–15
DMT, 171
Doors of Perception, The (Huxley), 22
Dostoevski, Feodor, 9
dramamine, 175
dreams, 112; and imagery, 79, 95–8, 100, 104, 110, 165–6; re-experiencing in therapy, 112–15, 179, 191–2, 194–6, 214
Drugs and the Mind (De Ropp), 174
dysfunctional personality patterns, 21

Eckhardt, Meister, 10, 109
ego-enhancement: and MDA, 65
egohood, 65–8
ego loss, 6
eidetic displays, 78–9; as feeling substitutes, 79
electroencephalogram, 143
Elkes, Joel, xix
encounter groups, x
"encountering," 119–21
Eros, 164
Esalen Institute, x
estrangement, 129
Ethnopharmacological Search for Psychoactive Drugs (ed. Holmstedt), xix

expression of feelings, 48, 59, 60, 97–9, 111, 140–1

Family of Man (Steichen) 177, 180
fantasy, therapeutic use, 59, 69–73, 96, 114, 123, 139–43, 145–9, 156–66, 172, 178–81, 188, 212–13
fantasy enhancers, xvii–xviii, 78
Federking, 4
feeling-enhancement   reactions, 100–2, 114–15
feeling-enhancers, xvii–xviii, xx
feeling substitution, 79
forgetting, 42
free association, 165
Freud, Sigmund, 43
frigidity, 165, 172
Fromm, Erich, 16

Gauguin, Paul, 9
Gershon, Samuel, 174
Gestalt psychotherapy, x, 101, 105, 111, 119, 177, 201, 214, 220
Greeks, 33
Grinker, Roy R., 4
group therapy, 29, 77; MDA in, 77
guided affective imagery, x
guided daydream, 15, 74–5, 143–50, 179, 181, 194, 214
guilt, 49, 72–3, 79, 86, 121, 163–7, 169, 185, 224

habitual patterns, interference of, 5, 87, 93
hallucinations, 27, 186
hallucinogens, 4, 5, 7, 27–8
harmaline, xix, xx, 5, 28, 40, 78, 186, 224; adverse reactions, 129–30, 170–1; and collective unconscious, 125–70; com-
bined with MDA, 171–2; effects, 5–6, 124–6, 129–32, 151–3, 170–1; and feelings of power and freedom, 65; and hallucinogens, 5–6; history, 124–6; and peak experiences, 130, 144; prevalent themes evoked by, 125–6, 133, 136–9, 154; subjective effects, research on, 125–6; therapeutic use, 124–73; and visual archetypal symbols, 76
harmaline-MDA, 126, 171
harmaline-mescaline, 126
harmaline-TMA, 126
Harvard prison rehabilitation project, 4
Heart of Buddhist Meditation, The (Thera), 227
Hegel, Georg Wilhelm Friedrich, 12
Hoffer, Abram, 4
Hoffmann, Franz, xvii
Holmstedt, Bo, xix
Homer, 81
Horsley, J. S., 4
Human Preference Test, 56, 58, 59, 61
Huxley, Aldous, 4, 6, 10, 22
hypermnesia, 27, 64, 71
hypnosis, 69, 71, 74–5, 77
hypnotic regression, 27

ibogaine, xix, xx, 5, 6, 27, 28, 78, 119; and aggression, 176, 185, 205–8, 212; characteristic imagery, 177, 184, 200, 207, 219–23; and childhood reminiscences, 176–7, 202, 214; effects, 5–6, 174–7, 186, 202, 214; and hallucinogens, 5–6; and impulse expression, 212; and instinctual forces, 176, 200, 221; and peak experiences, 188–90, 190–1, 194, 218, 225; prevalent

ibogaine (cont'd.)
  themes evoked by, 176–7,
  200, 205–7, 209; therapeutic
  use, 174–228
Icarus, 222
idealized image, 43, 85–7, 169.
  See also self-image
identification, 17, 114
identity shifts, 71–2
imagery, 125–8, 132–3, 186; as
  defense mechanism, 140–3,
  167, 172; and dreams, 112–
  23, 165–6; elicited by psychotropic drugs, 79, 95–8, 100,
  104, 110; exploration in therapy, 104, 110–11, 112–16,
  123, 131, 134–7, 140, 144,
  149, 154–6, 178–82, 194–6,
  208–12
imaginative representation in
  therapy, 15
impersonation, 48–50, 115–16,
  120, 172, 178–9, 186–7, 206,
  214, 220–2
incomplete therapy, evidence
  of, 54–5, 59–60, 152
initiation rites, 124, 151–2
insight, growth of, 16, 19, 85–
  7, 90, 94, 109, 114, 123, 167,
  180–1
instinctual forces, images of,
  170, 176, 201, 208, 210–12
integration, 6, 11, 17, 43, 99–100,
  226–7; and archetypal experience, 126, 142–3; and confrontation with unconscious,
  143, 210; and dissociation,
  71–3; and MDA, 65; and
  pathology, 11; and peak experiences, 22, 110
introjection, 212
iproniazide, 174 n.
isopropylamines, 78

Jantz, 4
Johns Hopkins University, xix
Jung, Carl Gustav, 4, 110, 126

Kabbalah, 220

Laignel-Lavastine, 3
Leuner, Hanscarl, x
Lowen, Alexander, x
LSD, x, xii, xix, 7, 15, 27, 66, 78,
  80, 172, 175, 194, 197, 202–3,
  211; and ego loss, 6; in
  psychoanalytic treatment, 4;
  and transcendence, 65

marathon sessions, x
Maryland State Psychiatric Research Center, xix
masks, use as defense, 38, 40–1,
  43, 44–5, 180
meditation, 18, 19, 21–2, 132,
  191, 227
Medusa, 98
mescaline, xii, xix, 6, 22, 27, 65,
  171
mesomorphic somatotonics, 143
MDA (methylenedioxyamphet-
  amine), xvi, xix, xx, 5, 26,
  78, 80, 132, 171, 175, 177,
  202, 211, 214; and age regression, 27–8; as "drug of truth,"
  76; effects, 5–6, 26–8, 39–40,
  54–5, 65–6, 76–7, 177; and
  enhancement of ego, 65; and
  group therapy, 77; and hallucinogens, 5–6; and hypermnesia, 27, 64, 71; and importance of sensations, 66;
  therapeutic use, 26–77, 202;
  toxicity, 77; verbal reactions,
  77
MMDA (3-methoxy-4, 5-methyl-
  ene dioxyphenyl isopropylamine), xix, 5, 6, 26, 65, 76,
  175, 177, 194, 201–2; effects,
  5–6, 78–81, 100–1, 110–11,
  122, 177; and everyday reality, 78–81, 88, 98–100; and
  exploration of present, 201;
  and feeling-enhancement, 78–

MMDA (*cont'd.*)
  9; and hallucinogens, 5–6,
    78–9; and peak experiences,
    79–80, 94, 97, 100, 110, 123,
    194; and psychosomatic
    symptoms, 79, 100, 105–10,
    112; therapeutic use, 78–123;
    visual imagery, 79, 95–8, 100,
    104, 110, 123
Middle Ages, 33
Minerva, 98
MAO (monoamine oxidase), 174
motor activity, significance of,
    66–7, 173, 187–8, 189, 190,
    207–9
Myerson, 4
myristicine, 26
mystery religions, 17
mystical experiences, sources,
    19–21
mysticism, 17–19, 109–10

narcoanalysis, 4
narcosynthesis, 4
Nehru, Jawaharlal, 156
Nicoll, B., 16
Nietzsche, Friedrich Wilhelm,
    81
nitrous oxide, 20
non-psychotomimetics, xvii, 6
nutmeg, 26, 78

Odyssey, The (Homer), 81
Oedipal situation, 200, 215
"original man," 17
Osmond, Humphrey, xviii, 4,
    5
otherness, issusion of, 72–3

"past-life memories," 71–3
pathology, enhancement of, 6–
    25
peak experiences, 3, 6–25, 79–
    80, 85, 110, 123, 130, 144,

188–9, 194, 202; and Christian
    grace, 24; dangers, 18–23; as
    guide, 91–5, 123; incomplete,
    94–5; and intrinsic values,
    7–10; and personality change,
    19, 23; and personalization,
    65; stabilization of, 97–101;
    therapeutic implications, 20,
    85, 90–2
Peganum harmala, 124
pentobarbital, xviii
Perennial Philosophy (Huxley),
    92
Perls, Fritz, x
personality change, 19, 28; and
    peak experiences, 21, 23, 123
"personalization," 65–6
Perseus, 98
personality types, 6–7, 189
peyotl, 92
phenylisopropylamines, 5
phobias, 23, 154–9
photographs, use in therapy, 58,
    61, 67–8, 70, 98, 177–9, 193,
    197, 201, 214
physiological insusceptibility, 31
pineal gland, 125
polycyclic indoles, 5
prenatal memories, 69
projection, 114, 141, 167, 169,
    194, 216
psilocybin, xii, 4
psychedelics, xvii–xviii, xx; and
    behavior change, 4–5; "hea-
    ven and hell" of, 6–8; prop-
    erties, xix; and self-discov-
    ery, 13; spiritual value, 4;
    therapeutic use, xix, 5, 16
Psychopharmacology, xix
psychosomatic symptoms, 10,
    79, 100, 105–10, 112, 131
psychotherapy: goals of, 17, 39;
    and psychotropic drugs, 16;
    and spiritual traditions, xii,
    16–17
psychotic experience, value of,
    3
psychotomimetics, xvii–xviii

psychotropic drugs, 3–6; and setting, 7; and types of personality, 6–7
puberty rites, 124

Ramakrishna, 132
reactive formations, 11
reality, confrontation of, 20, 41, 66, 98–100, 104–5
reconditioning, 14
Renaissance, 33
repression, 11, 43–4, 54–5, 66, 79–80, 94, 149, 163–4, 201, 211, 212
resistances, 22, 31, 41, 110, 131, 171, 204
rêve éveillé, x
Rite of Spring, The (Stravinsky), 178
role-playing, 40–1
Rolf, Ida, x
Romans, 33

safrol, 26
samadhi, 18
Sandison, 4
scopolamine, xviii
"screen memories," 71–3; therapeutic use, 74–5
self-acceptance, 13, 17, 39, 149, 171; and mescaline, 171
self-actualization, 129
self-concept, 17, 43, 56, 85, 128–9. See also self-image
self-defeating fantasies, 149
self-discovery, 127, 129, 181, 187
selfhood, awareness of, 65–6, 71, 73, 152, 181–2, 193, 210, 220
self-image, 40–3, 55, 192, 212, 221. See also self-concept; idealized image
self-knowledge, 13, 33, 39, 65, 86–7
self-realization, 17
self-rejection, 13, 101, 149–50
seratonin, 125

shamanism, 3, 92, 124, 140, 152, 181
Sheldon, W. H., 7
sodium amytal, 4
somatotonic, 7
South American mythology, 140
spiritual traditions, xii, 18–19, 21, 24; and contemplation, 12; and magic, 18; and psychotherapy, 16–17
spontaneity, 41, 87, 93, 150, 152
Stokowski, Leopold, 8
Stravinsky, Igor, 178
substitutive symbolic expression, 11, 72–3, 104, 140
super-ego, 105
symbols, recurrent, 17–18, 125–6, 130, 133–4, 140–3, 154, 170, 224
symptom substitution, 74

Tabernanthe iboga, 174
telepathine, 124
10-methoxy-harmaline, 125
Thanatos, 164
Thera, Nyaponika, 227 n.
therapeutic intervention, 7, 14, 31, 91–2, 94–5, 96–7, 100, 106, 111, 114–15, 122, 132–4, 140, 143–4, 149, 155, 189, 204–5
time regression, 71, 176–7, 202, 214
TMA (trimethoxyamphetamine), 126 n., 176
Tofranil, 174 n.
"top dog," 105, 211–12
transcendence, feelings of, 65, 84
transformation as goal, 12
tryptamines, 4
Turner, William, 5

unconscious, access to, 5, 20

Van Gogh, Vincent, 9

via activa, 15
via contemplativa, 15
via purgativa, 13, 18; psychological disharmony as, 24
via unitiva, 18
Virgil, 14
viscerotonic, 7, 180
Vivaldi, Antonio, 103

Watts, Alan, 16

"Weckanalyse," 4
wish-fulfillment fantasies, 149
writing, use in therapy, 44, 98–9, 163

yage, xi, 124
yoga, 18

Zen Buddhism, 18

About the Author

Claudio Naranjo is a Chilean psychiatrist and the author of several books and monographs on psychology and meditation. He has studied at Harvard and the University of Illinois on a Fulbright Scholarship, and in 1966 went to the University of California at Berkeley on a Guggenheim Fellowship. In recent years he has been a major figure at the Esalen Institute and in spiritual teaching programs in California.